PARIS
CONTRASTS

PARIS
CONTRASTS

Vasyl Prokopyshyn

CONTENT

Paris is a very photogenic city, if I may say so. From the first daguerreotypes of Paris in 1839 something of a love affair developed between Paris and photography, a romance that grew more passionate as it lasted the decades.

Paris has been a source of inspiration for countless artists and writers down the ages. But not least it is the home and constant muse of a relatively young art: photography. Since the earliest days of the photography right up to our time, renowned photographers such as Joseph Nicéphore Niepce, Henri Cartier-Bresson, Robert Doisneau, and Jeanloup Sieff lived and worked in the city of lights. They were creating a remarkable record of the metropolis and a telling history of a new art form. Paris has remained an inexhaustible source of inspiration for all photographers, those "poets of light'.

This book is my modest attempt to show modern Paris, so different, contradictory, full of contrasts. My homage to the world's most beautiful city. Real Paris is about people that don't afraid to express their feelings and emotions. They create the unique atmosphere of the French capital. I tried to create atmospheric black-and-white photos, which show everyday scenes from the life of real people. In some photos I tried to refer to the classical masterpieces of photography, the attentive spectator will be able to notice them.

All photos in this book are spontaneous, snatched moments from the real life on the streets of modern Paris. I invite you to stroll with me through Paris with a camera in hand.

LOVE IN PARIS

Everybody knows that Paris is the city of Love and Romance. Paris is said to be one of the most beautiful cities in the world. A city whose beauty strikes us at every corner, with its elegant architecture, iconic monuments, and the subtle combination of art, history and nature, creating the perfect canvas on which love can be conceived and painted into its own masterpiece. Historically, Paris was the center of ideas, art, poetry and revolutionary politics in Europe. The best painters, writers, poets gathered in Paris and glorified it in their artworks. Numerous movies over the years have embedded a certain idea of love in the French capital. Hollywood movies had idealized Paris for many years. It is the perfect place for the couples that love each other more and more every day, and say "I love you" for thousands times a day.

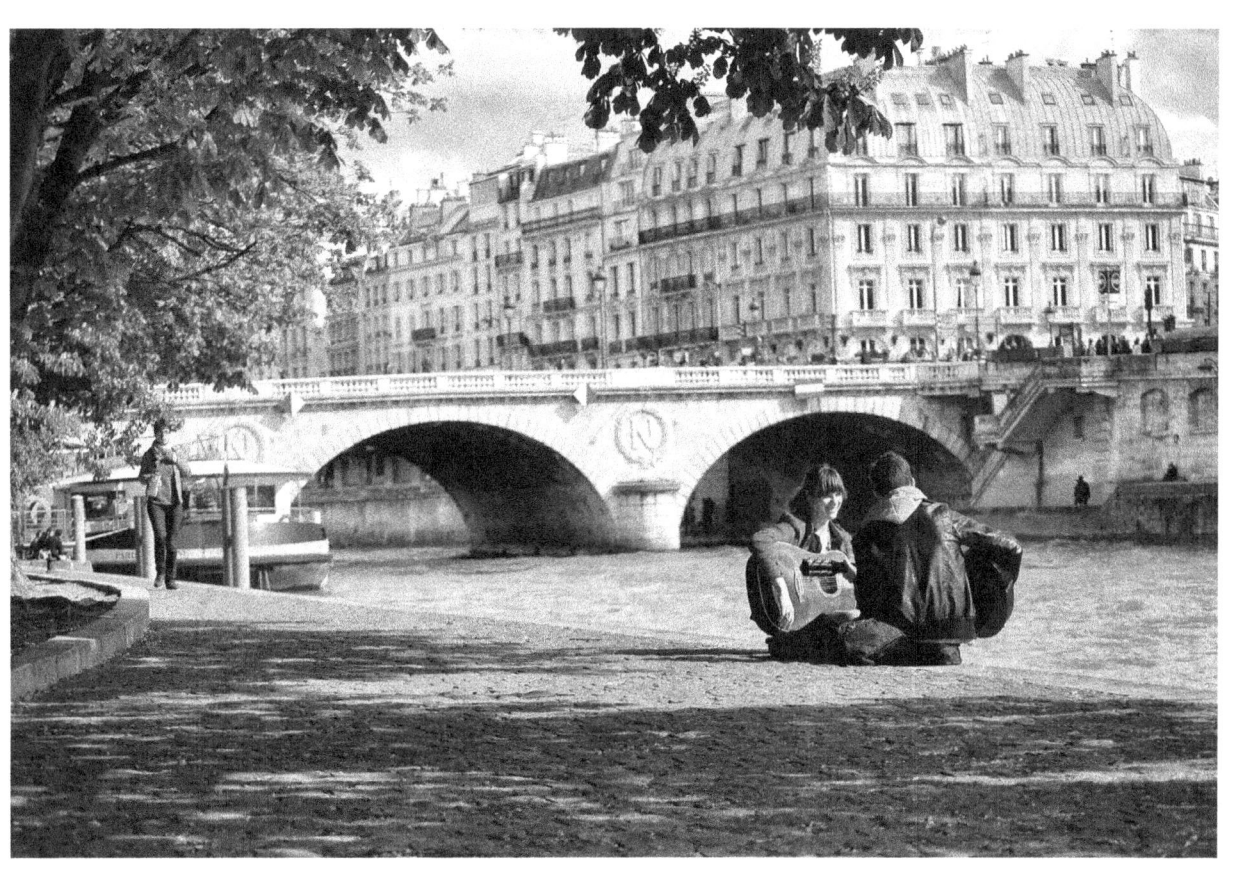

Love song on the banks of the Seine, 2012

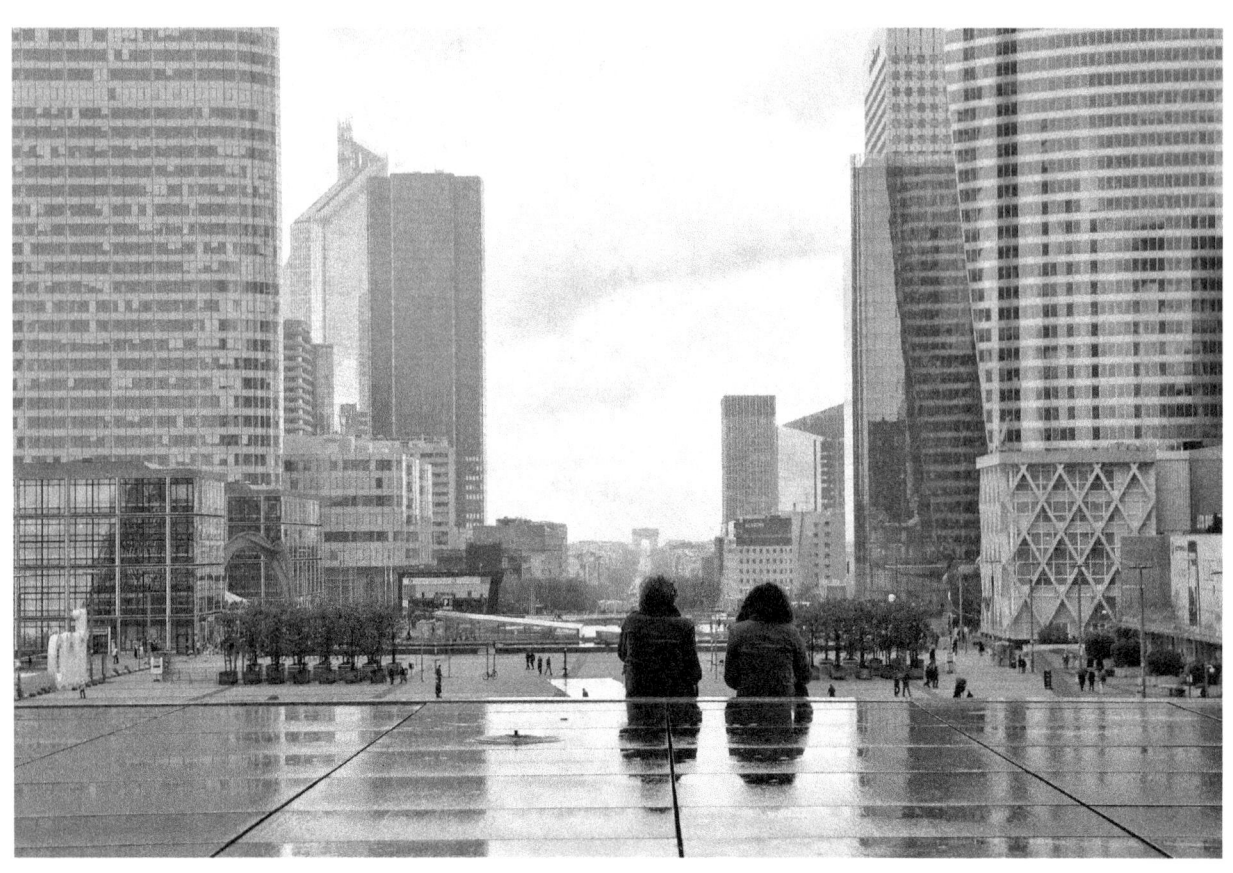

Rainy Défense, 2012

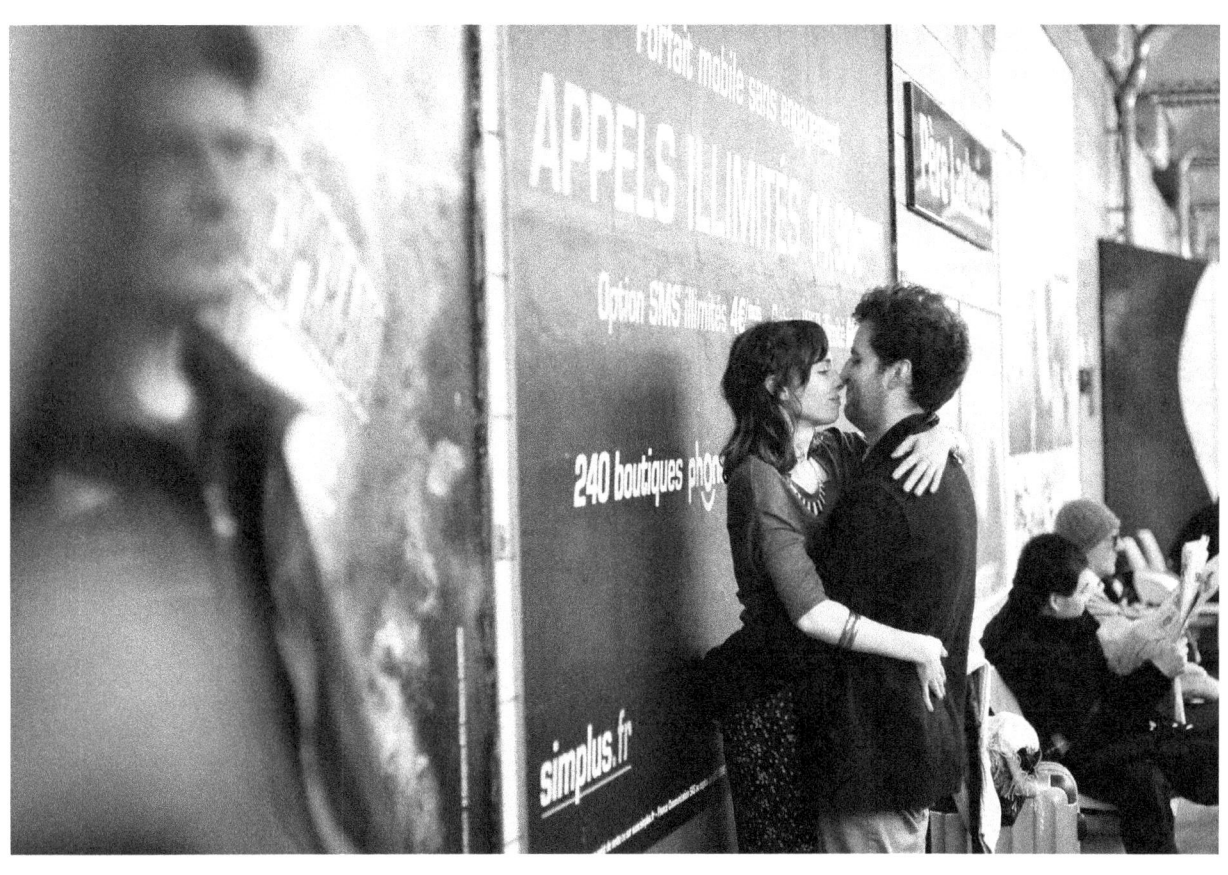

Lovers in the underground, 2012

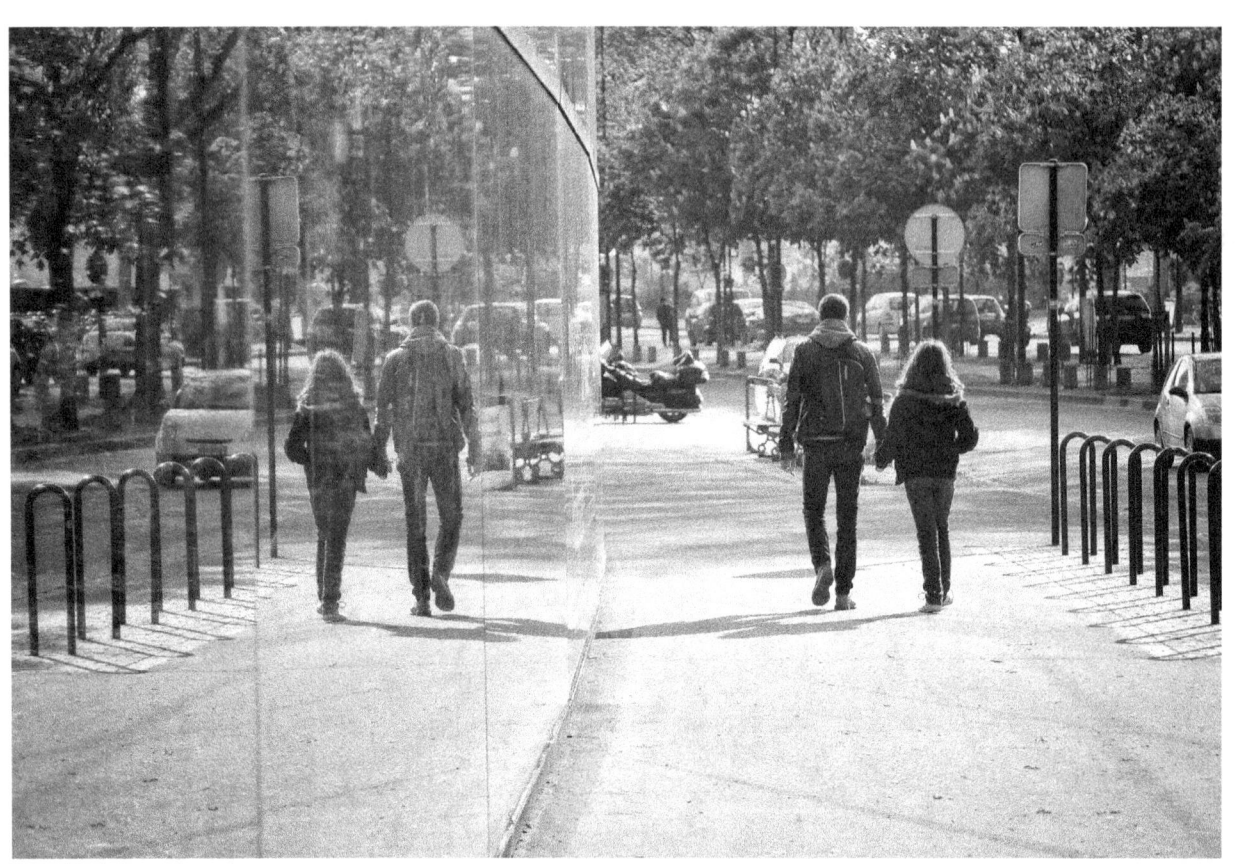

Reflection, 2012

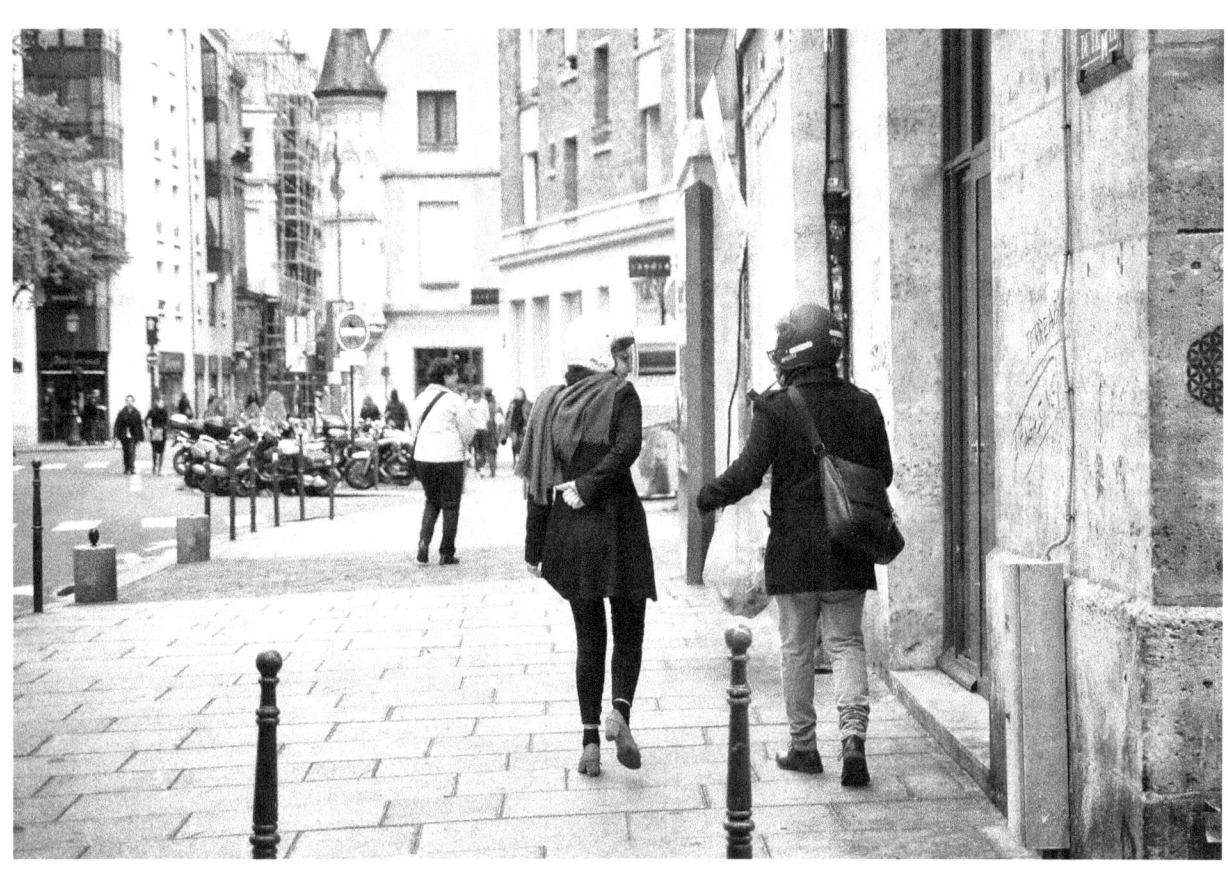

Head protection is useful, 2012

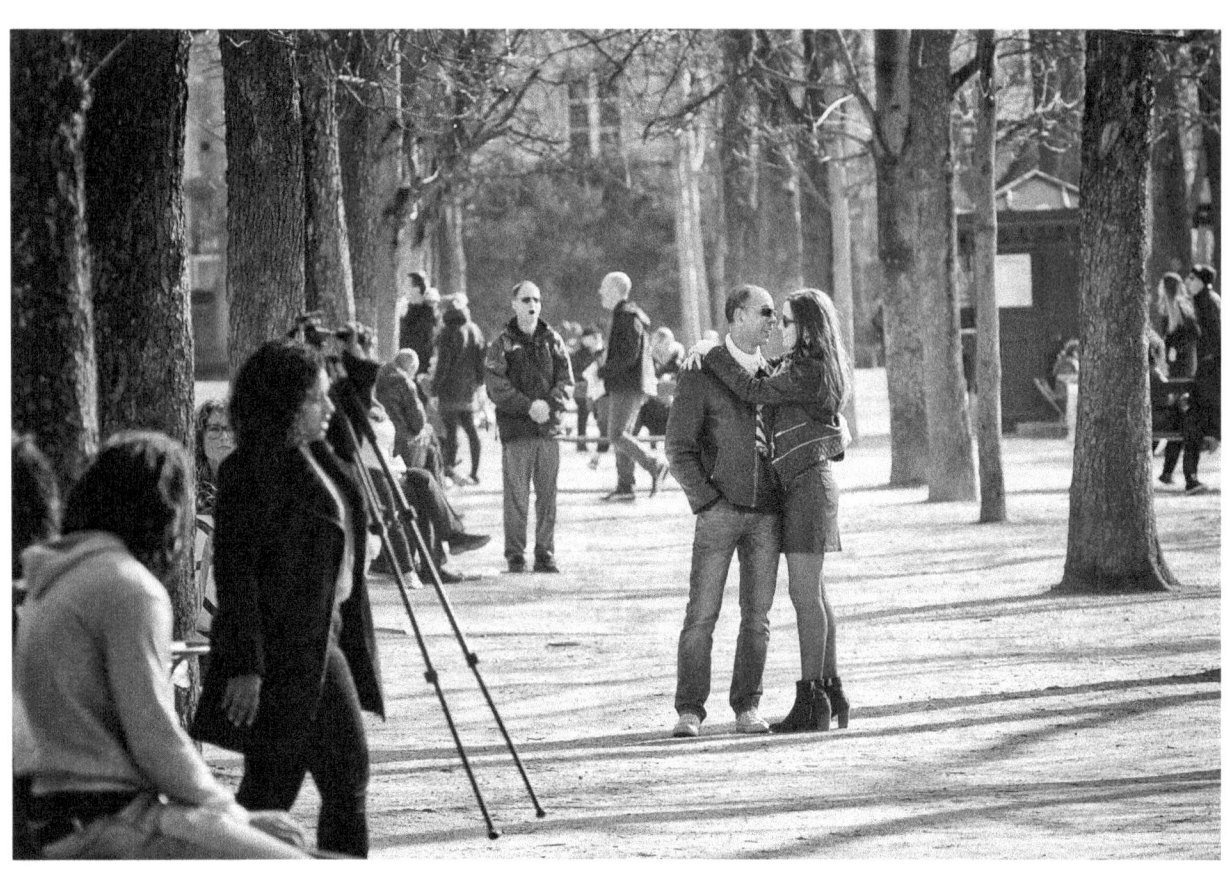

In the park, 2016

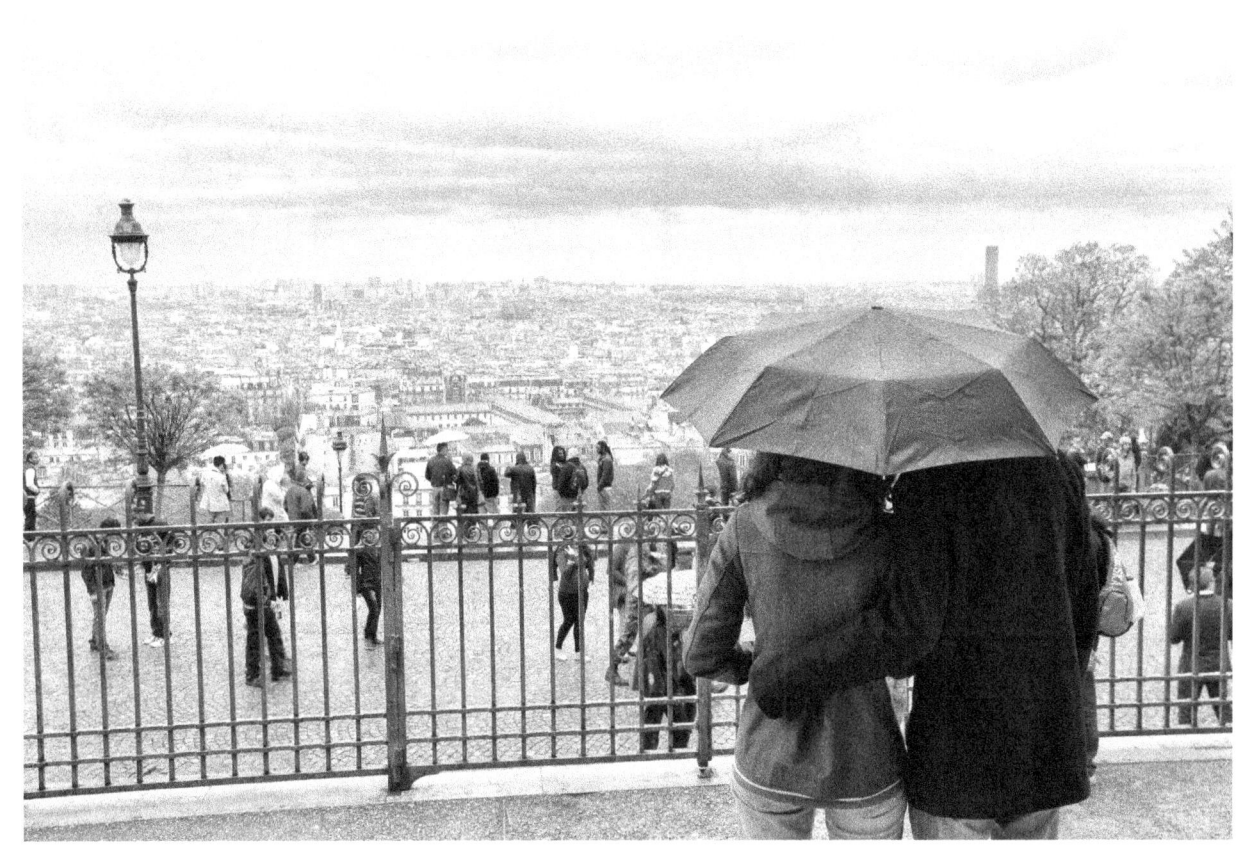

Under the umbrella, 2012

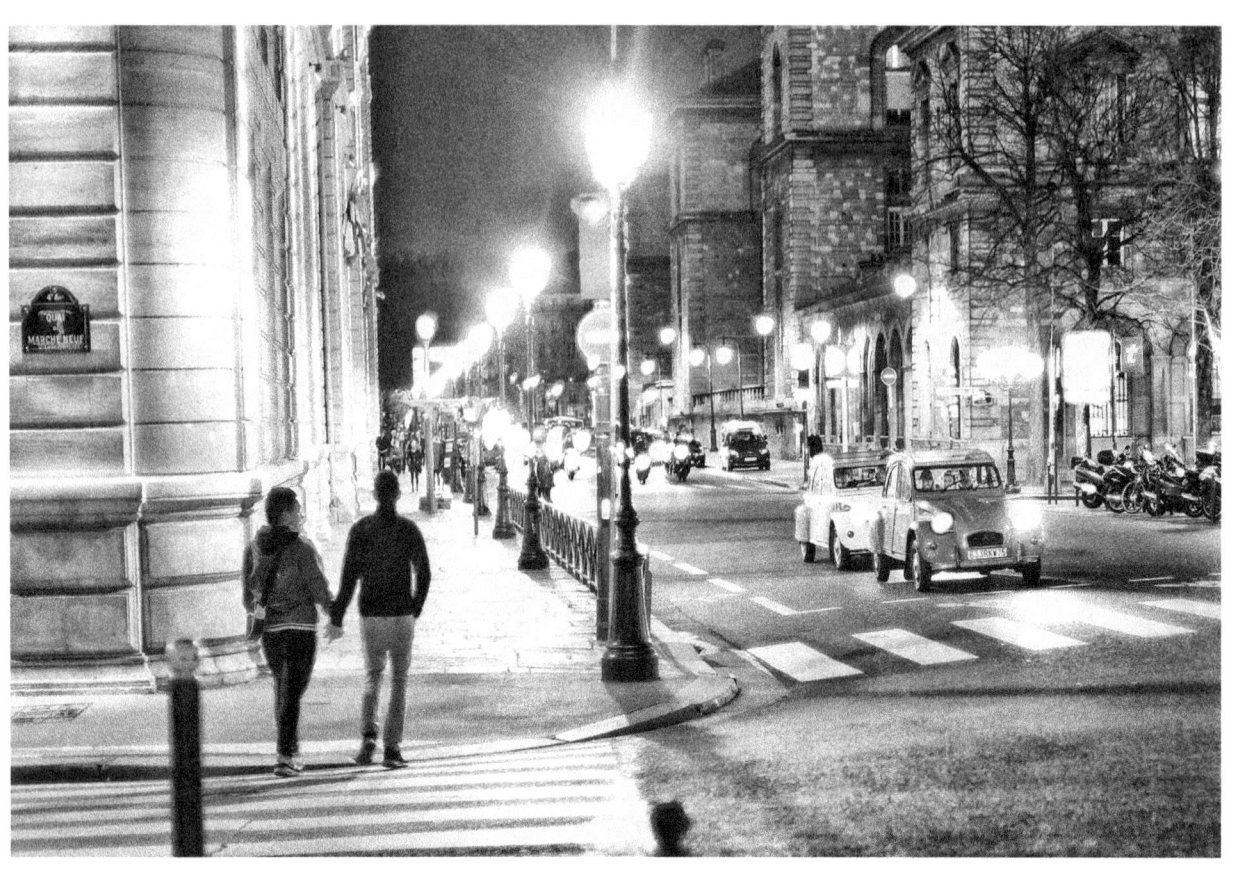

Two in the evening lights, 2016

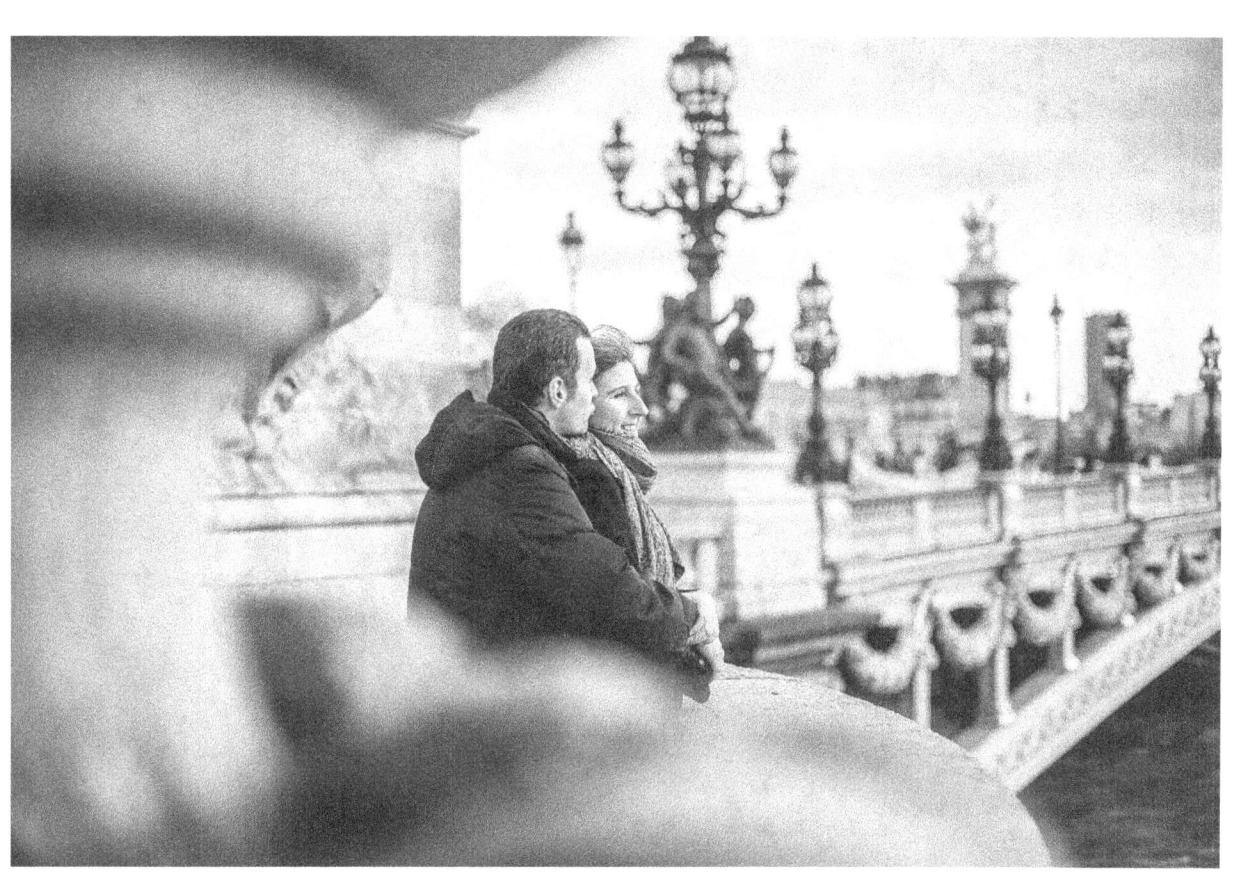

Lovers on the bridge of Alexander III, 2016

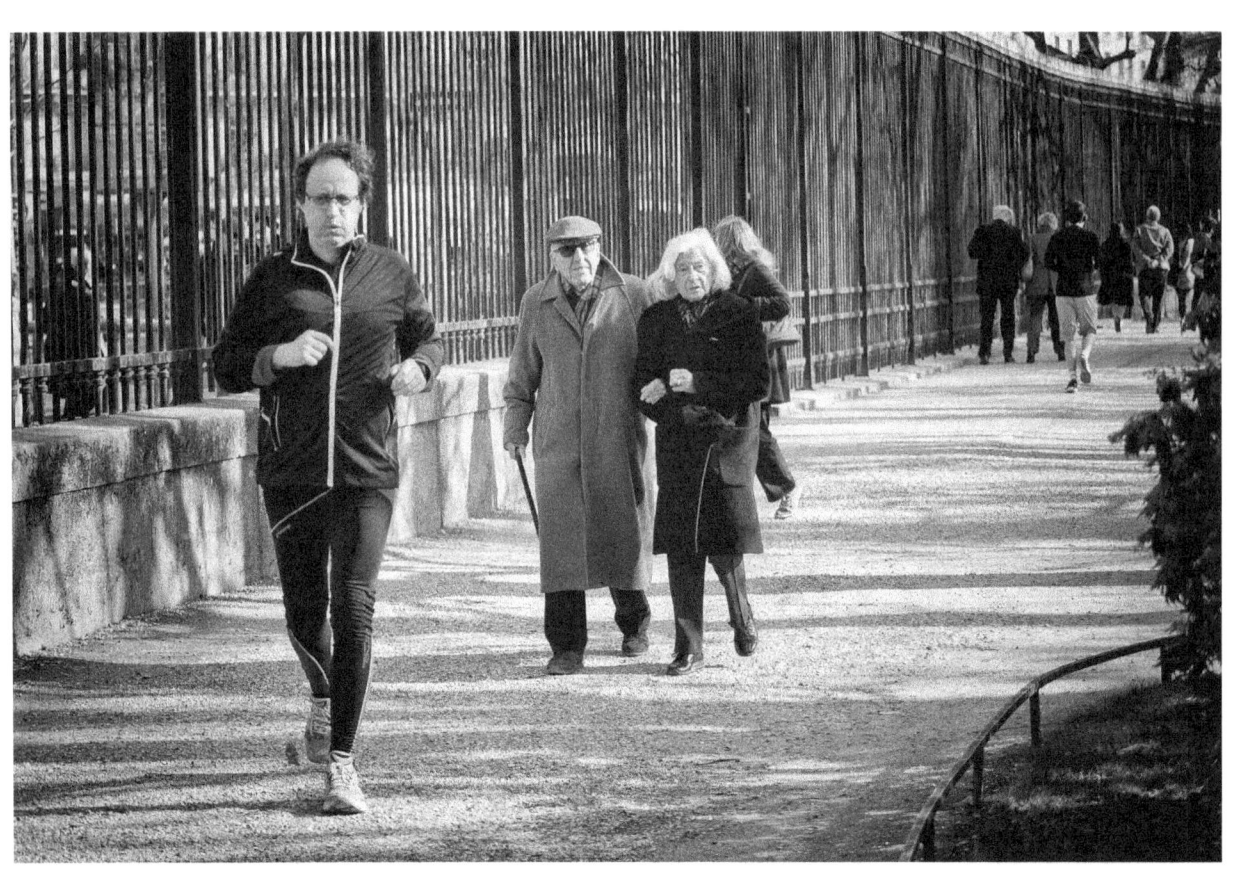

Love through the years, 2016

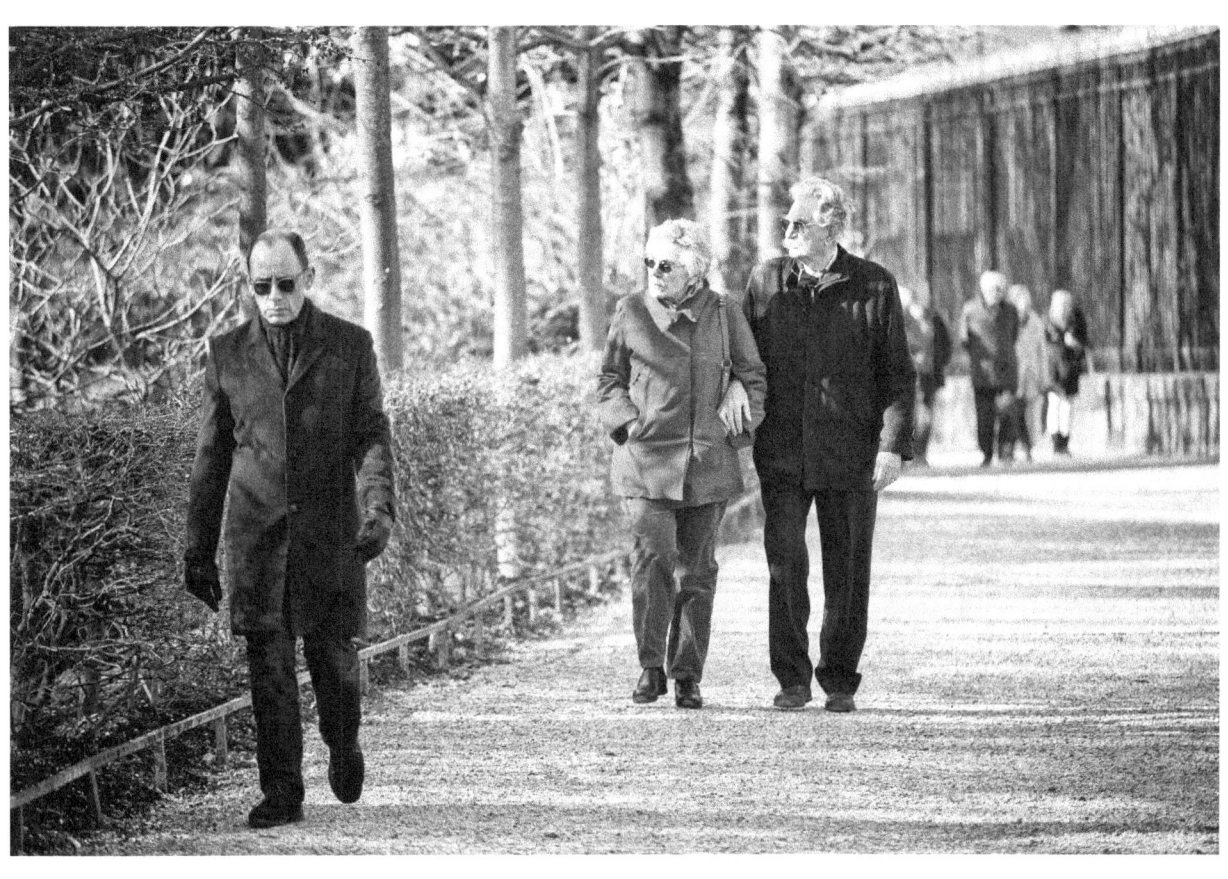

Look in one direction, 2016

ART AND PARIS

Paris had acquired a reputation as the "City of Art". For centuries, Paris has attracted artists, writers, poets from around the world, arriving in the city, to seek inspiration from its unique atmosphere. They lived in Paris and glorified Paris in their art works. Impressionism, Symbolism, Art Nouveau, Neo-Impressionism, Divisionism, Fauvism, Cubism, Art Deco and Abstract art movements evolved in Paris. Painters such as Vincent van Gogh, Paul Cézanne, Pierre-Auguste Renoir, Claude Monet, Édouard Manet, Edgar Degas, Henri de Toulouse-Lautrec, Pablo Picasso, Henri Matisse, Amedeo Modigliani, Salvador Dali and many others became associated with Paris. Many of them showed the life of Paris of their time on their canvases.

Paris is a home of many museums now, both large and known as the Louvre and Orsay, as well as small or dedicated to the work of individual artists as Picasso Museum or Museum of Romantics.

You will find a lot of street artists ready to create your portrait in different genres or to sell their ready artworks, on the streets of Paris.

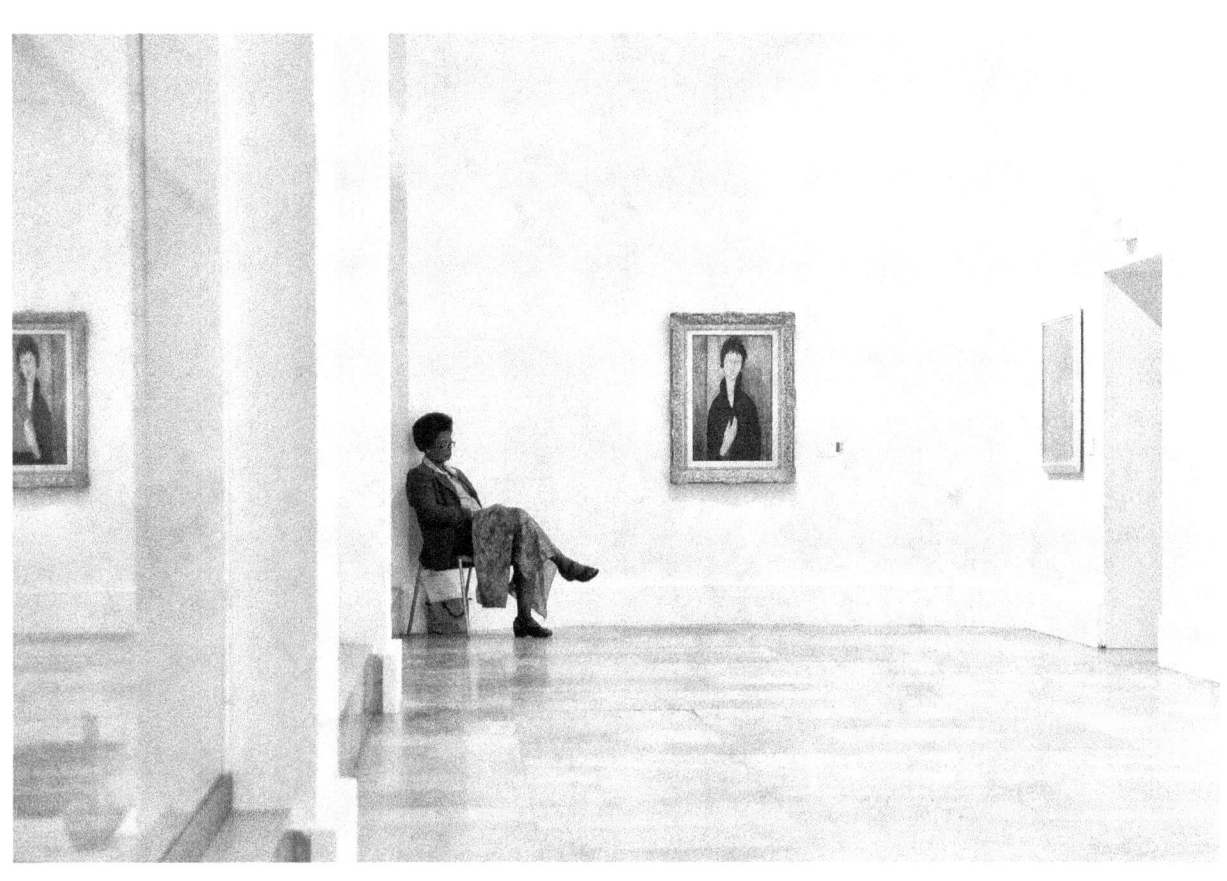

Guard of Modigliani, 2012

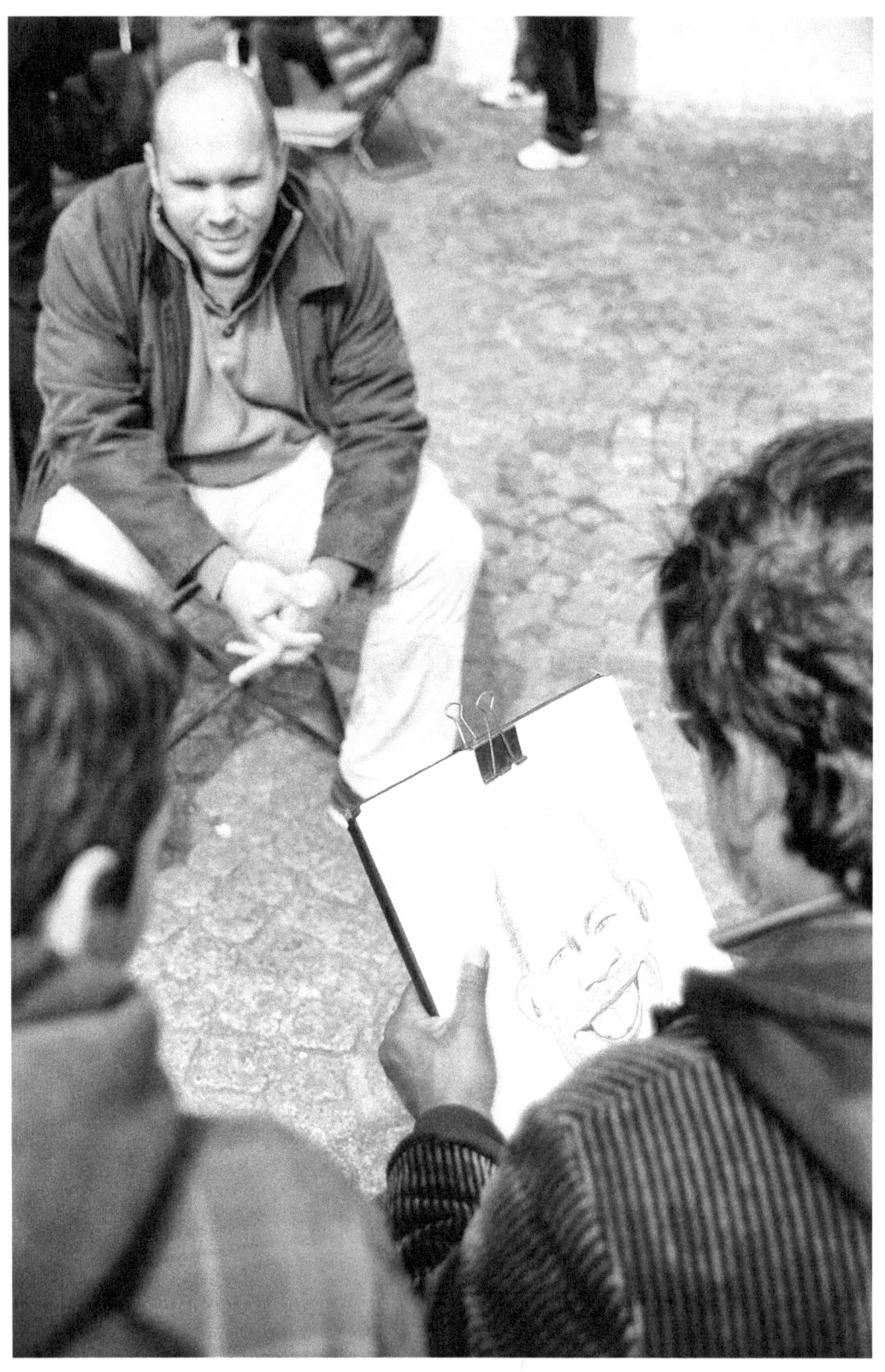

Smile, 2012

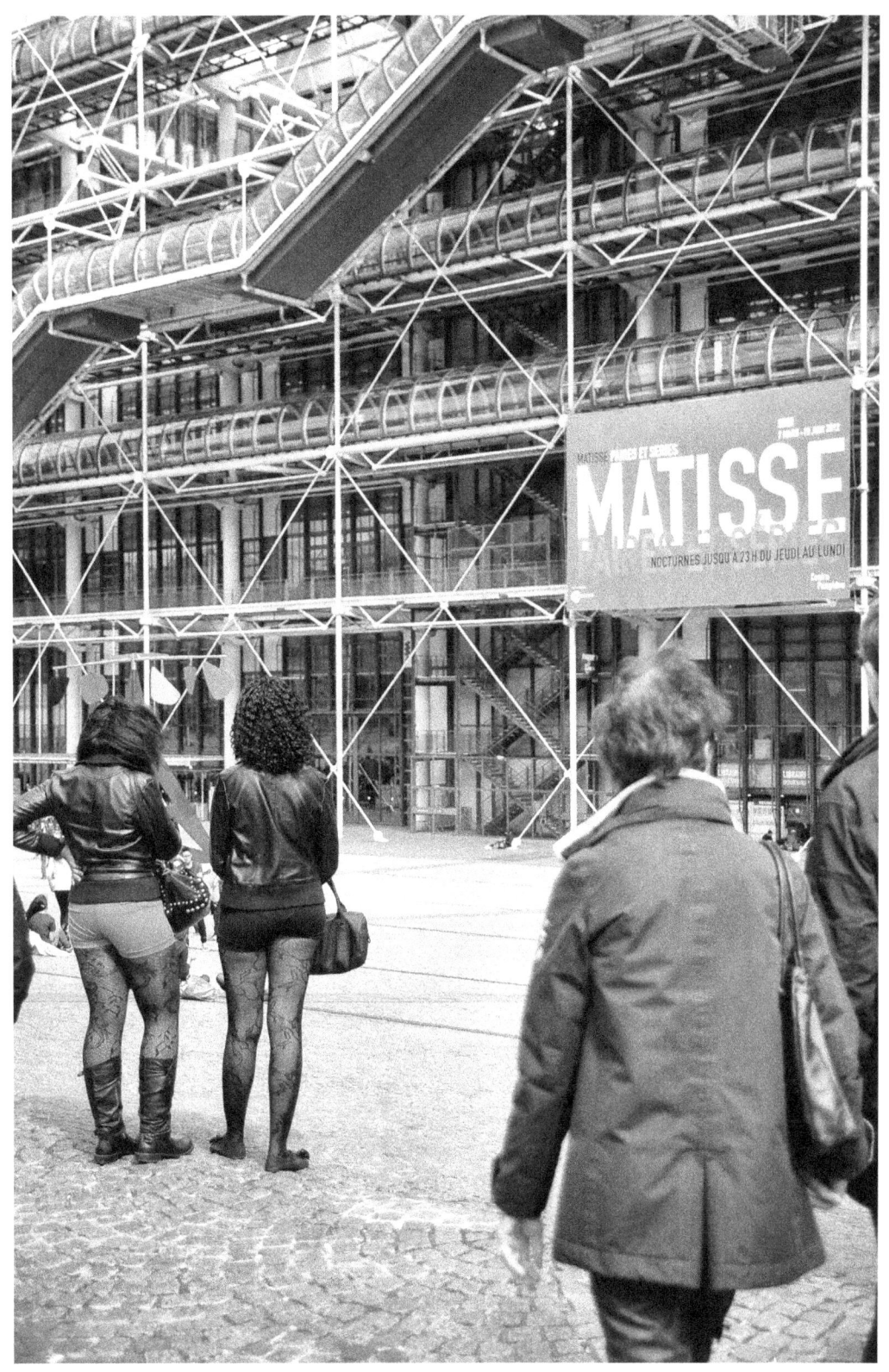

Matisse and modernity, 2012

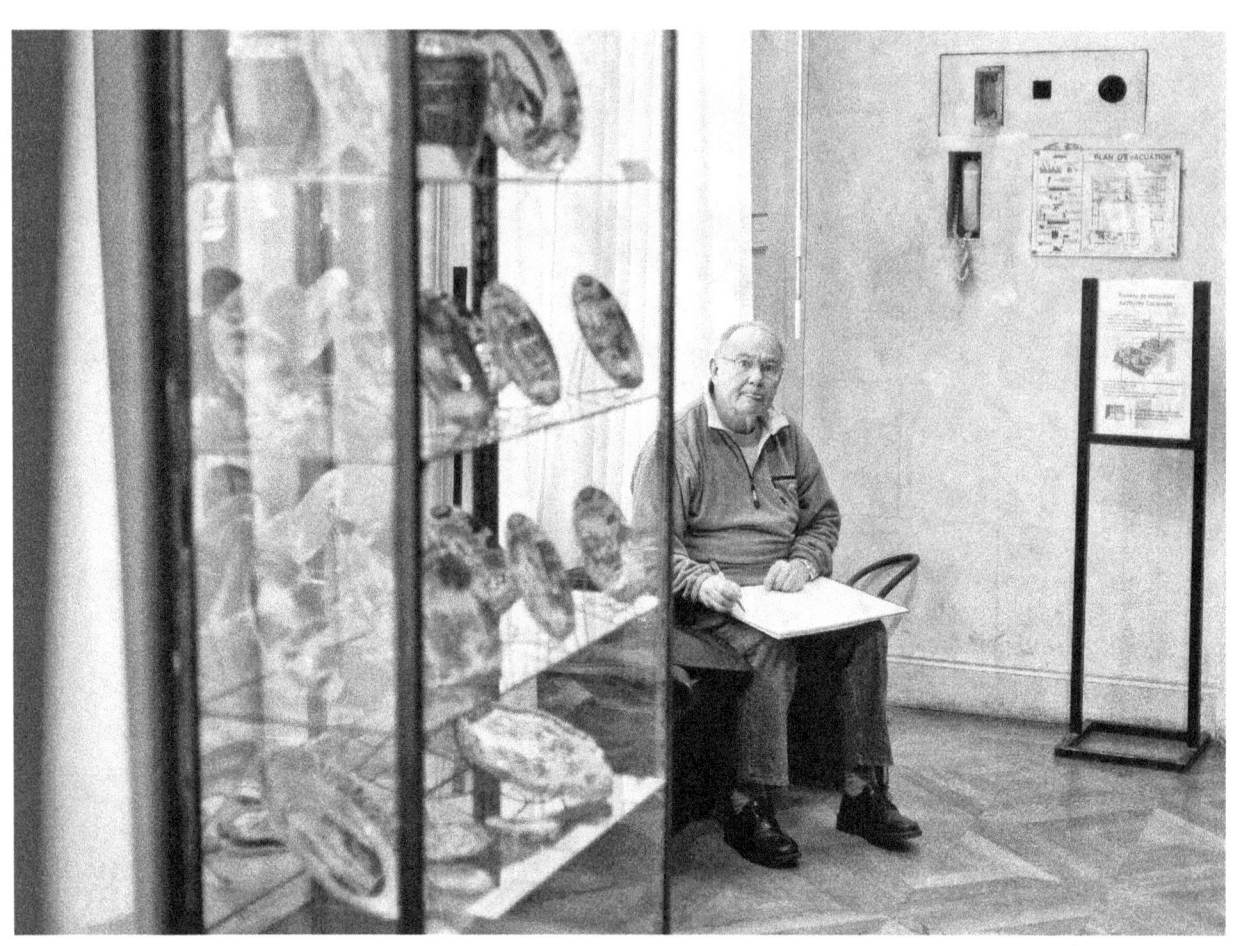

Fascinated by the process, 2016

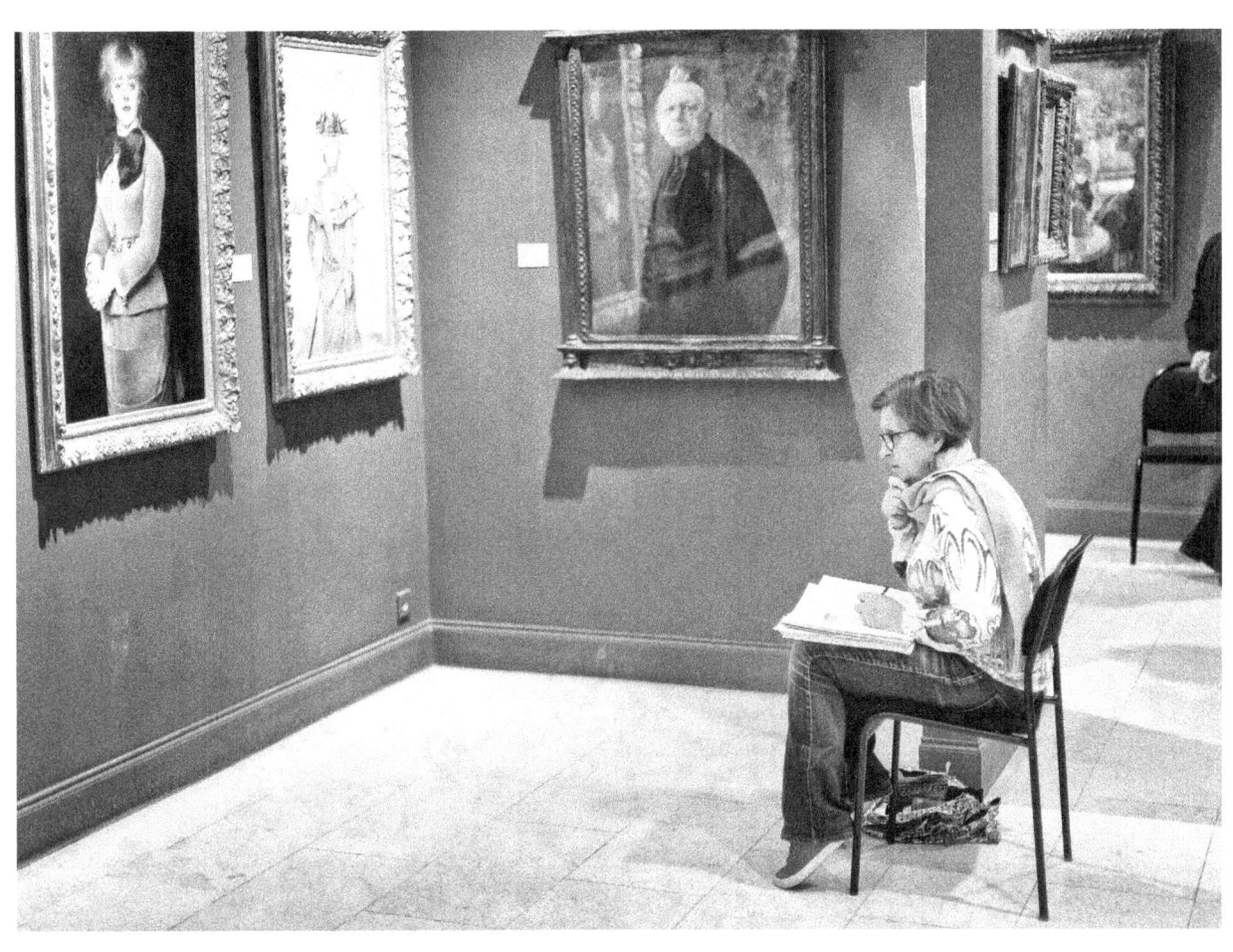

Inheriting the classics, 2016

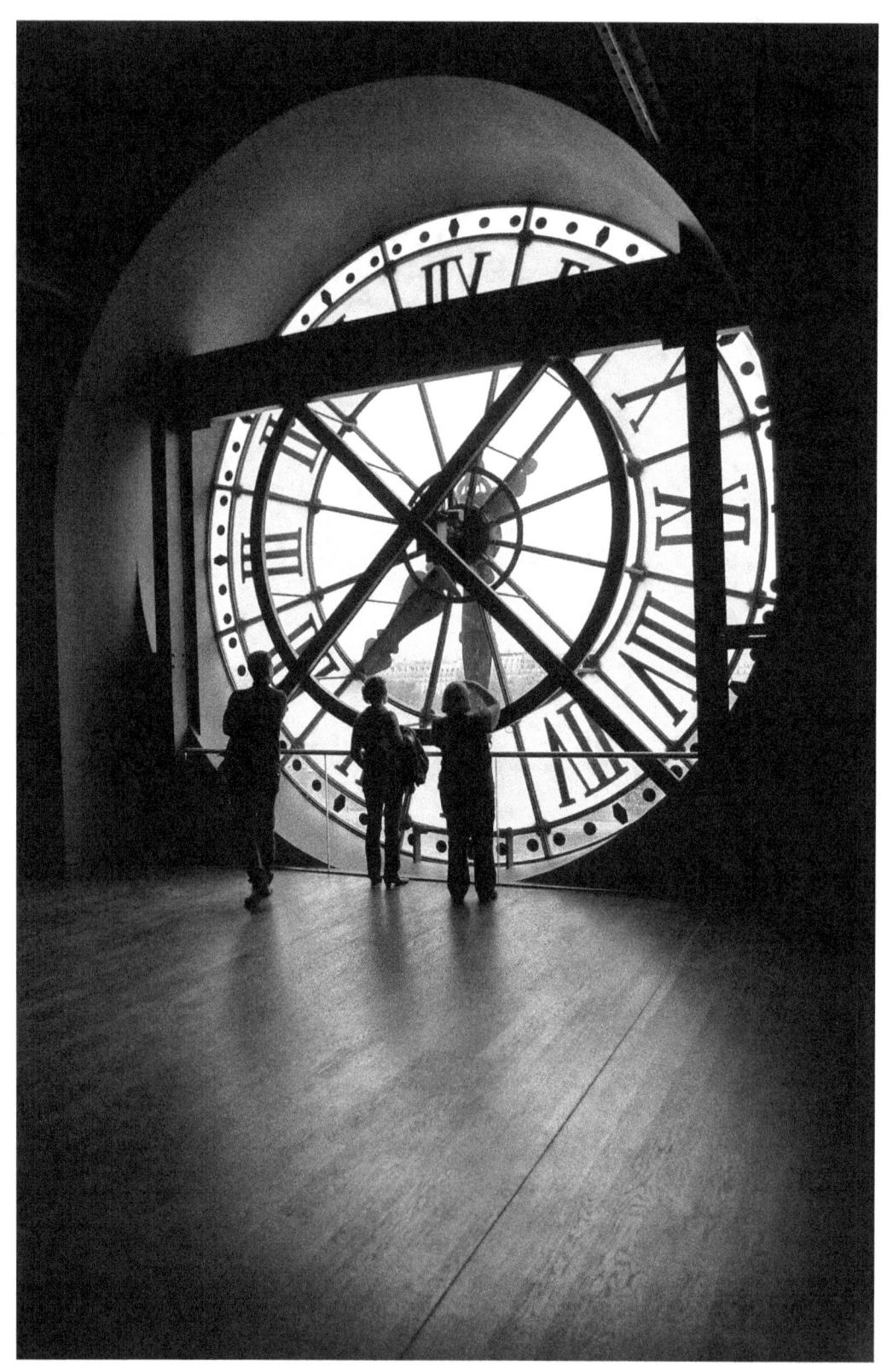

Time has stopped in Orsay, 2012

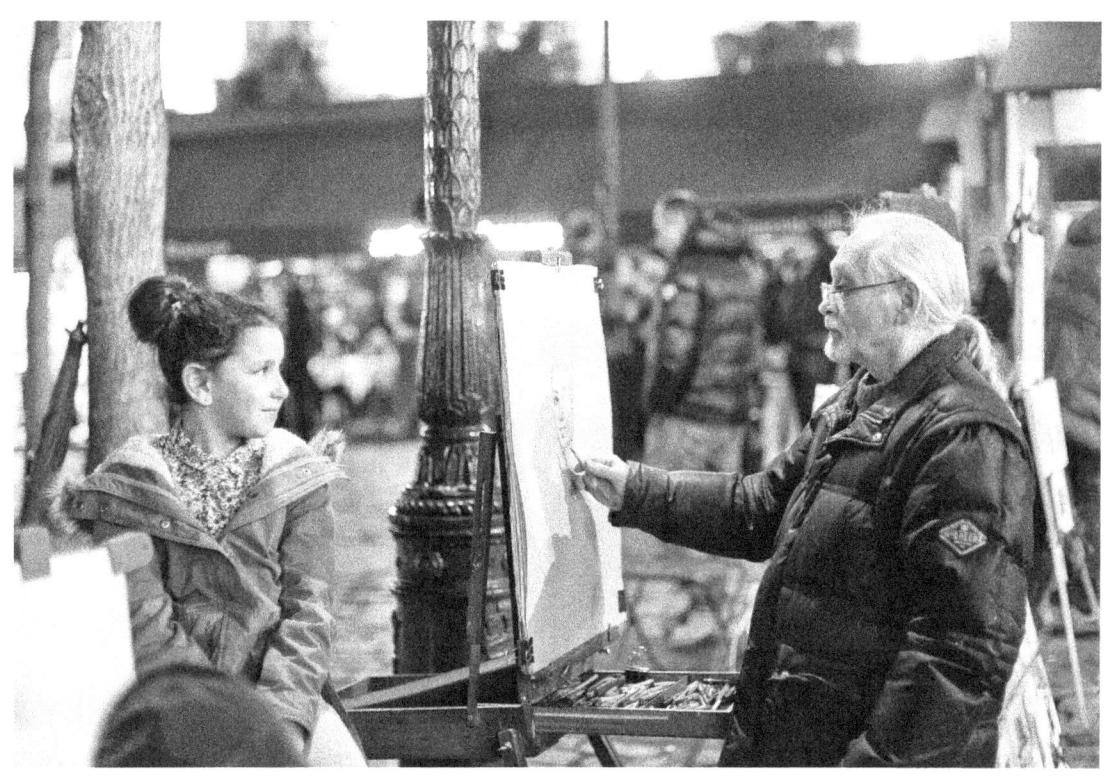

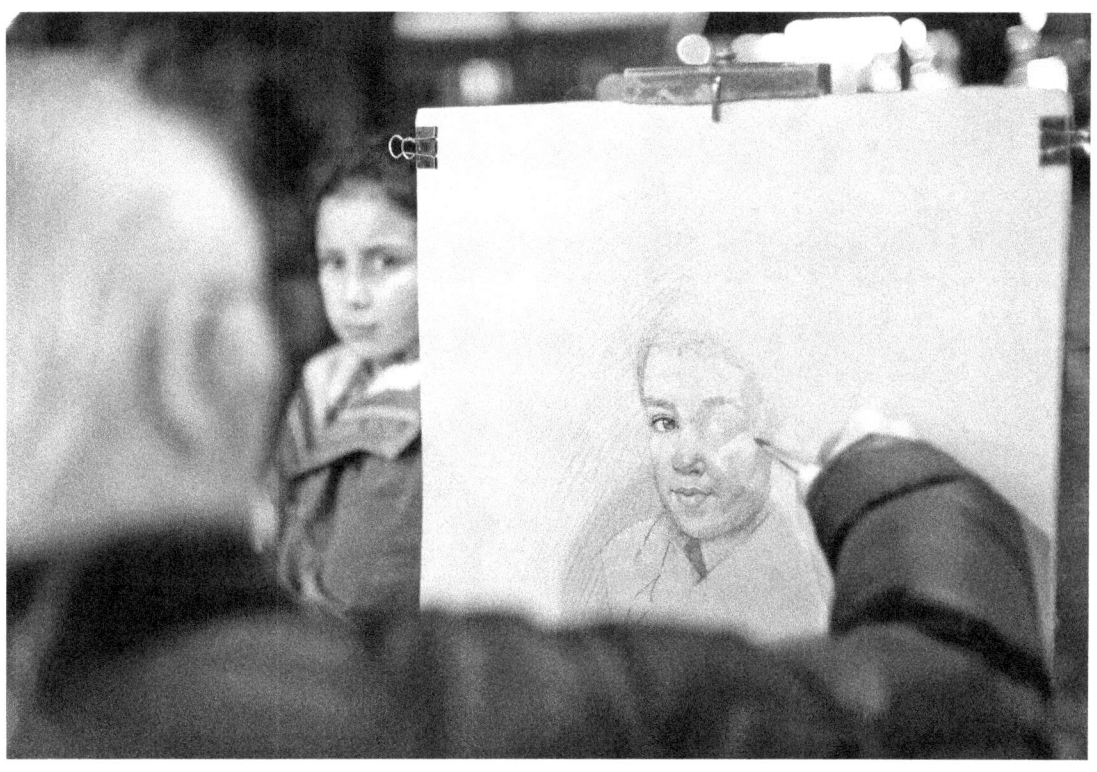

Portrait in memory of Montmartre, 2016

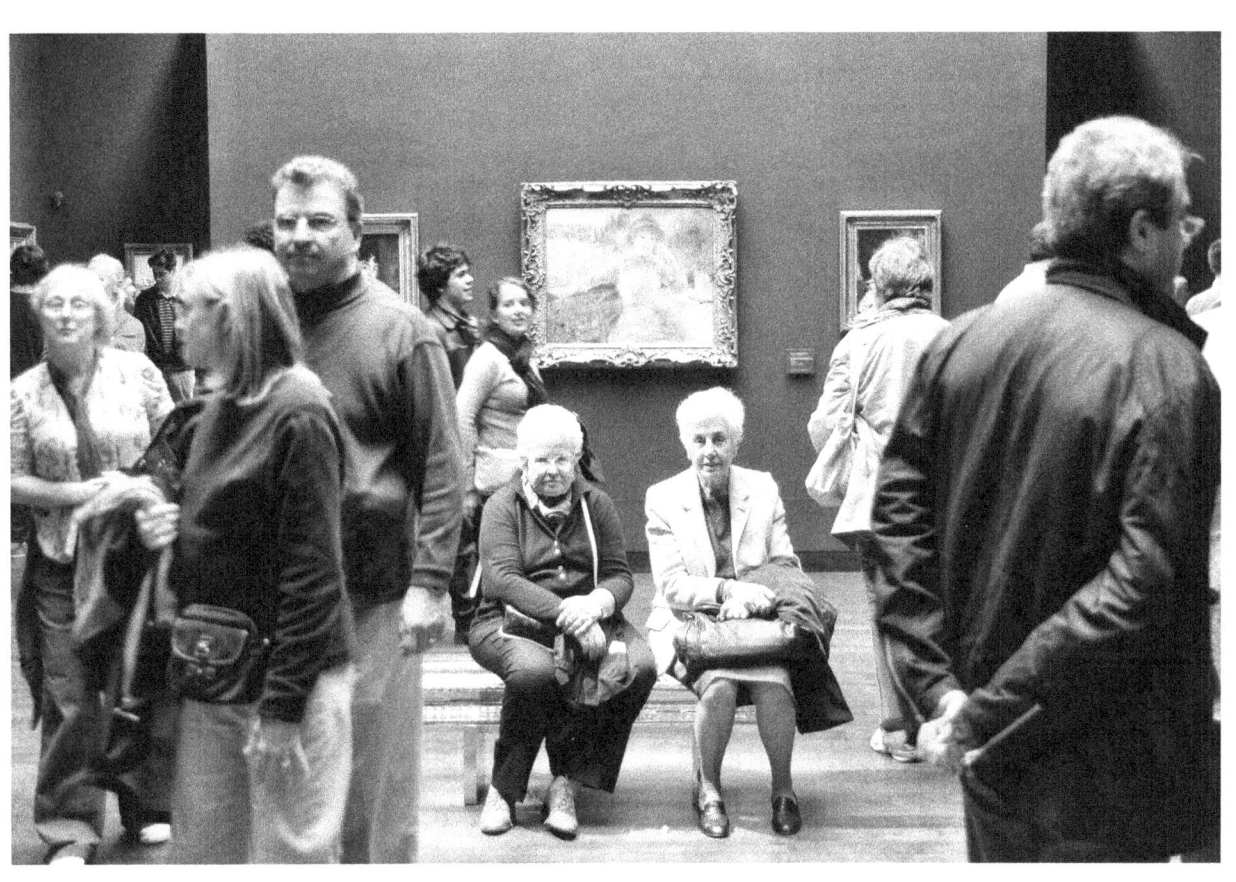

Three ladies, 2012

READERS

Famous novelists, poets, and playwrights from France and all over the world were living and working in Paris: Moliere, Voltaire, Honoré de Balzac, Jean-Jacques Rousseau, Victor Hugo, Émile Zola, Marcel Proust, Alexandre Dumas, Stendhal, George Sand, Gustave Flaubert, Jules Verne, Guy de Maupassant, Charles Baudelaire, Paul Verlaine, Arthur Rimbaud, Oscar Wilde, Ernest Hemingway, James Joyce, Erich Maria Remarque, F. Scott Fitzgerald, Milan Kundera, Jean-Paul Sartre, Simone de Beauvoir, Ezra Pound, Albert Camus... From the pages of their works we read about Paris, and now we can visit a lot of places where they spent time themselves or heroes of their works.

It's no wonder that Parisians like reading and doing it everywhere: on the streets, in transport, in libraries, in parks and gardens, in cafes and bistros...

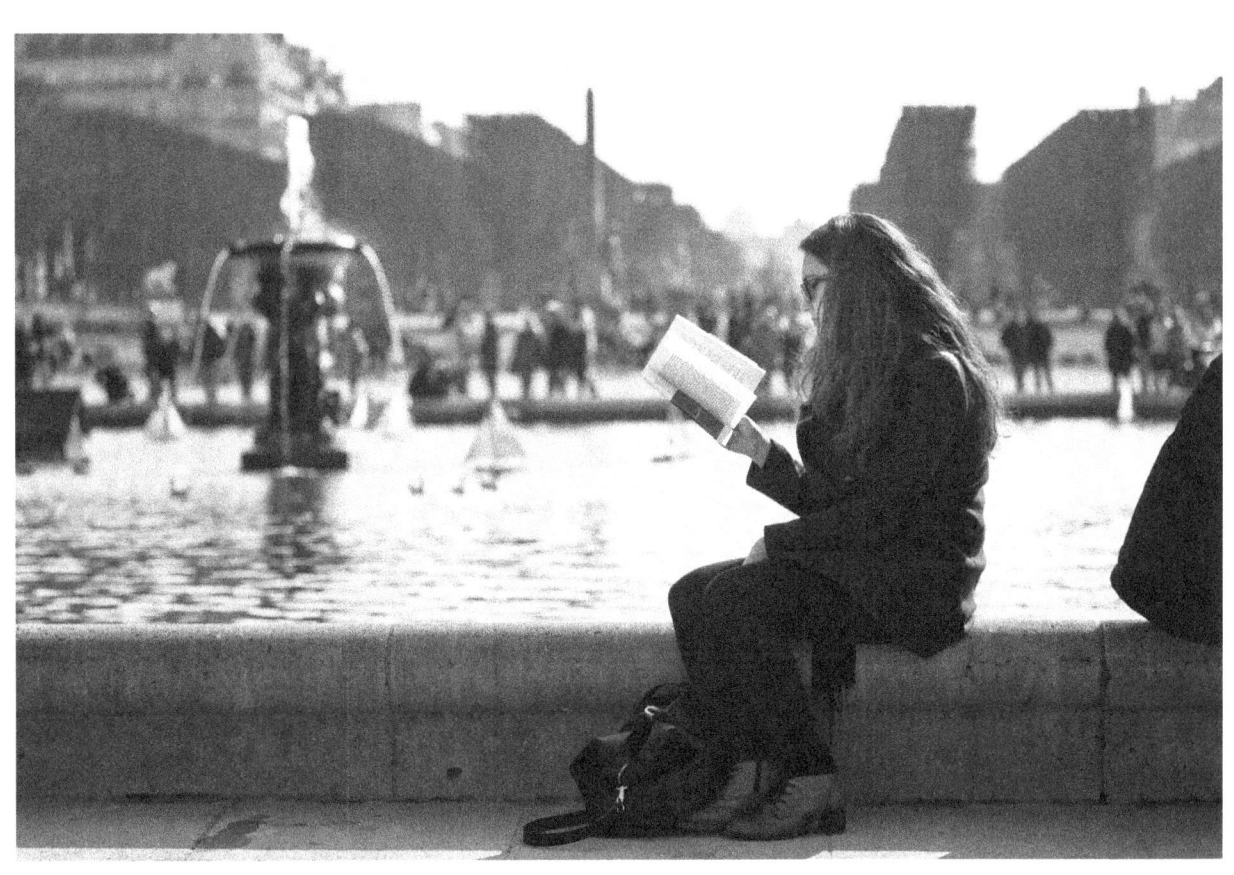

A girl reading in the rays of the spring sun, 2016

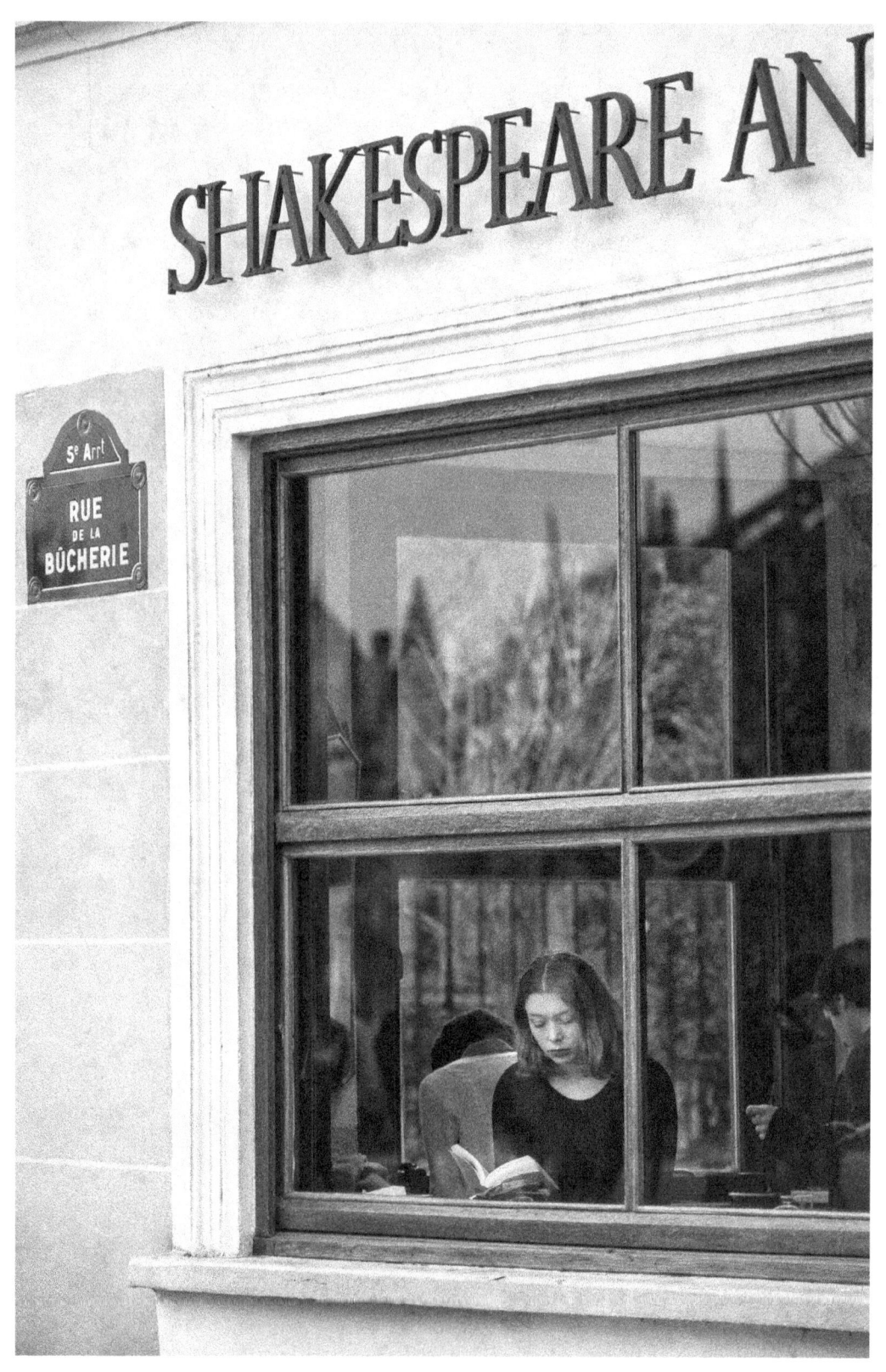

The spirit of Shakespeare, 2016

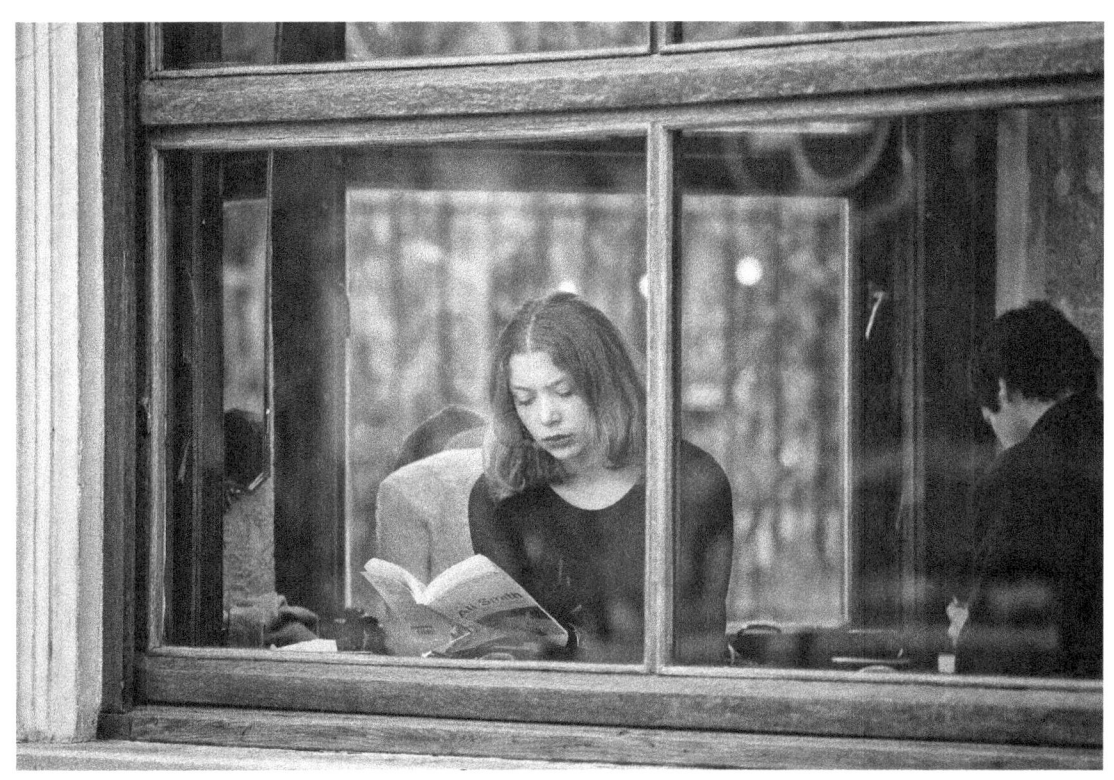

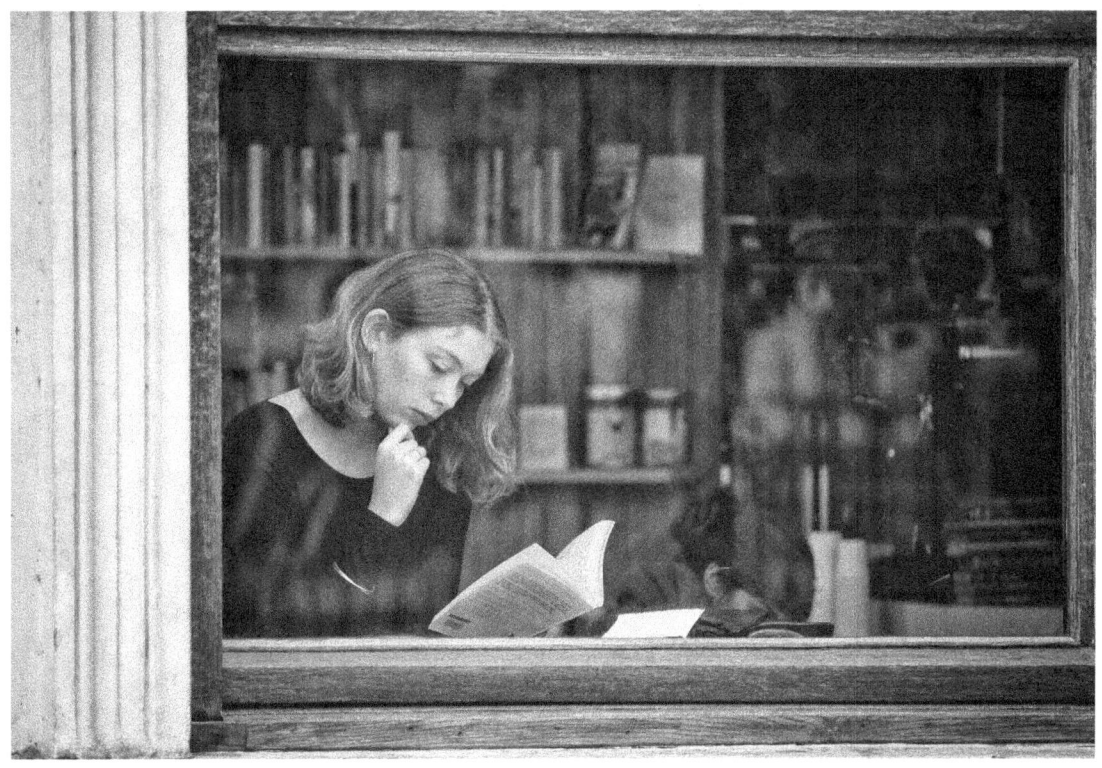

Very interesting book, 2016

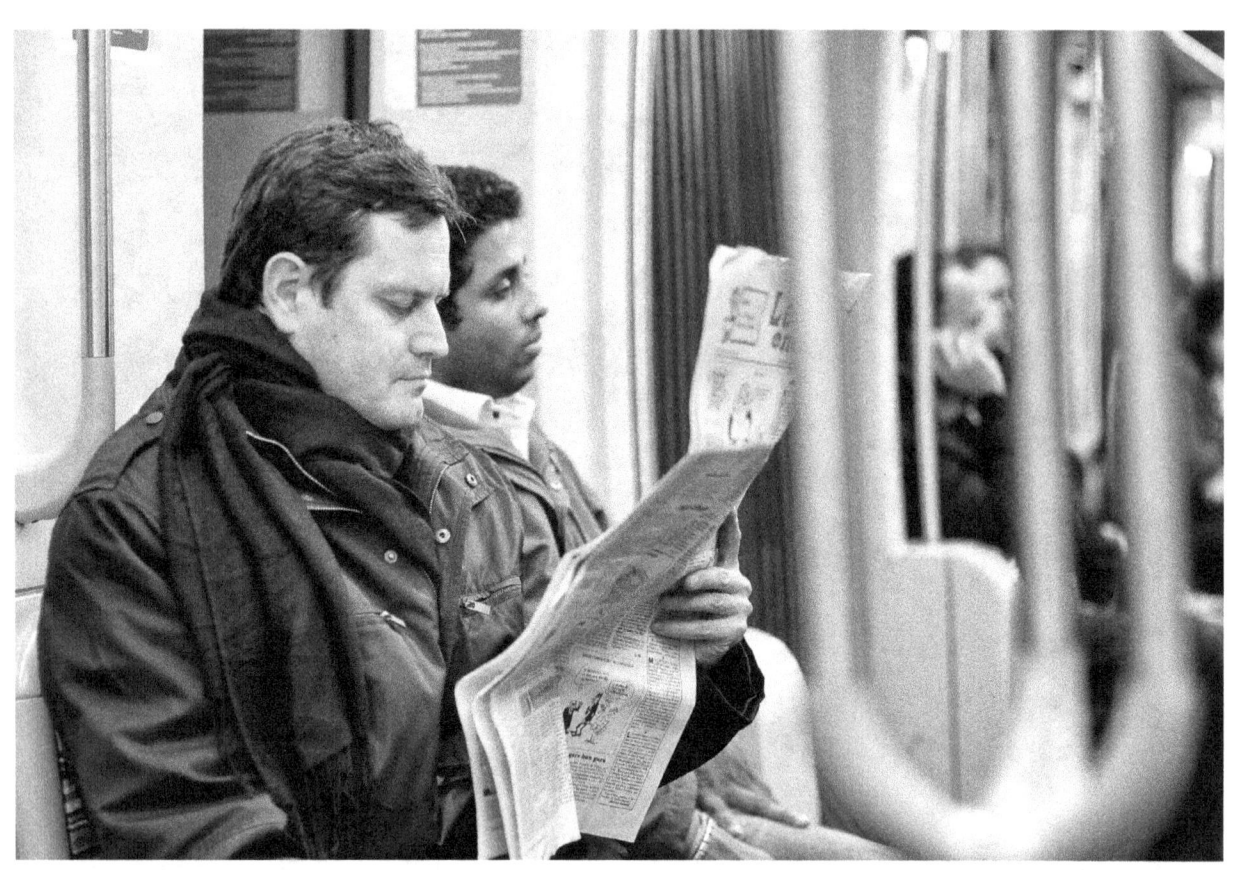

On the way home, 2012

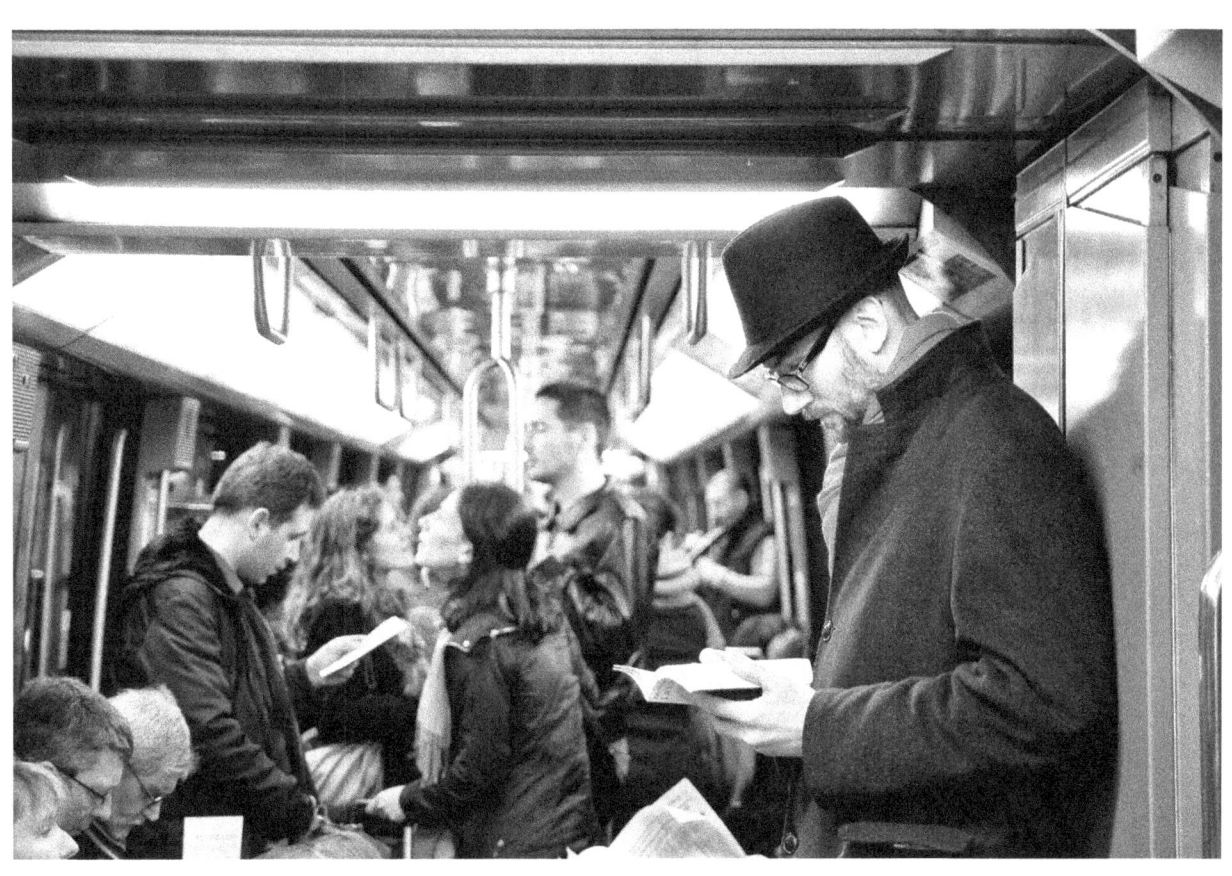

Exciting plot, 2012

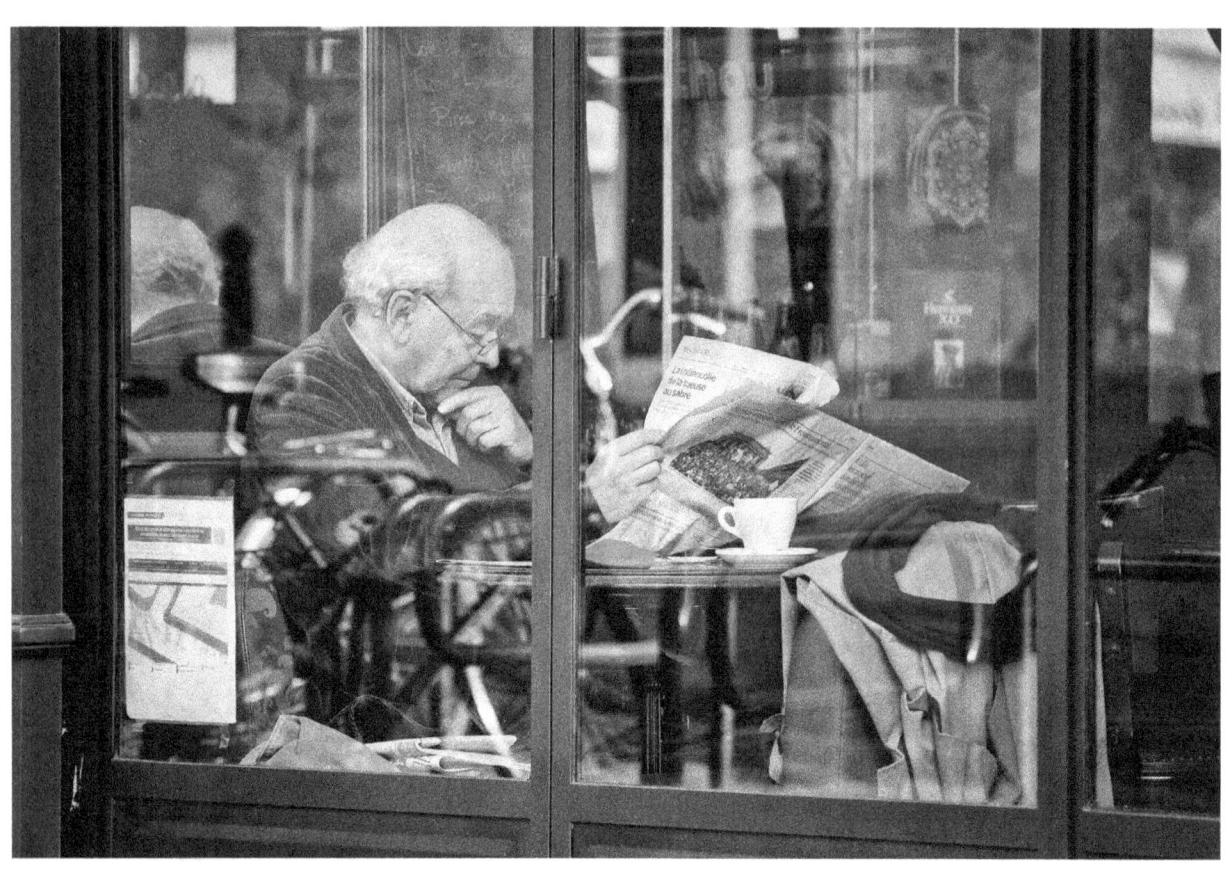

In the cafe, 2016

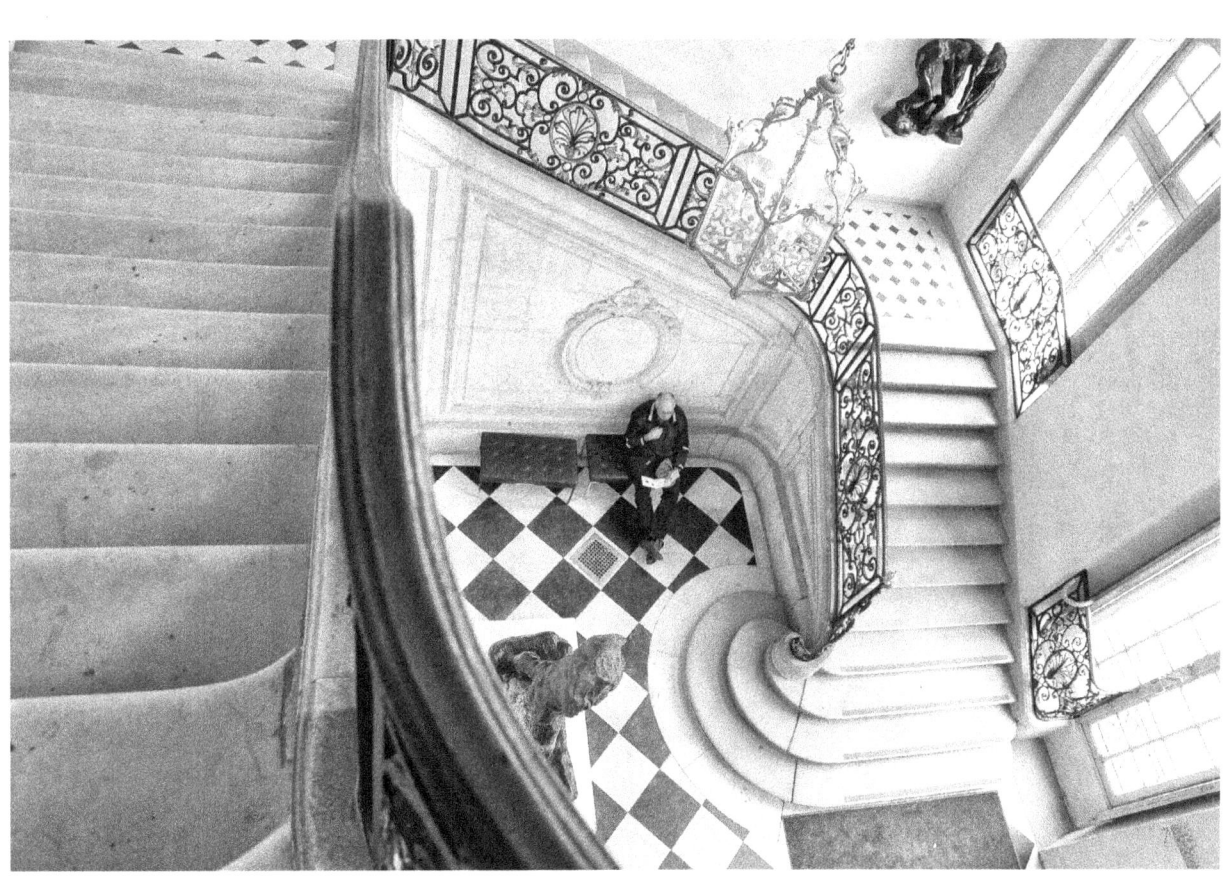

In the Rodin museum, 2012

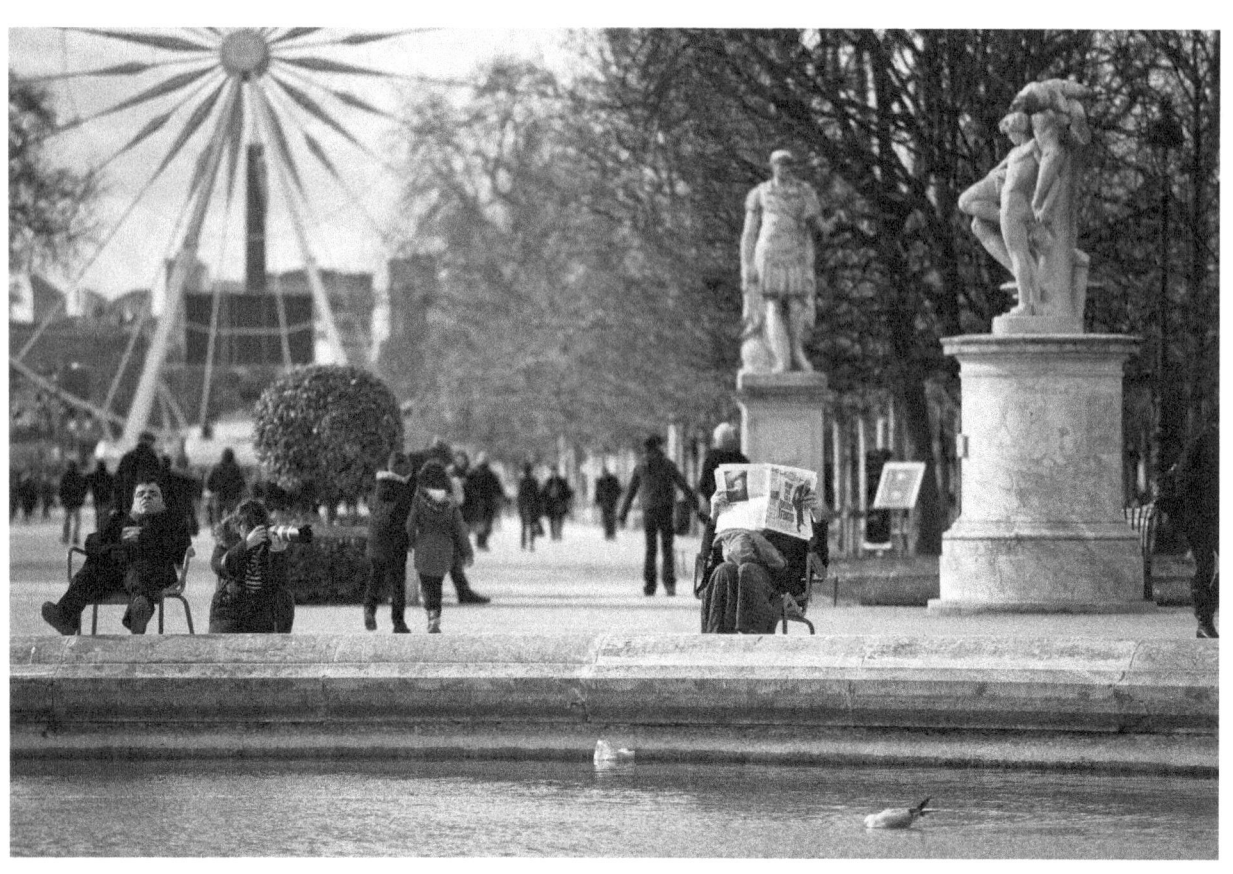

I don't see you!, 2016

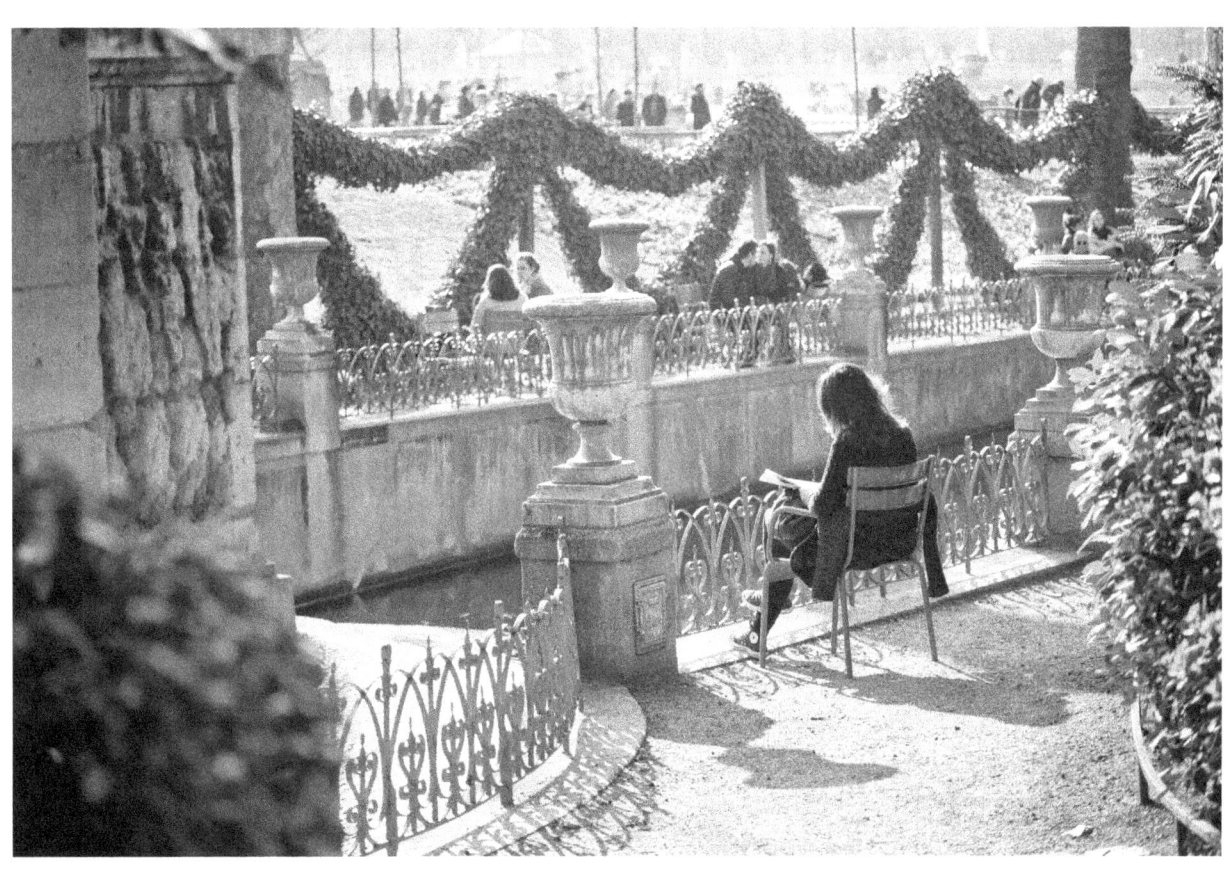

Nice place to read, 2016

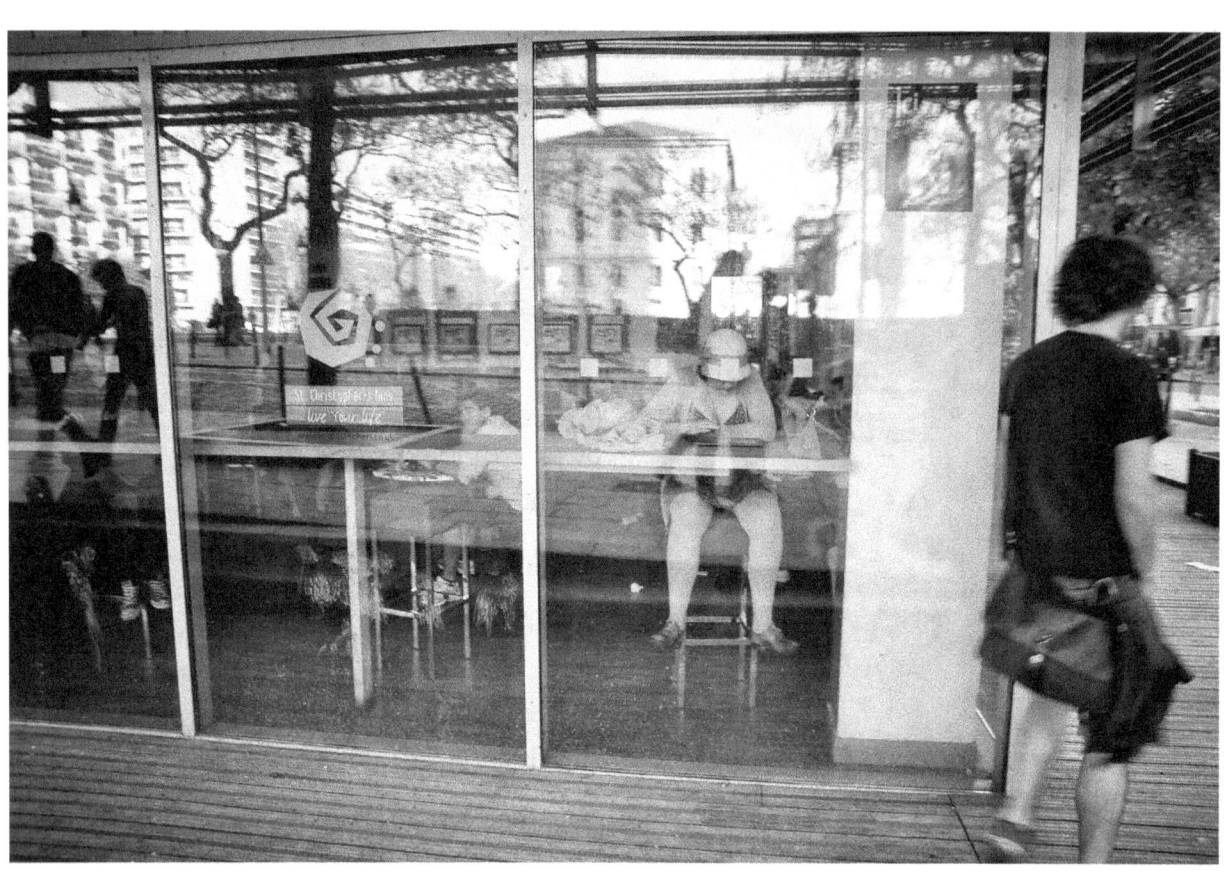

Nothing else matters, 2012

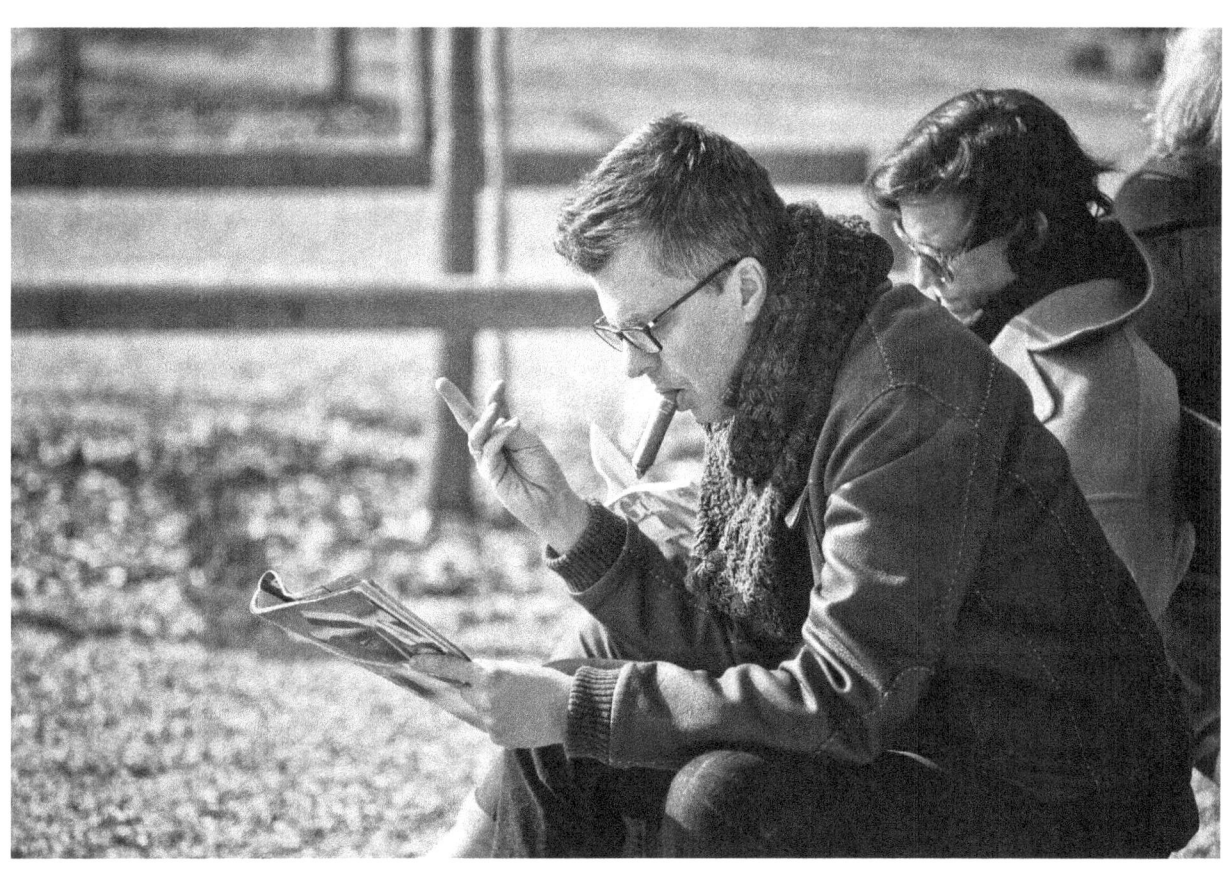

Time to relax, 2016

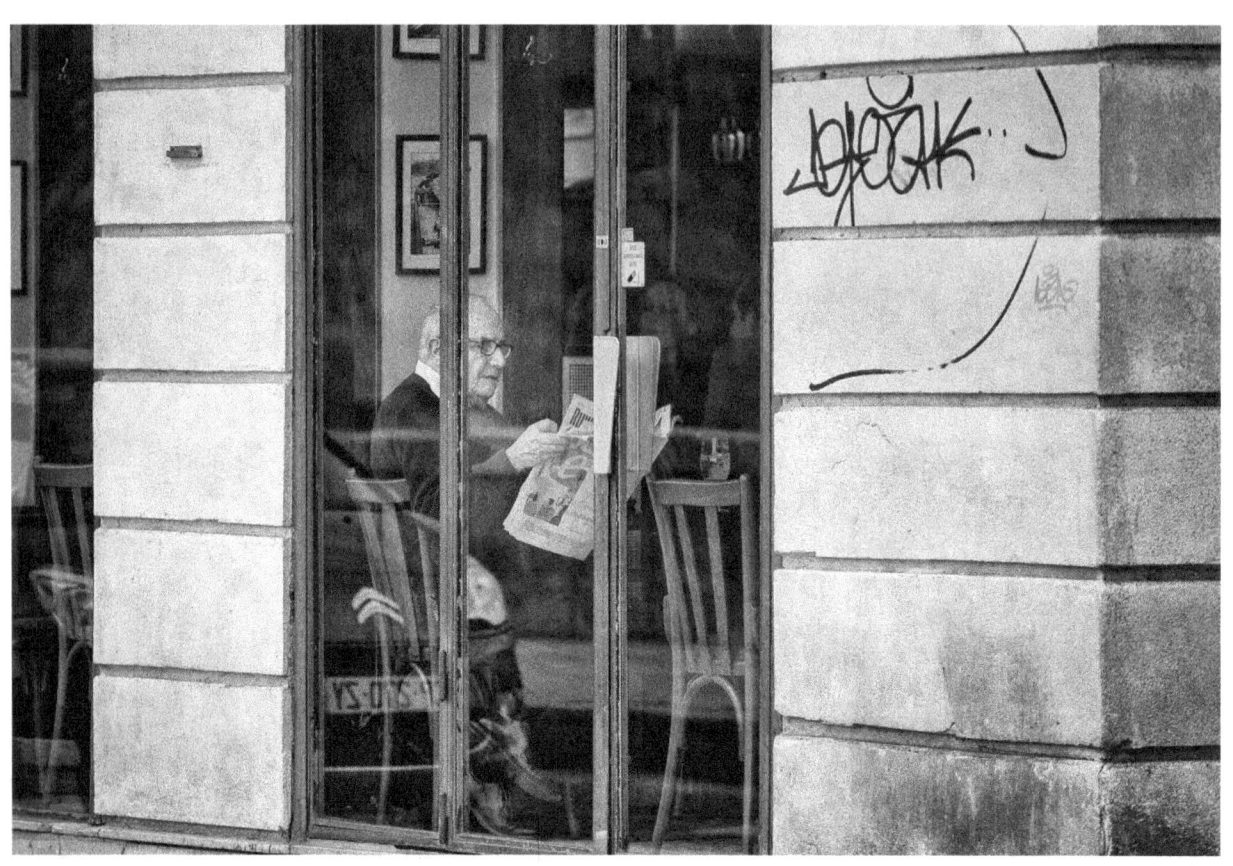

Tradition, 2016

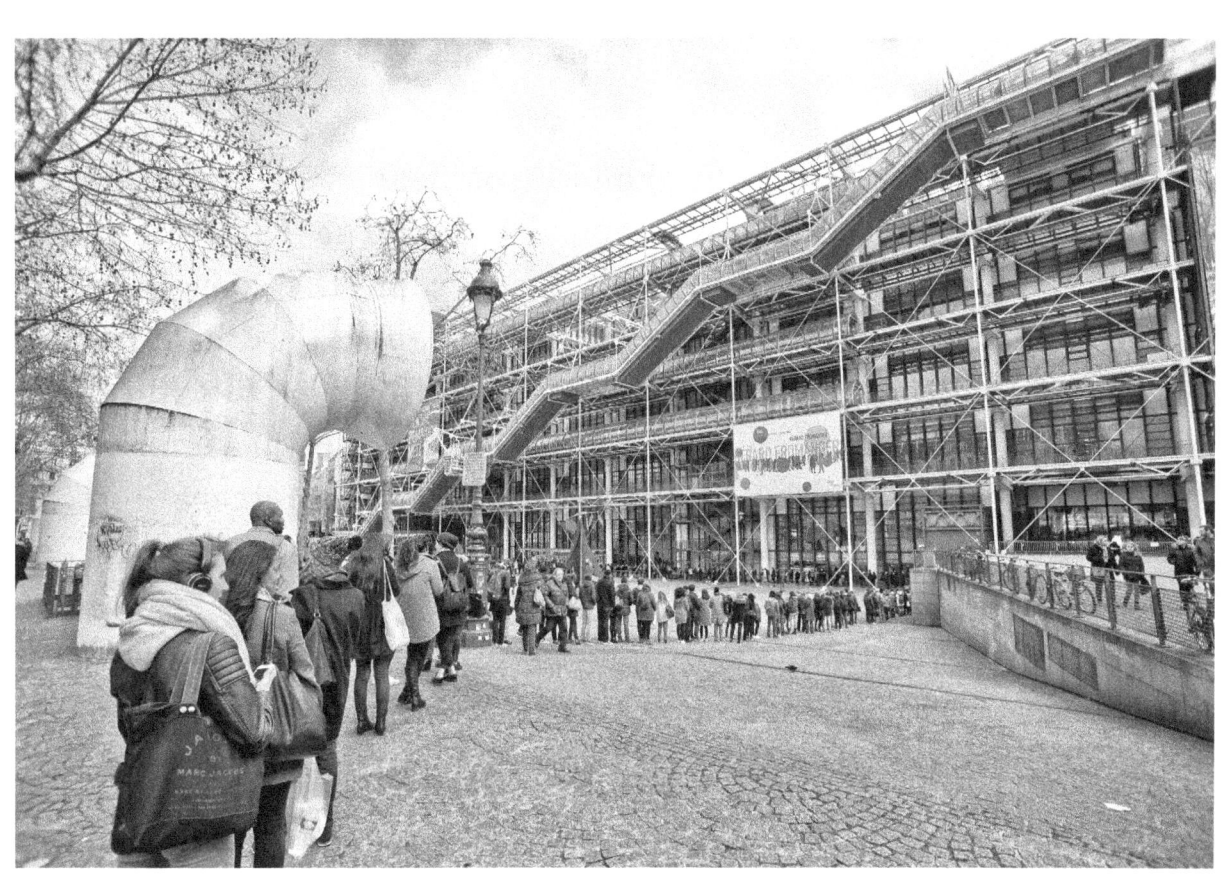

A queue to the library, 2016

METRO

The Paris metro is special and recognizable. You can see it in many movies and on many famous photos. The Paris Metro or Métropolitain had opened in 1900 and became the coeval for the stormy 20th century. One of the symbols of the city, it is noted for its density within the city limits and its uniform architecture, influenced by Art Nouveau. The Métro has a cultural significance that goes well beyond the city of Paris. The name Métropolitan (or Métro) has become a generic name for subways and urban underground railroads.

You will definitely remember the white tiles on the walls of stations. You will not meet as many extraordinary personalities in no other metros as here. And, of course, musicians in underground passages...

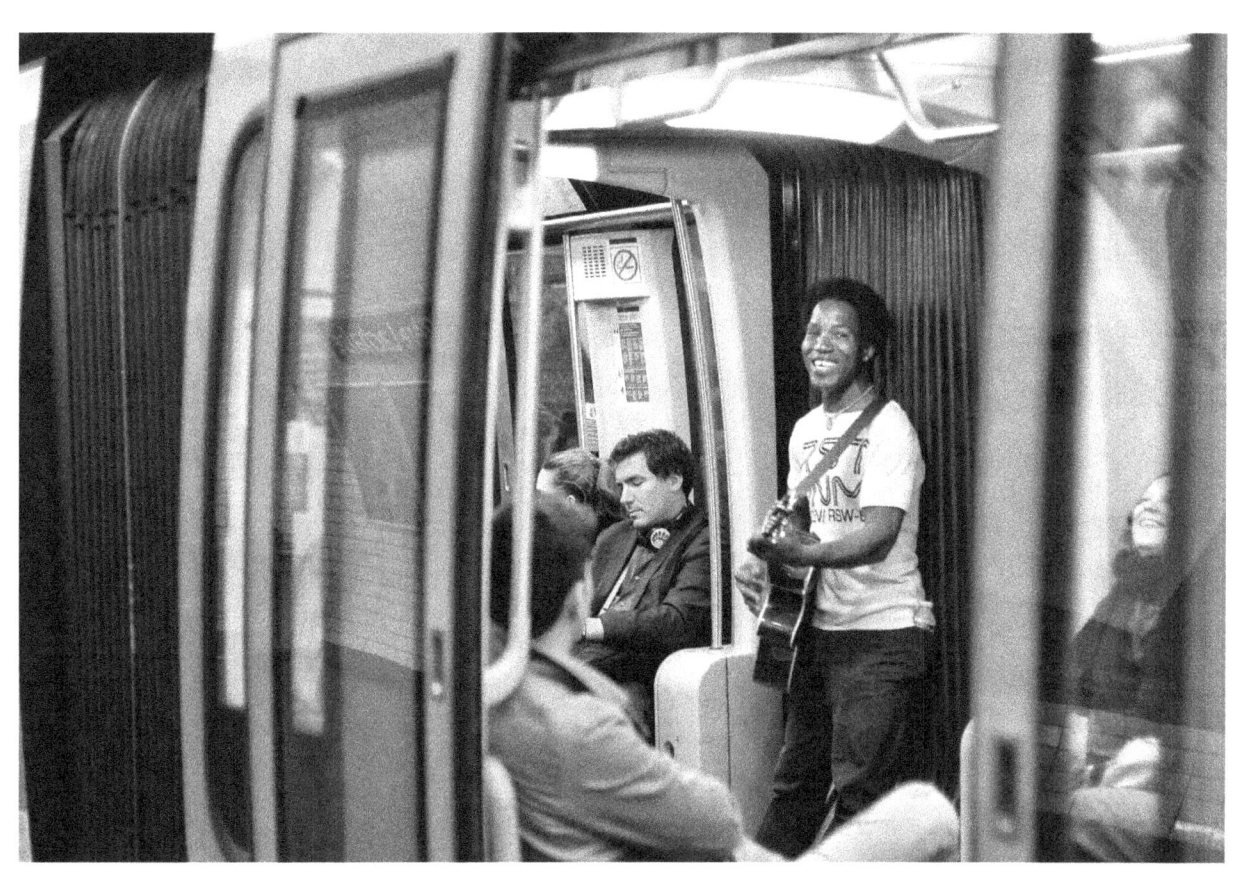

Happy singer, 2012

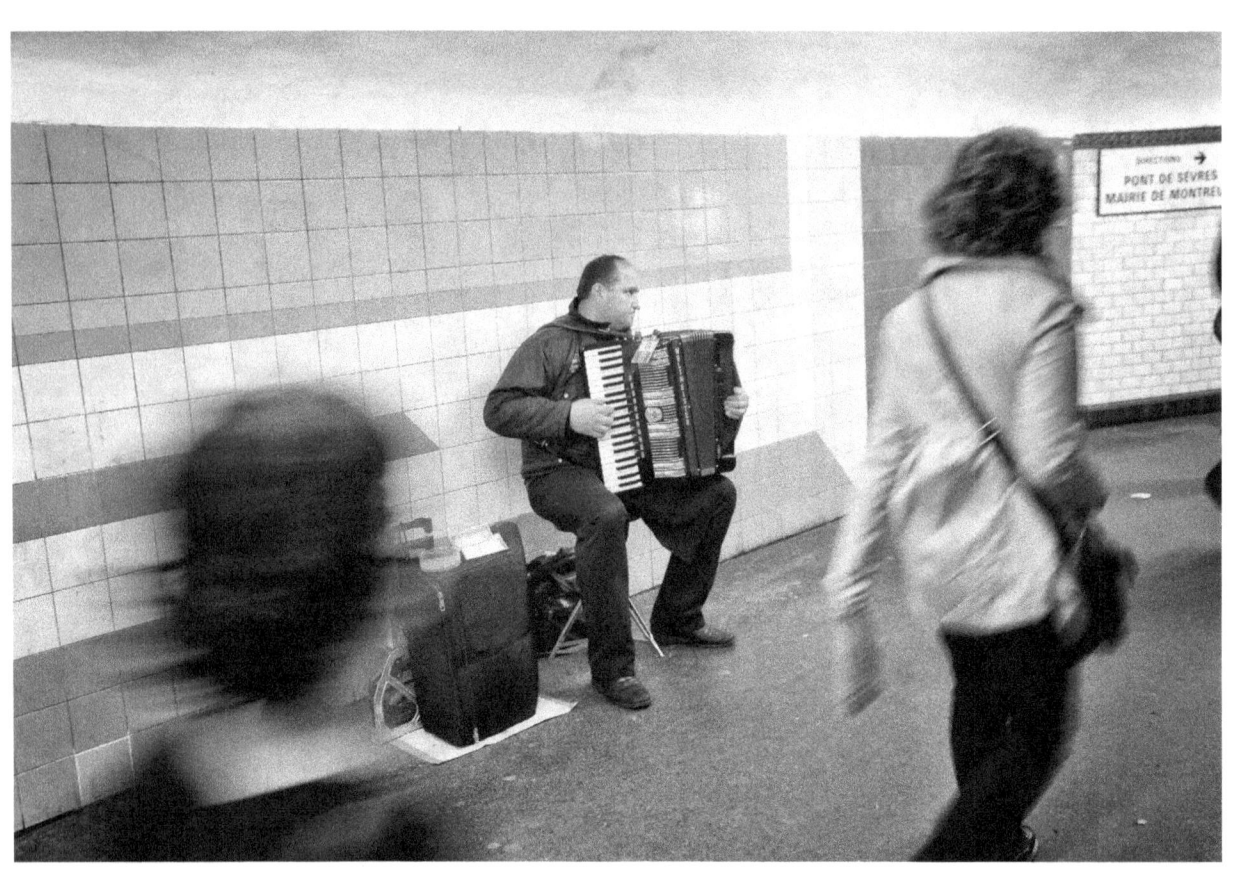

Melancholy, 2012

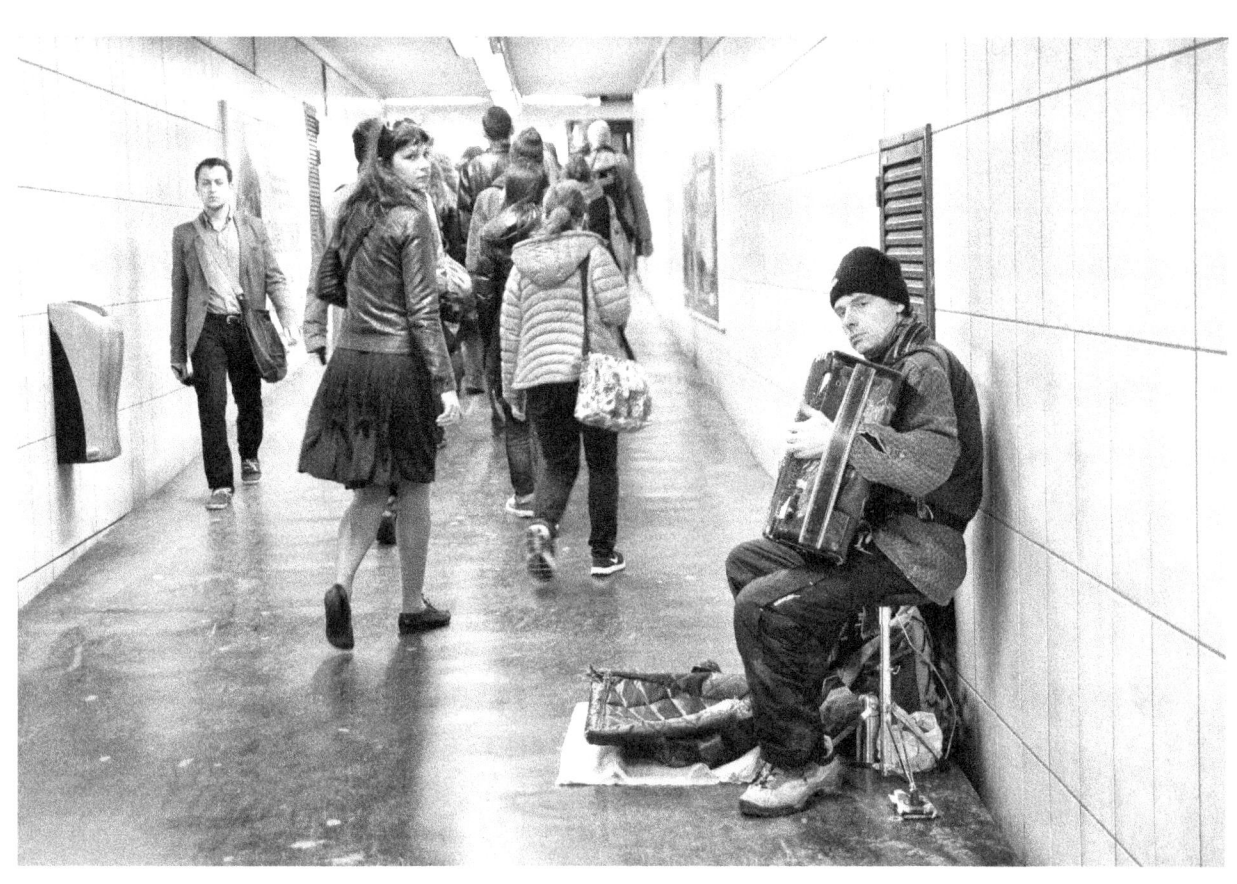

Melancholy 2, 2012

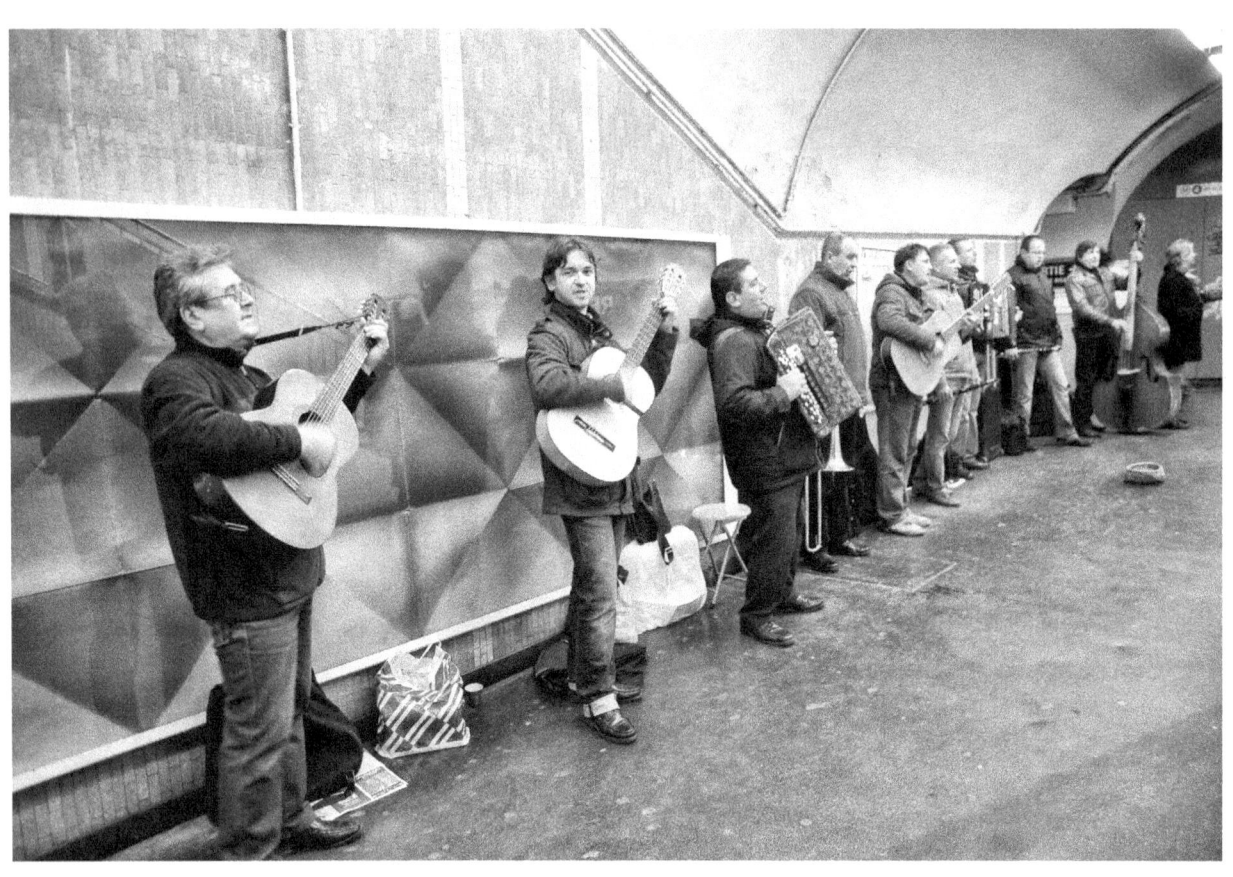

Spanish melody, 2012

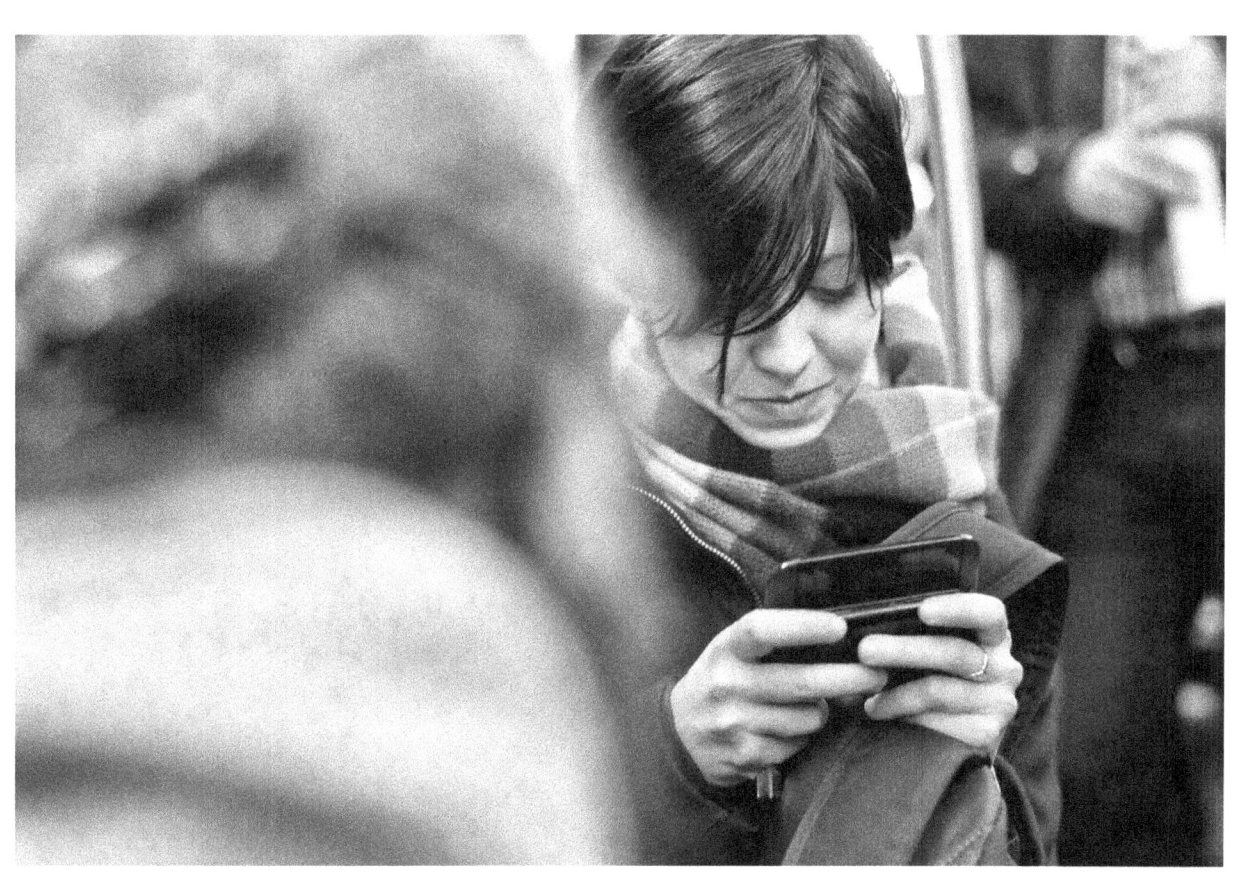

He has written!, 2012

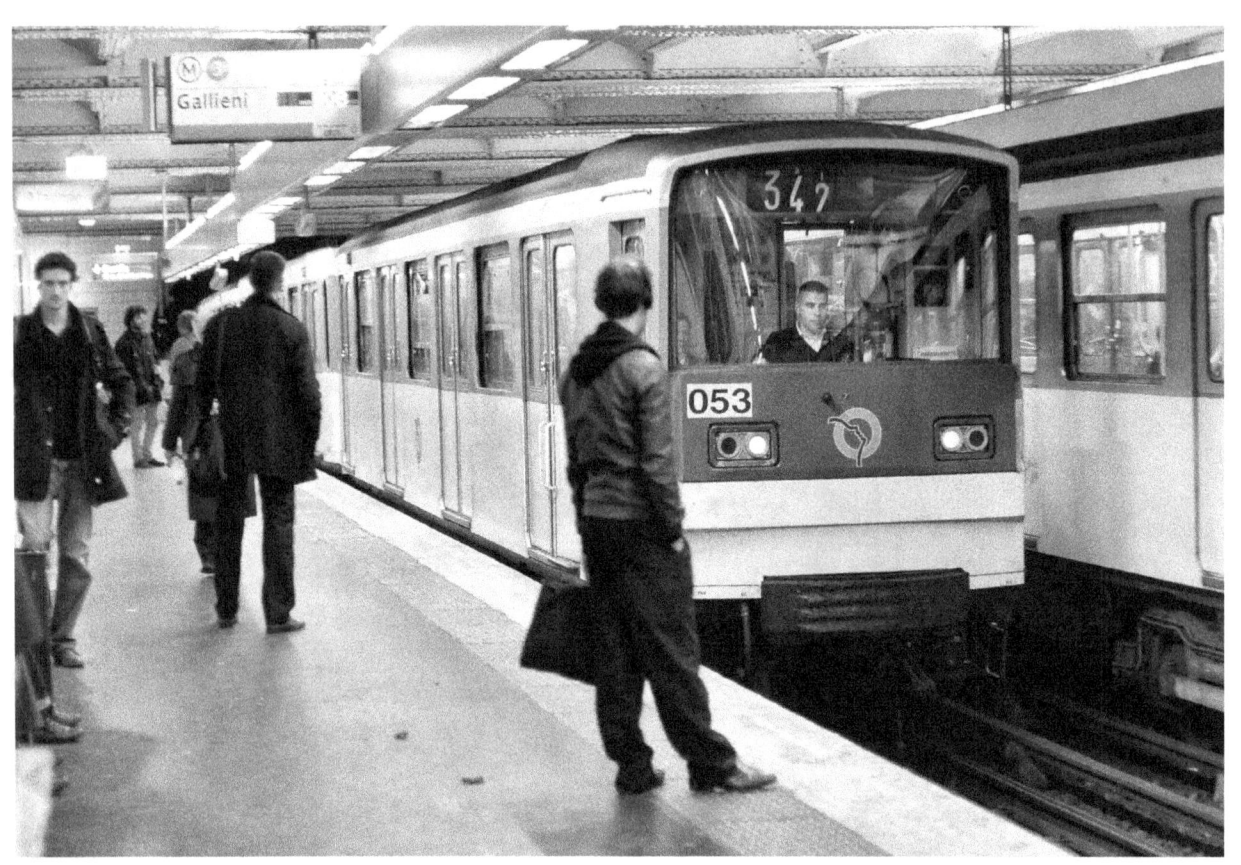

Gallieni, 2012

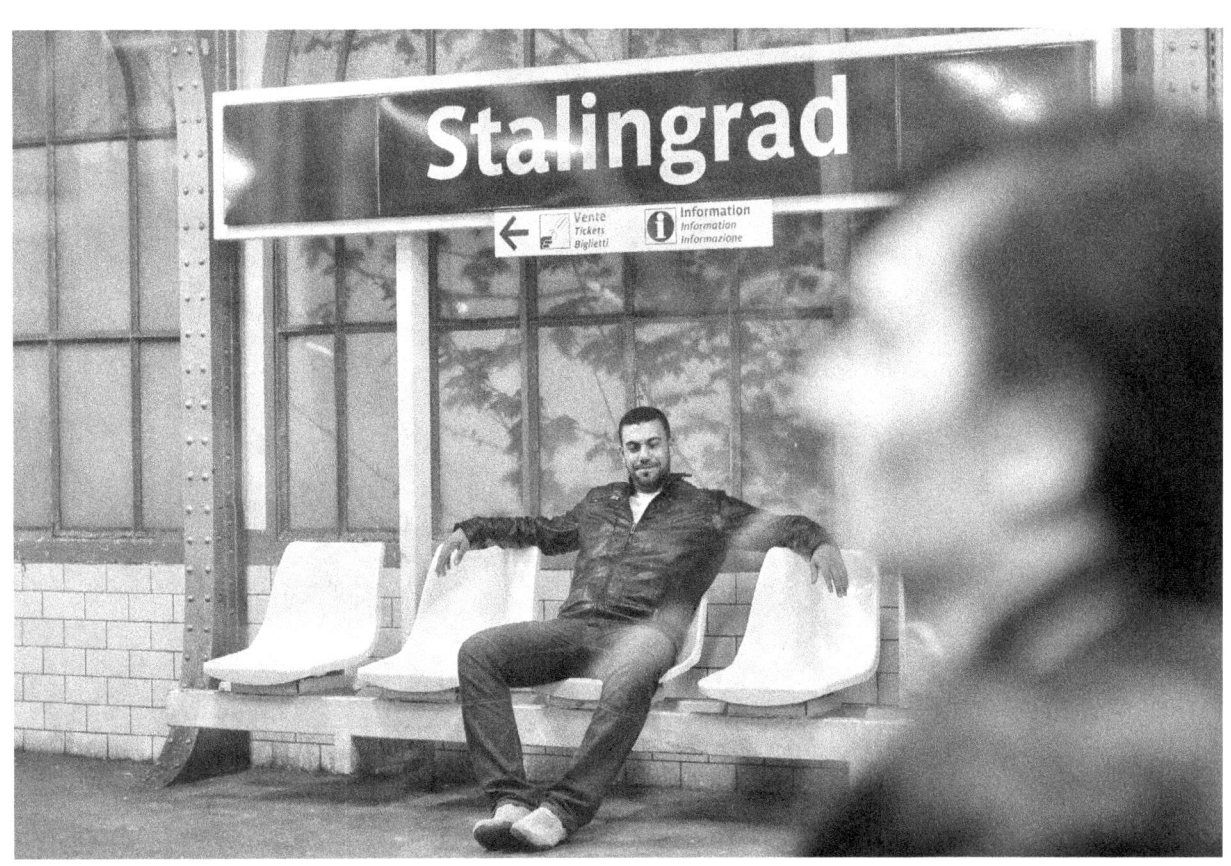

New Stalingrad, 2012

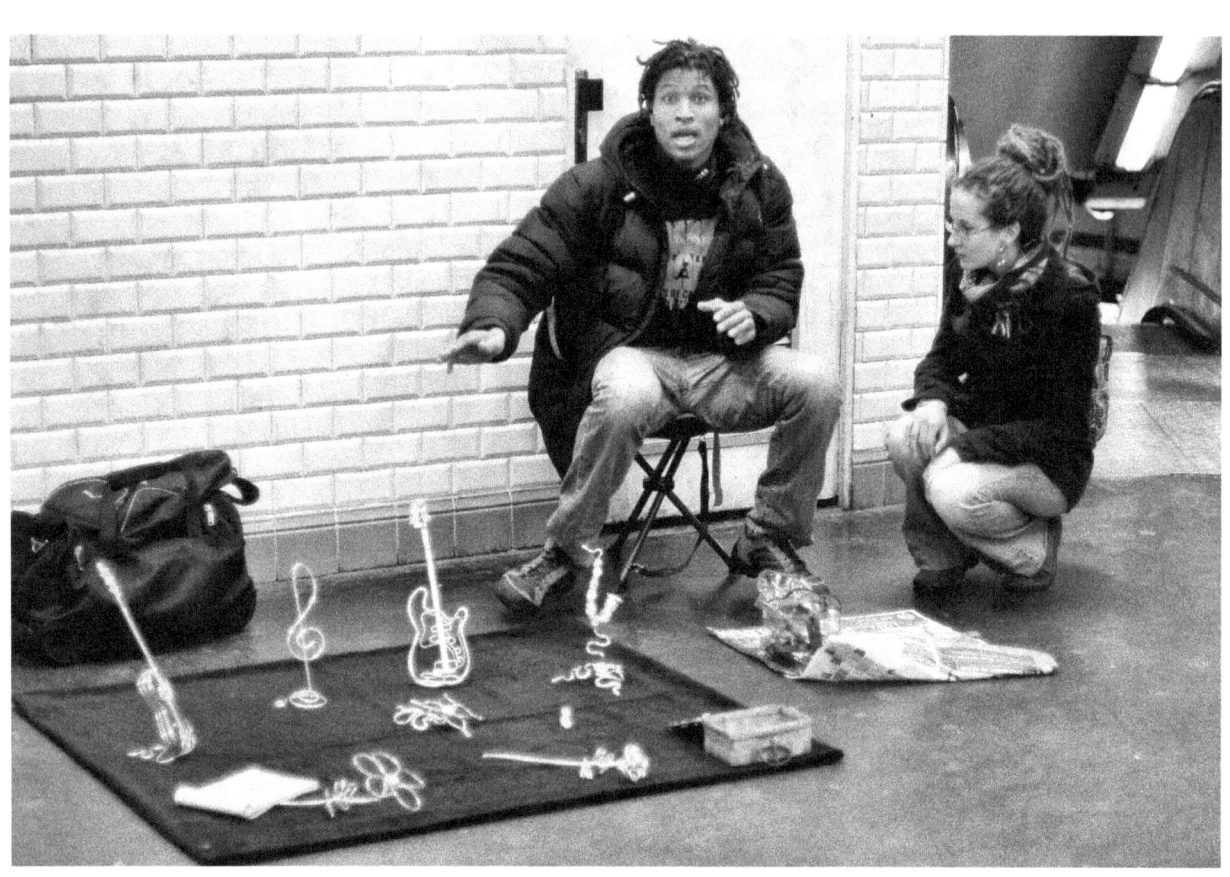

No photos!, 2012

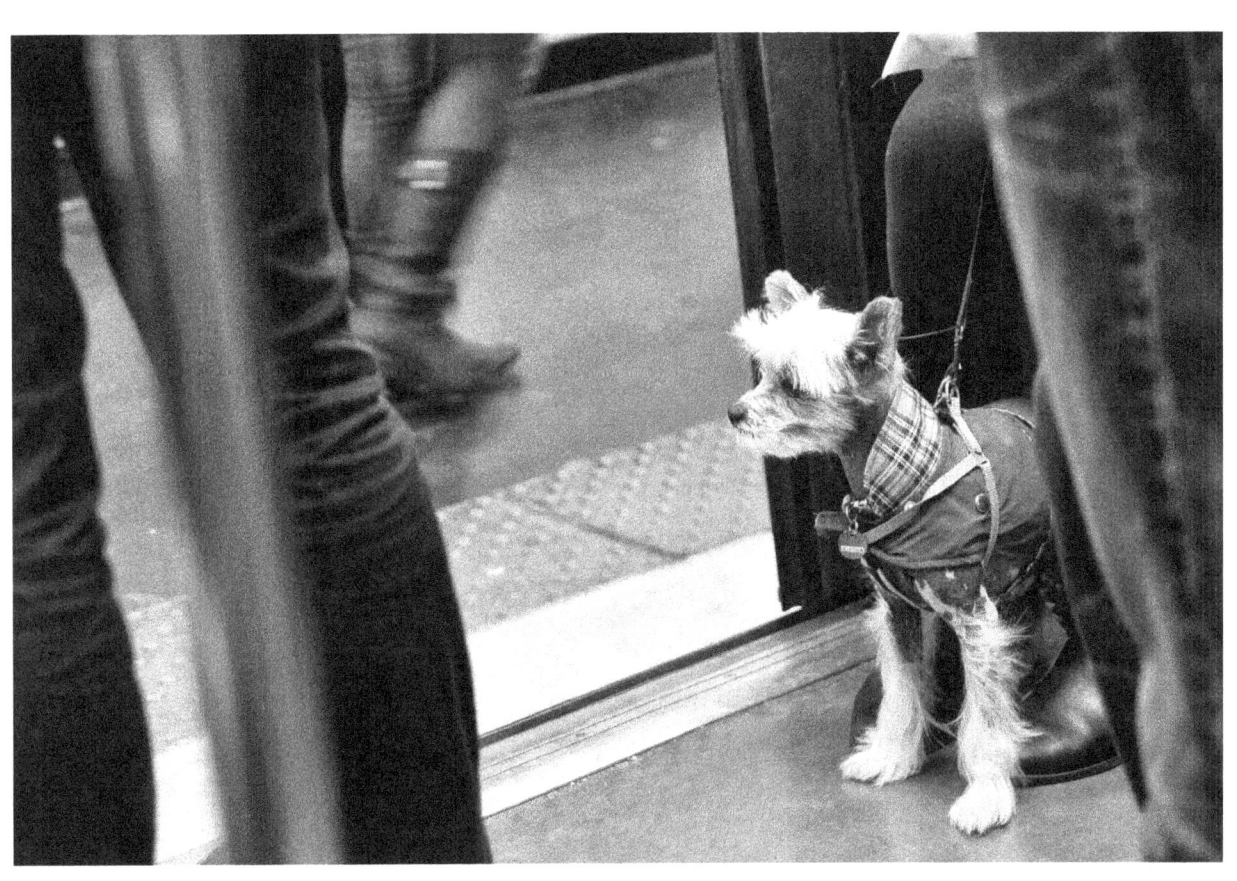

A lot of legs, 2012

BISTROS

French cuisine is considered the best in the world. There are countless restaurants, cafes and bistros in Paris, and Parisians like spending a lot of time there. Although the grand French gastronomic meal has just been beatified by Unesco, that gives little indication of the sheer variety of places to eat you can find here in Paris, from haute-cuisine temples to all-day cafés, eccentric wine bars, vintage bistros and the new "bistronomiques" serving affordable modern cuisine in a casual setting.

Cafes, restaurants and bars, are on almost every street corner, which just goes to show that food and drink is an essential part of Parisian culture. A big part of the enjoyment of Paris cafes is to linger and people watch, and there is always so much to see.

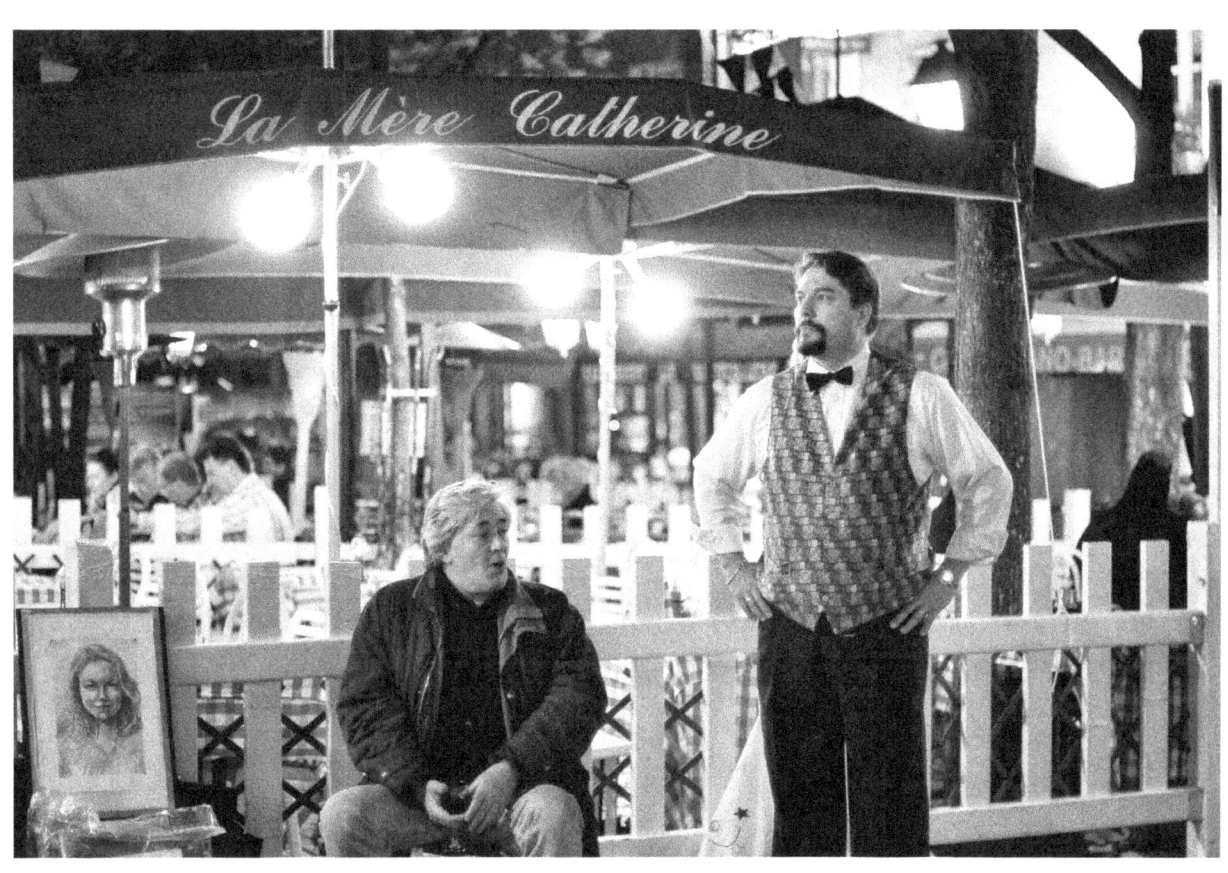

Street artist and the waiter, 2012

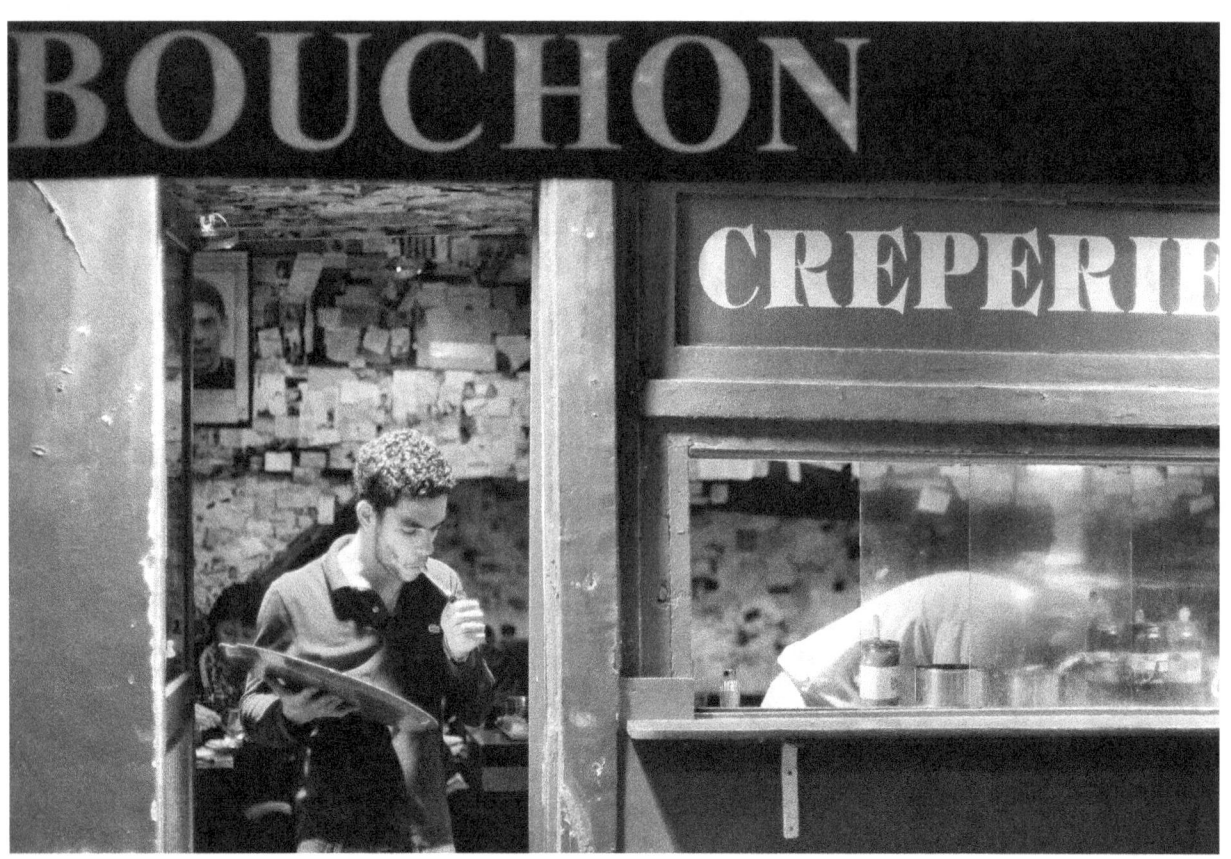

Smoke break, 2012

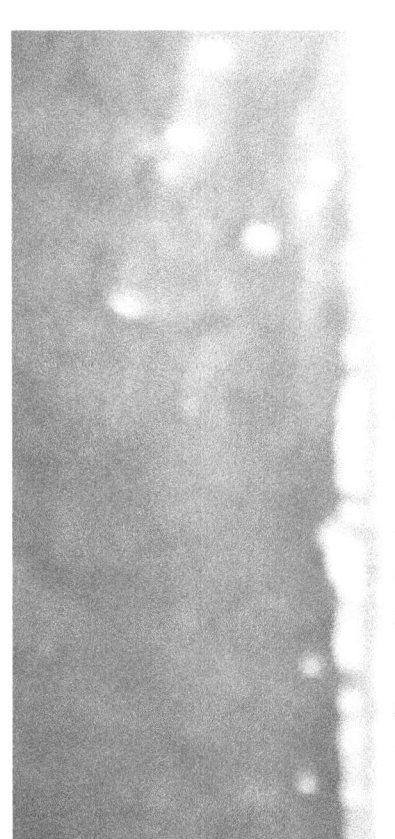
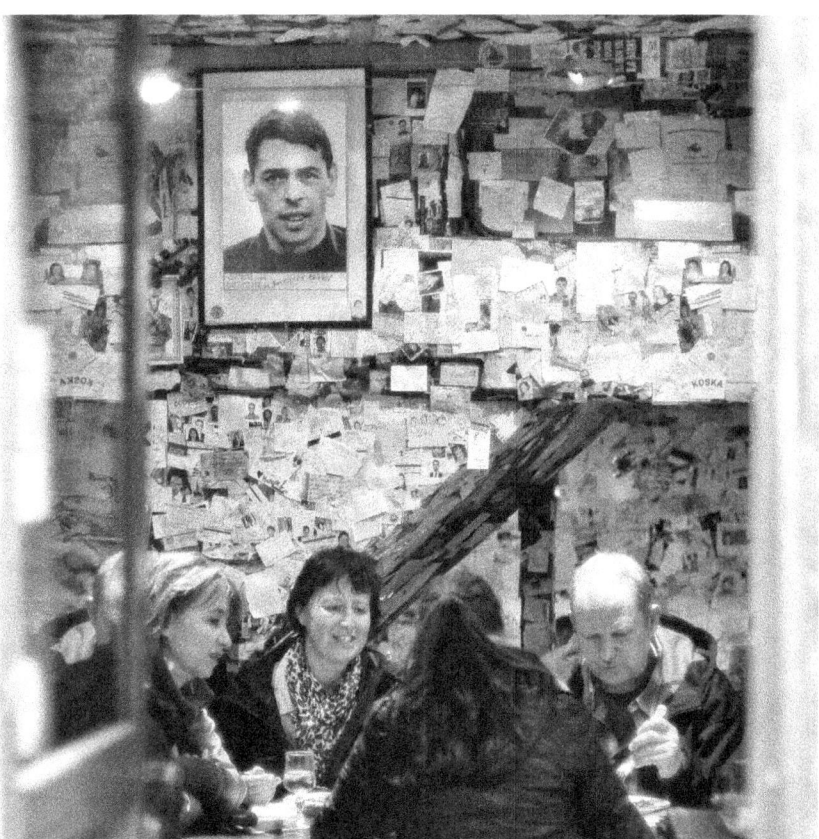

A pleasant evening with Jacques Brel, 2012

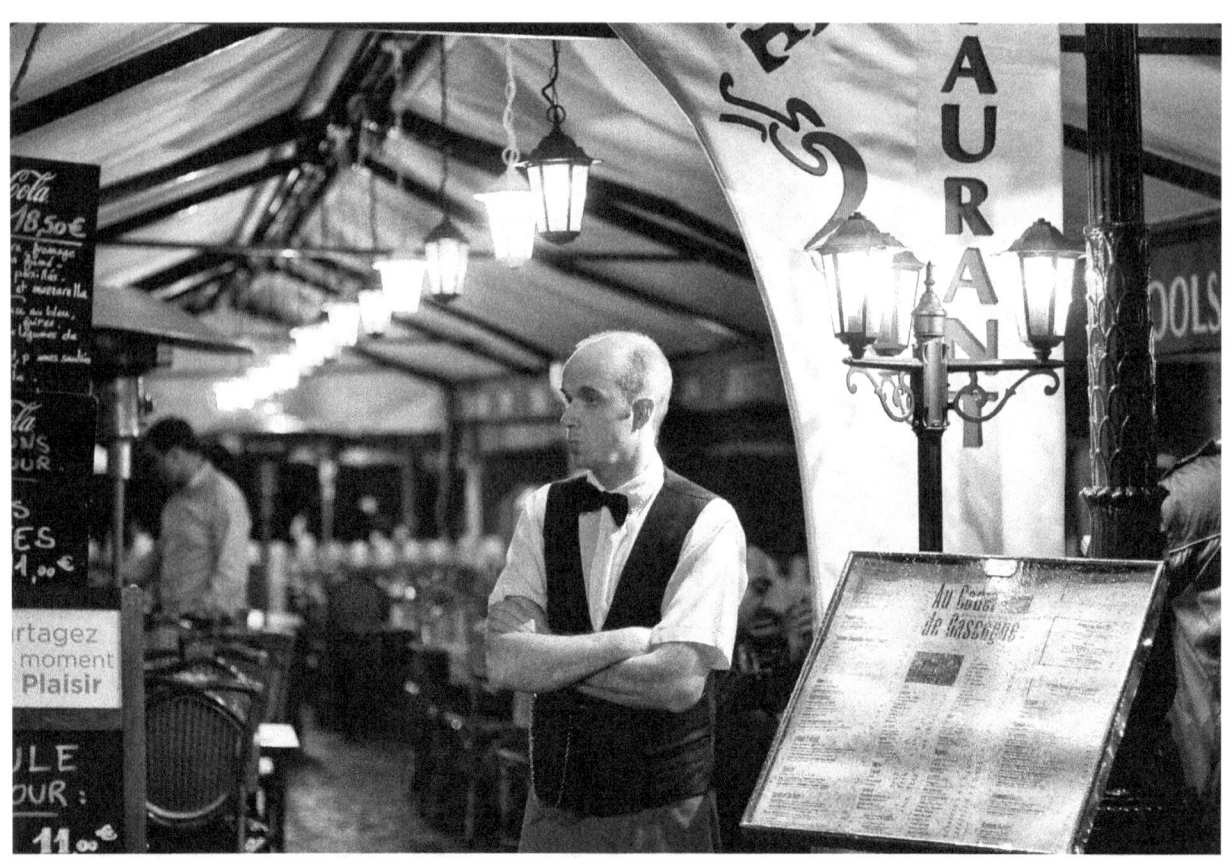

Waiting for customers, 2012

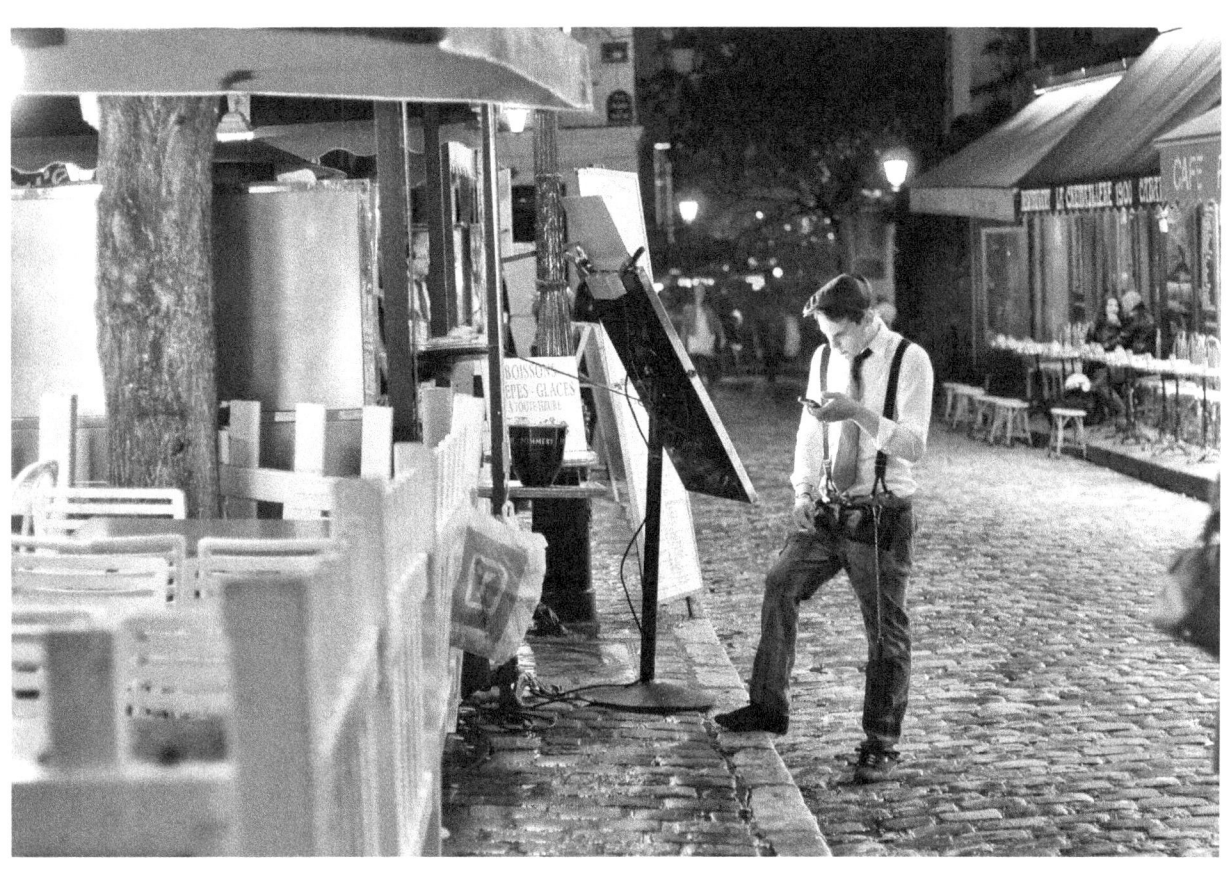

At the end of the shift, 2012

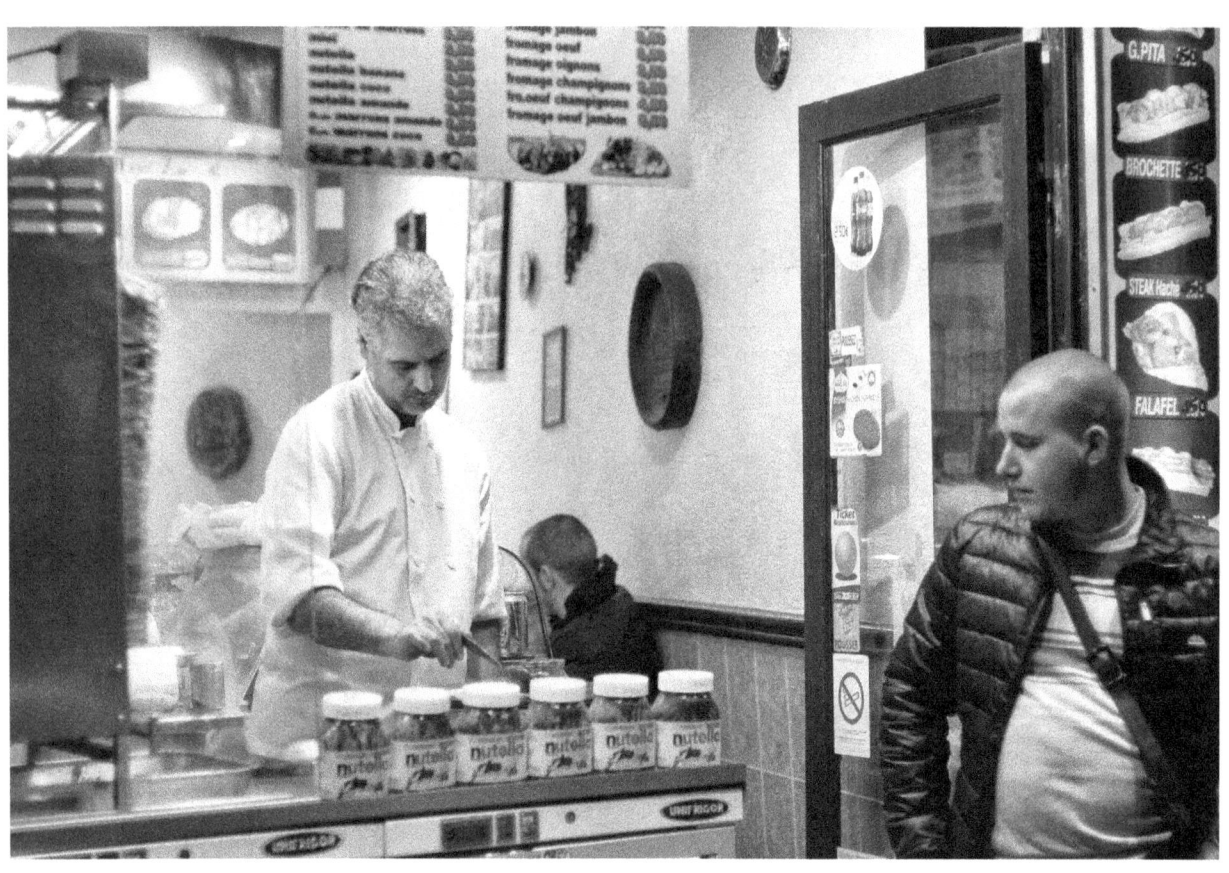

Pancake with Nutella, 2012

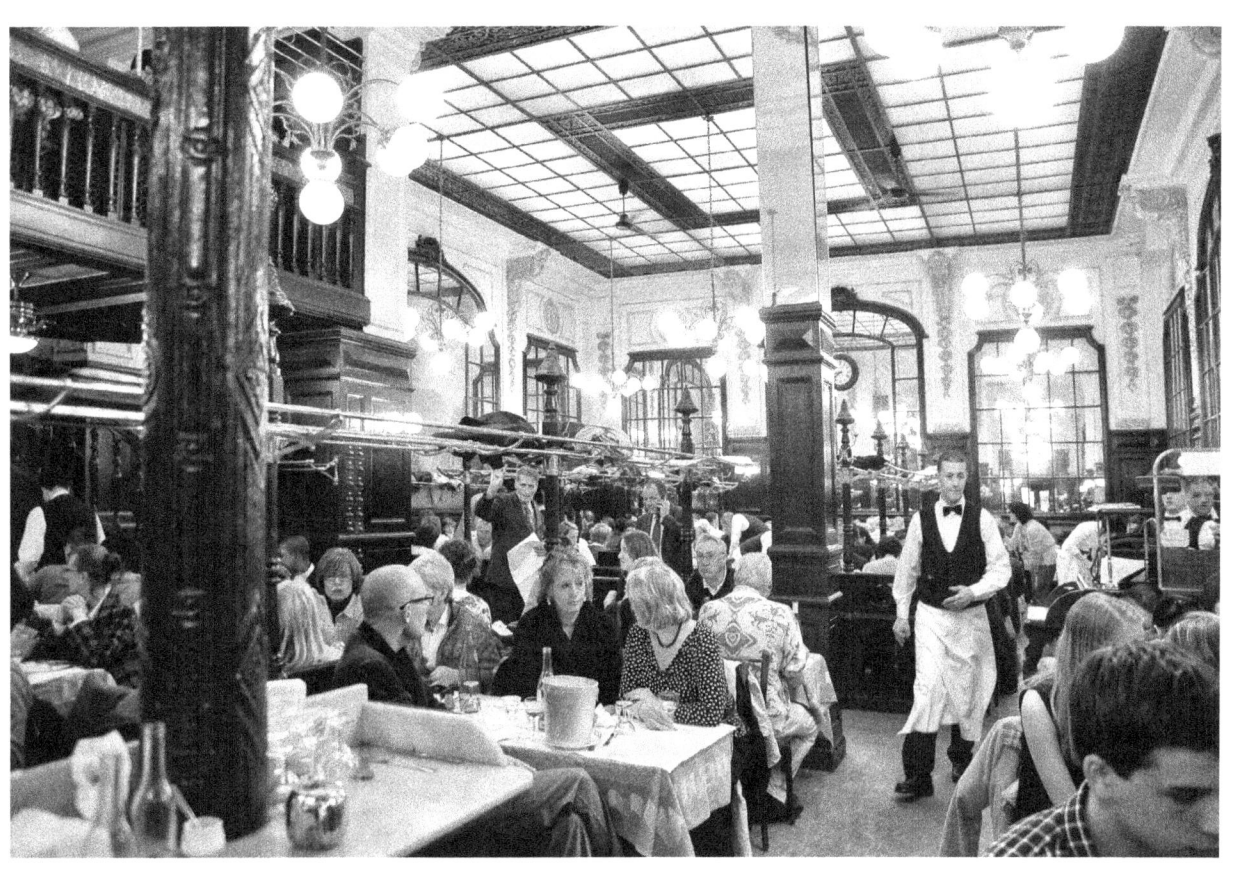

Le Bouillon Chartier, 2012

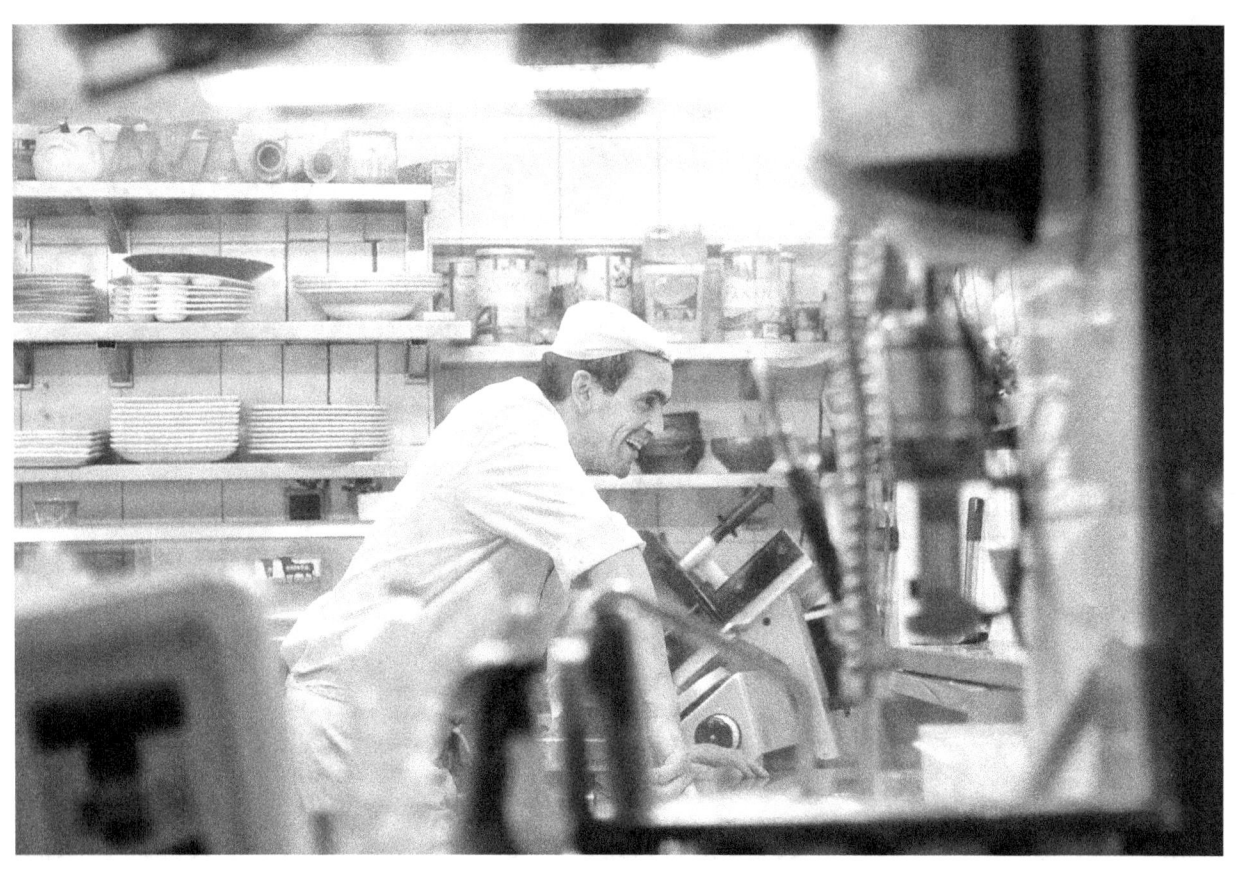

Work with pleasure, 2012

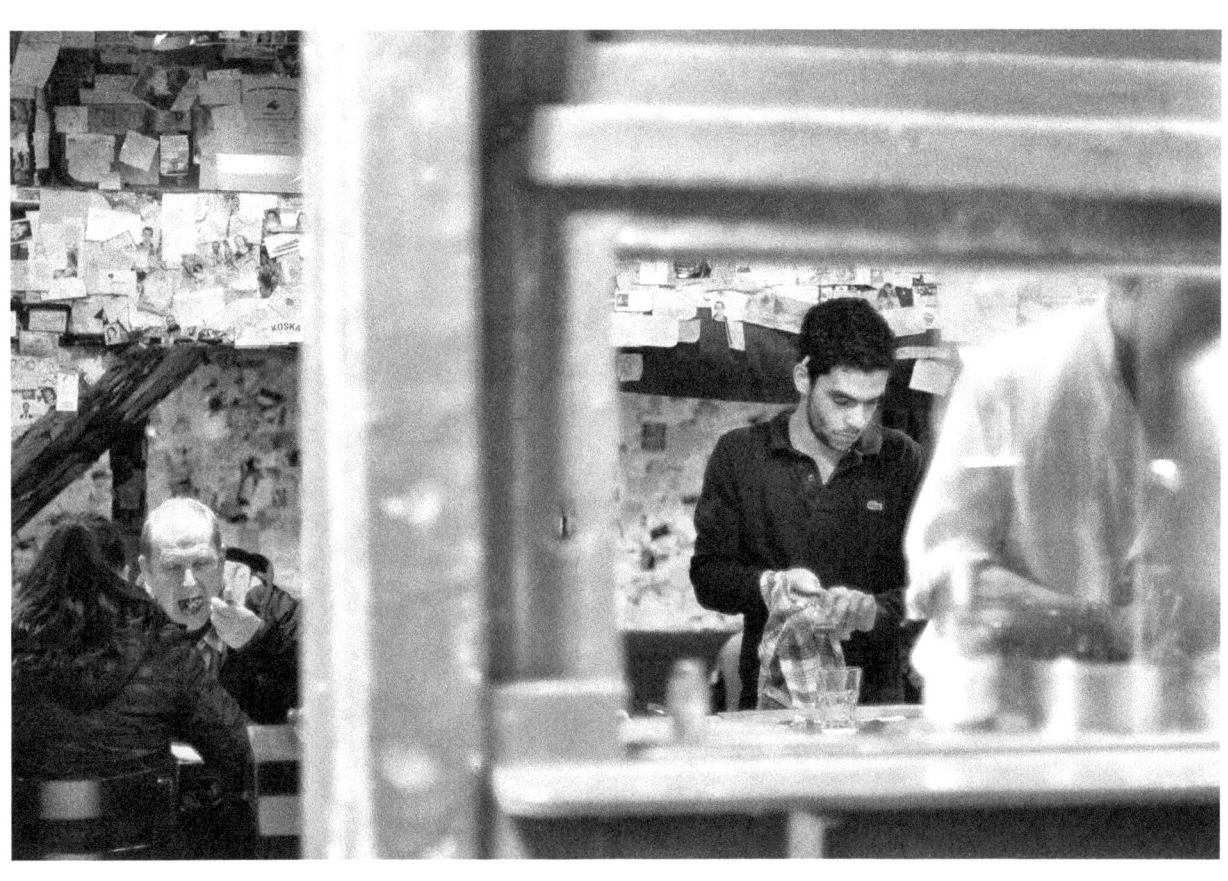

Cigarette behind the ear, 2012

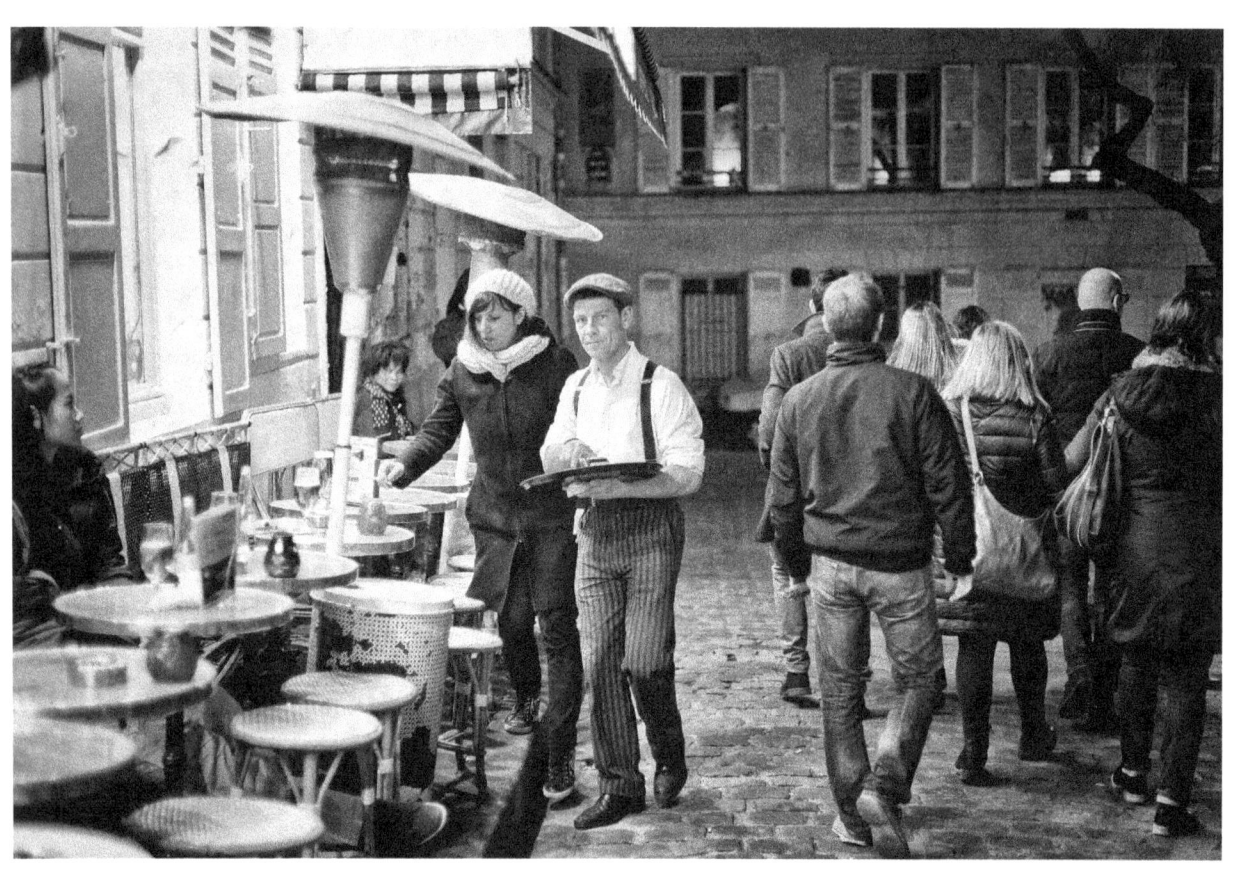

Montmartre, 2016

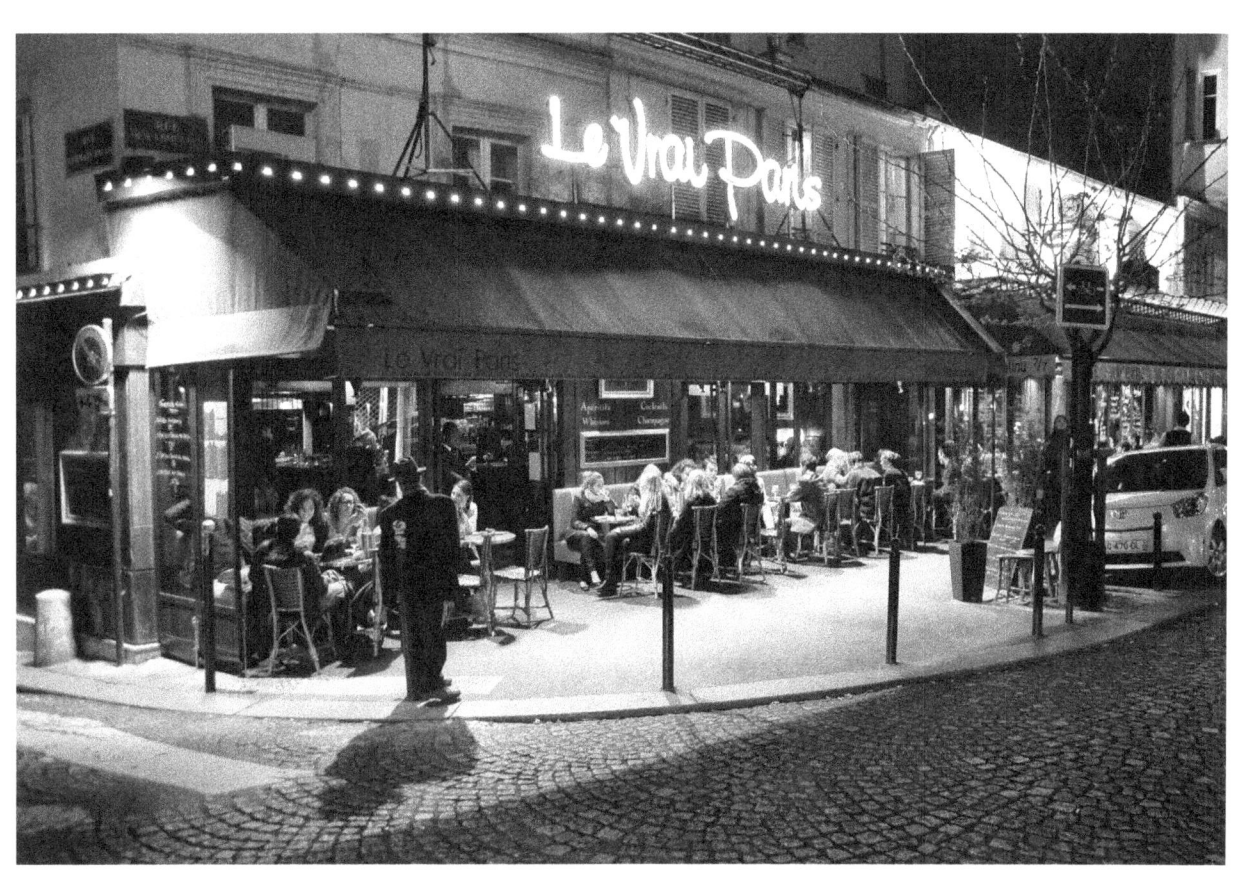

Real Paris, 2012

IN THE PARK

There are many parks and gardens in Paris, they are beautiful and well-groomed. Parisians like to rest there, to walk with children, feed the birds, read and sunbathe, run, do different sports, play petanque or chess. This is a part of the Parisian culture.

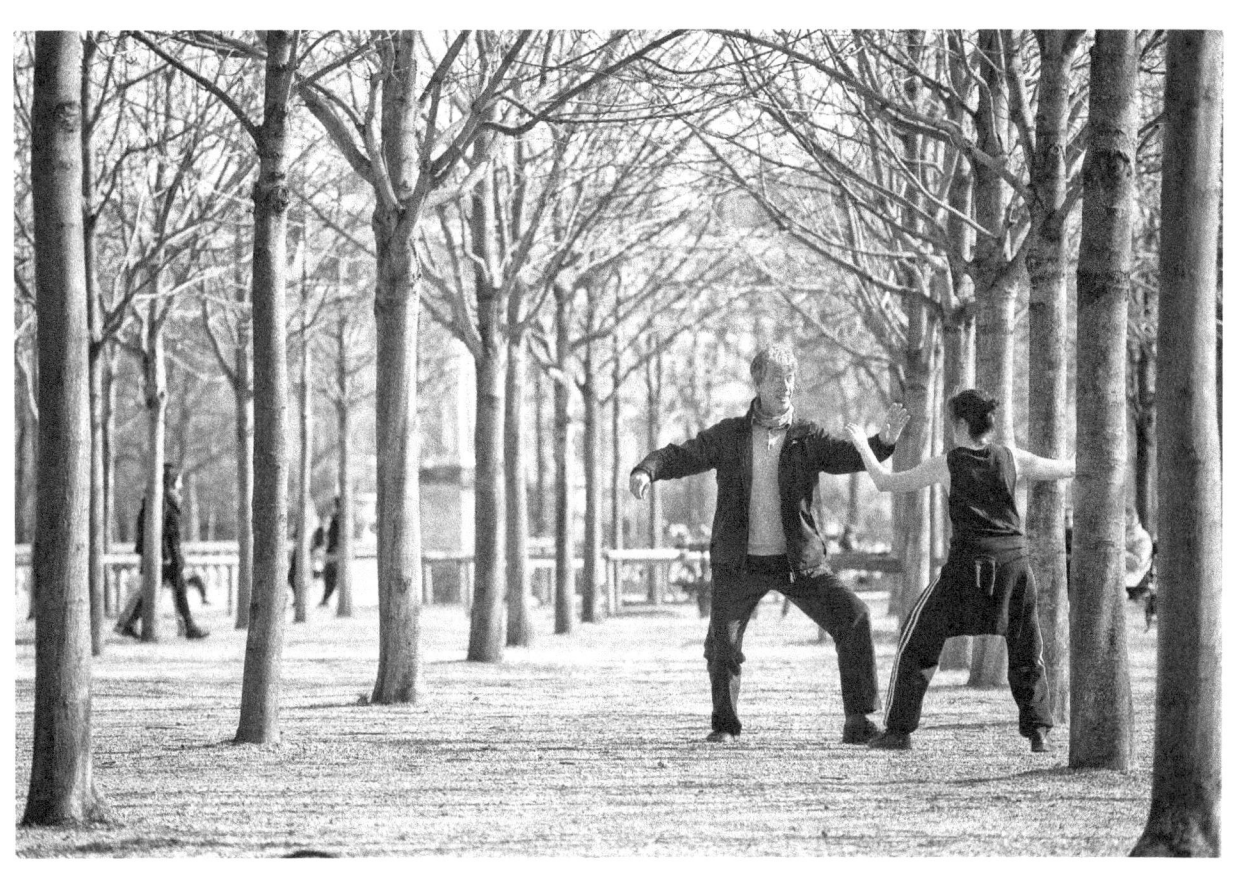

Harmony, 2016

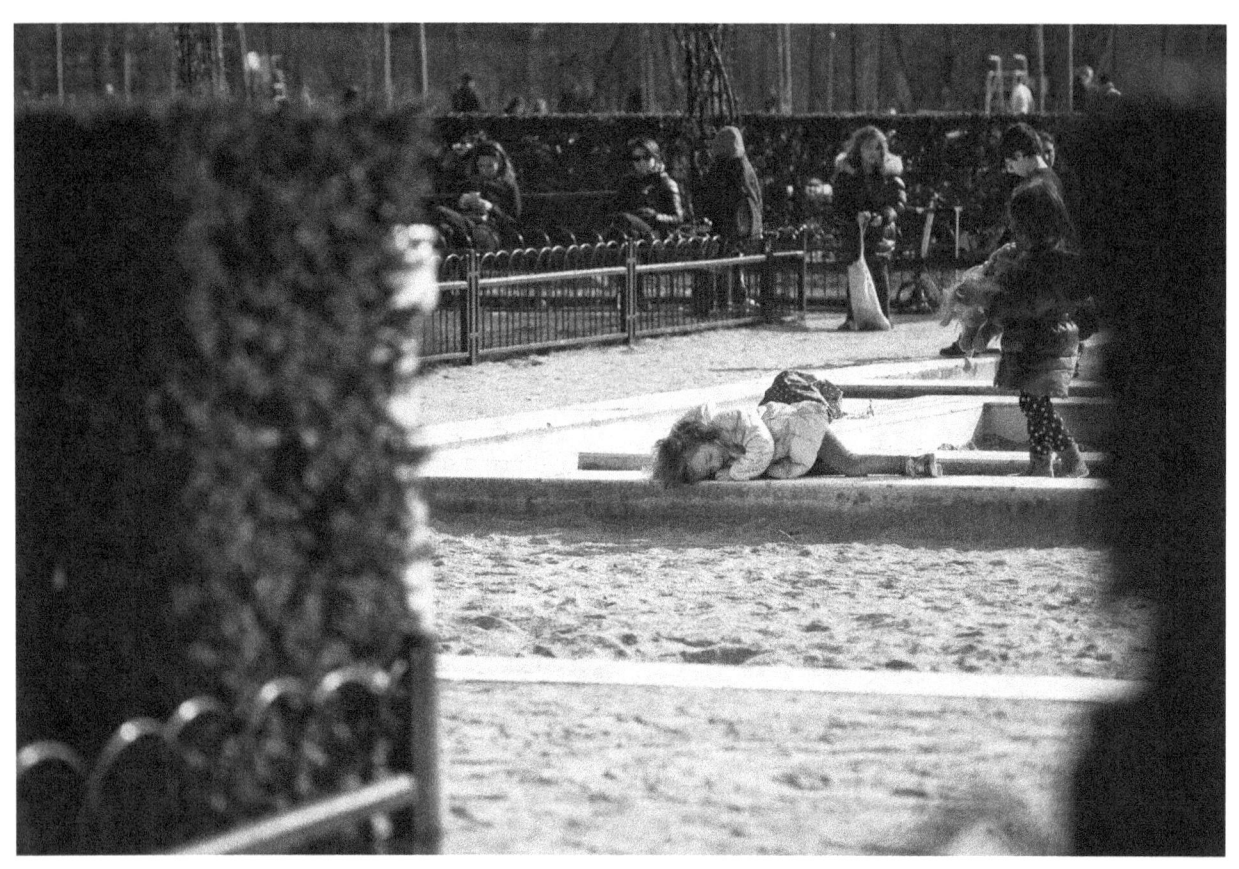

I'm tired, 2016

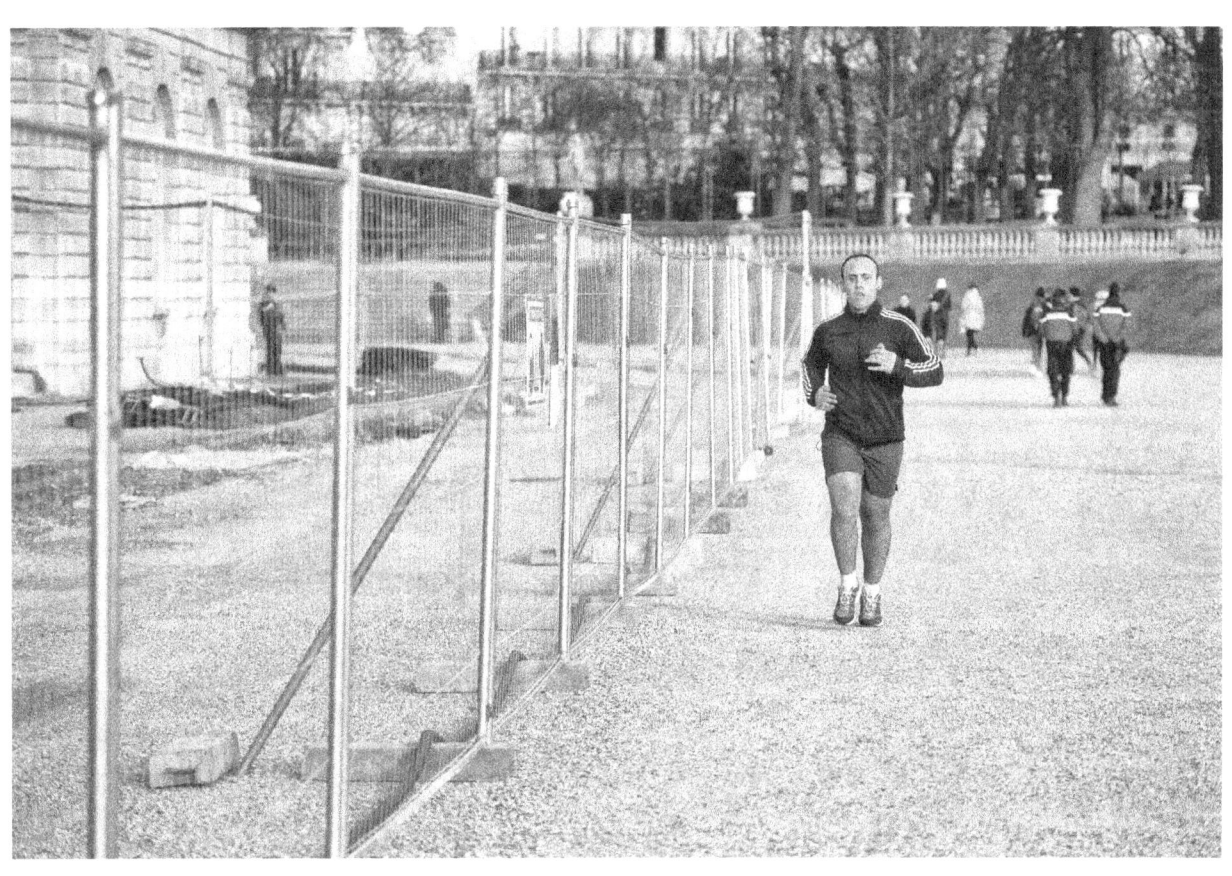

Running for health, 2016

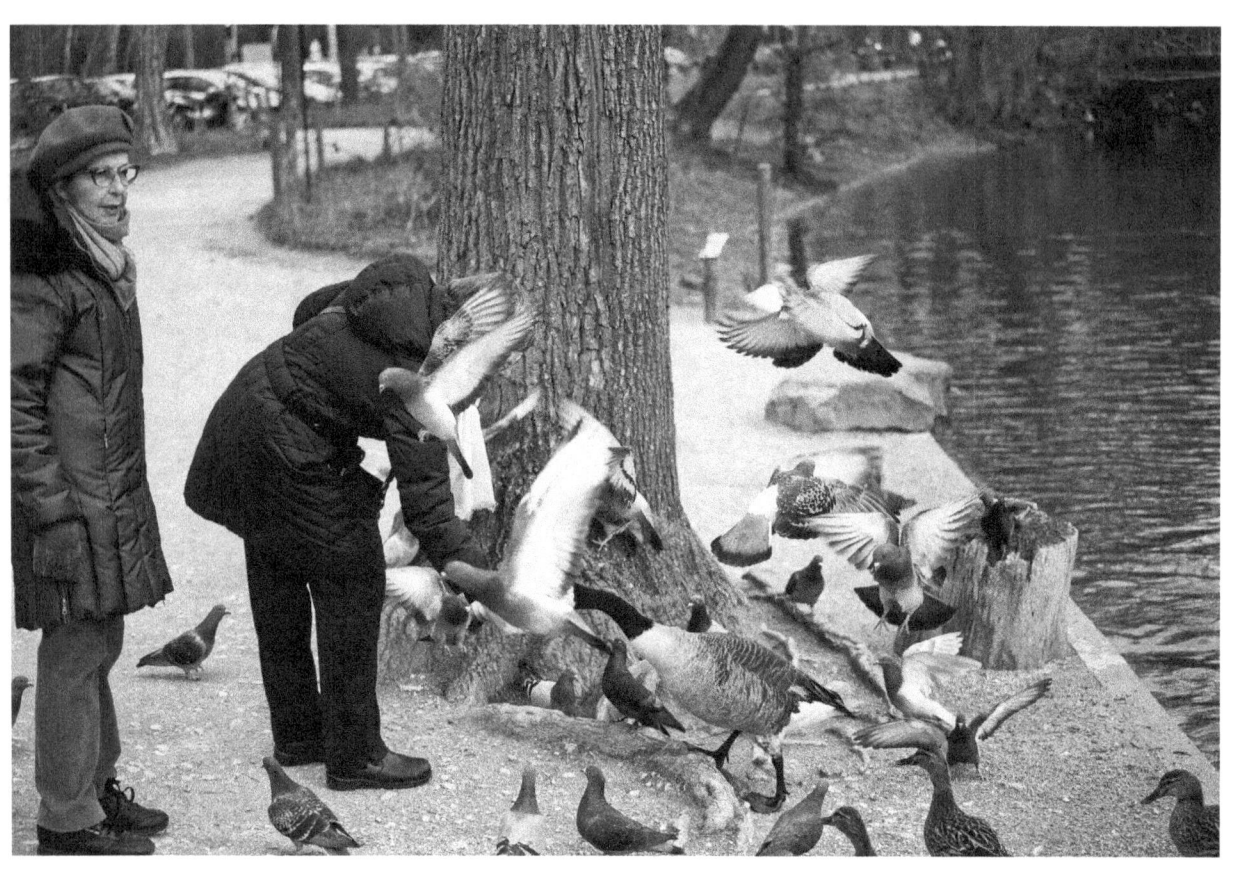

Dinner, 2016

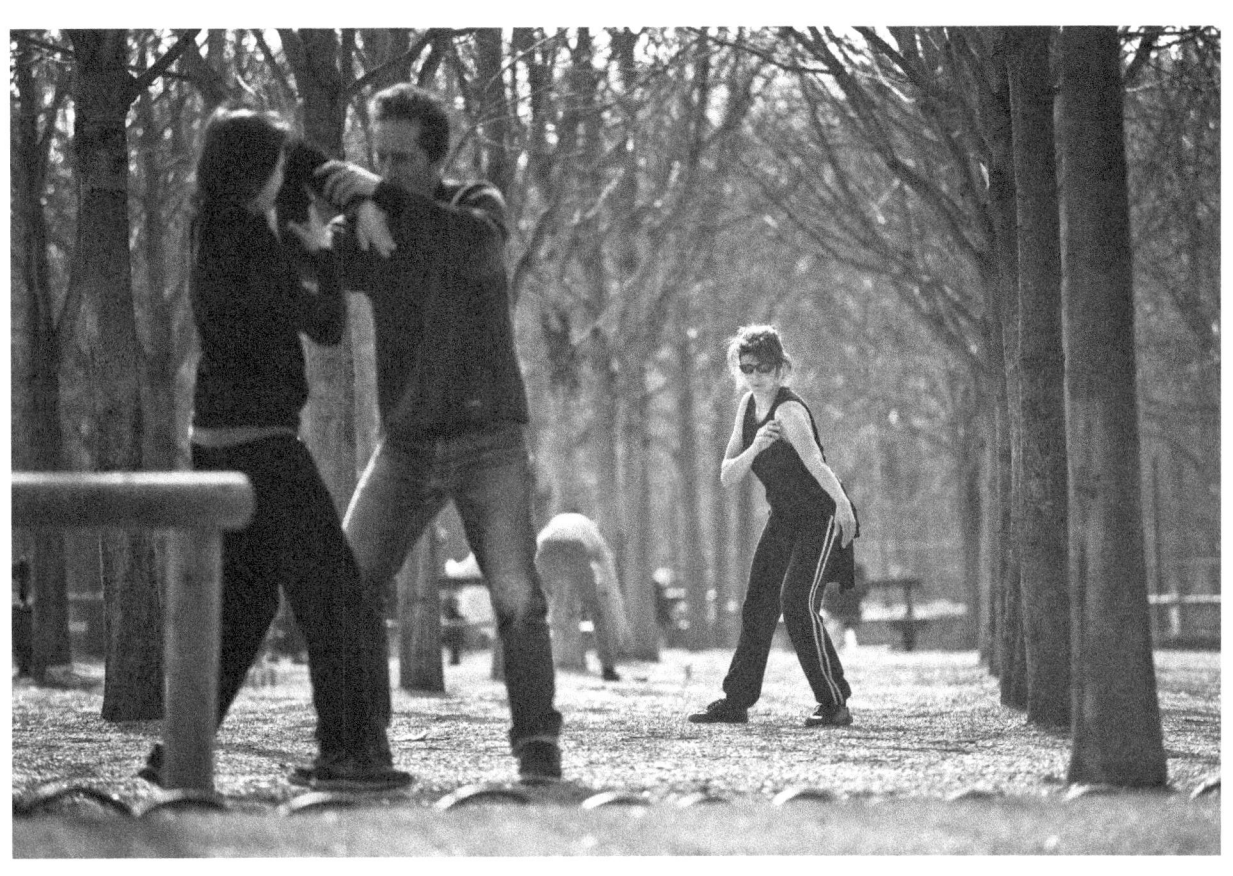

Virtual fight, 2016

BIRDS

There are a lot of birds in Paris. These are, of course, pigeons and gulls, but in the parks, you can find a lot of different geese, ducks, swans, crows and ravens, as well as the birds whose name you will not know. Parisians like birds, many come to parks especially to feed them.

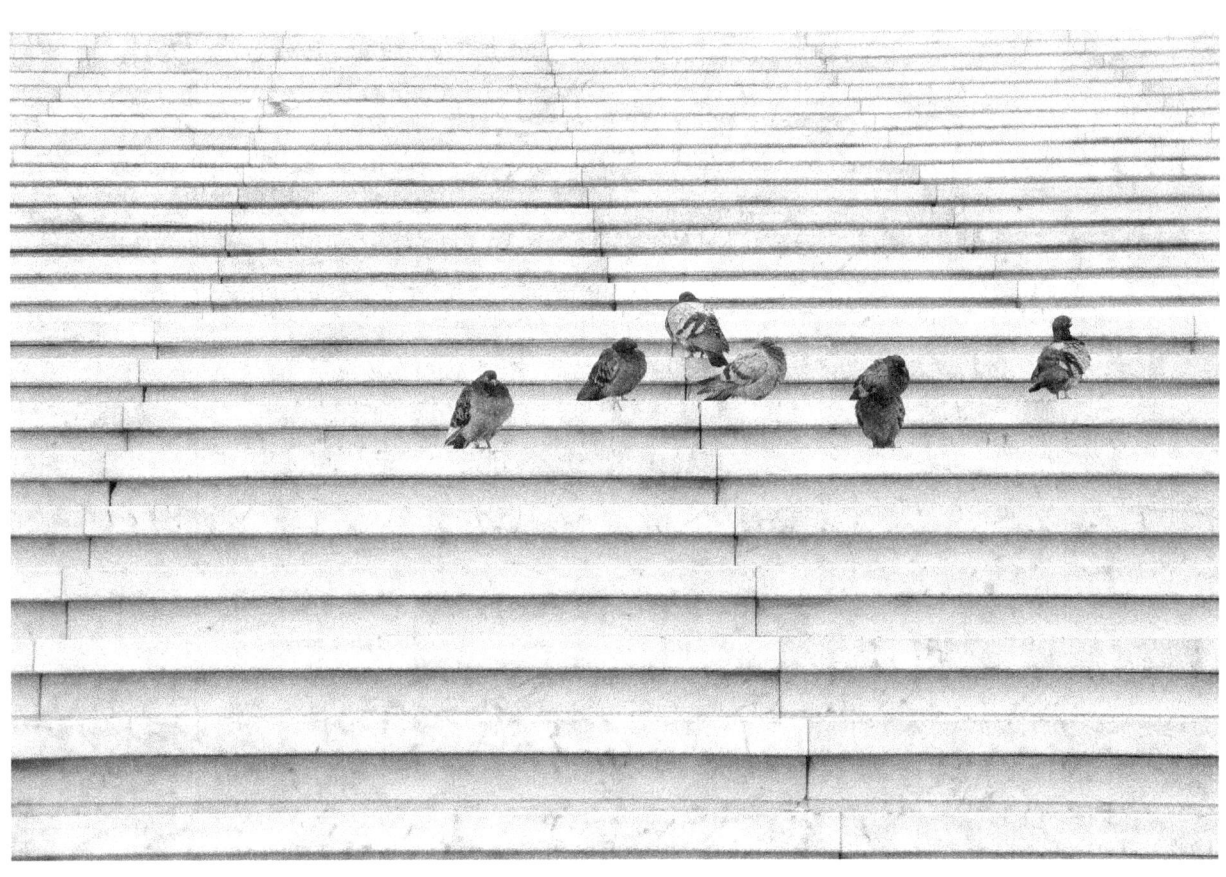

Do, re, mi, re, do-o, re-e, 2012

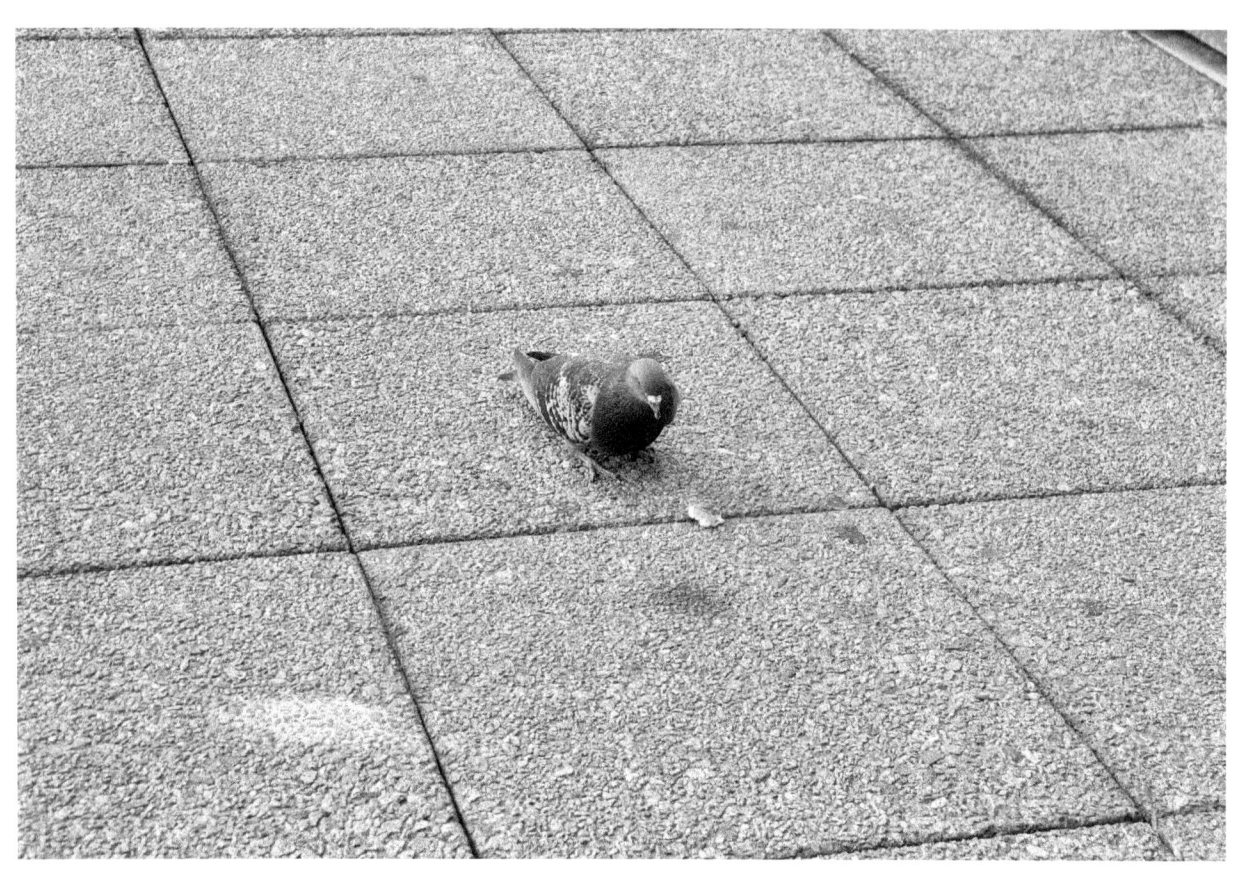

At the intersection, 2012

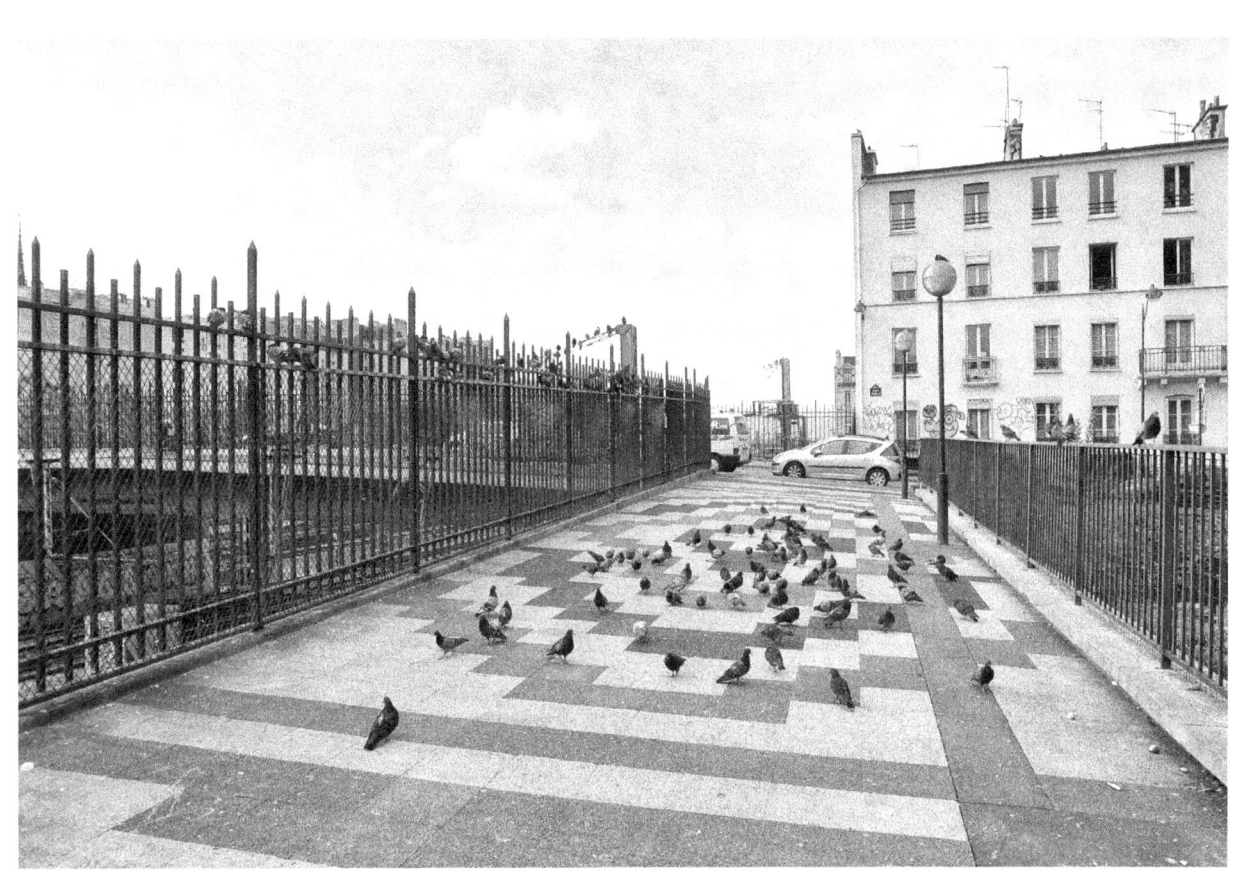

Playing Go, 2012

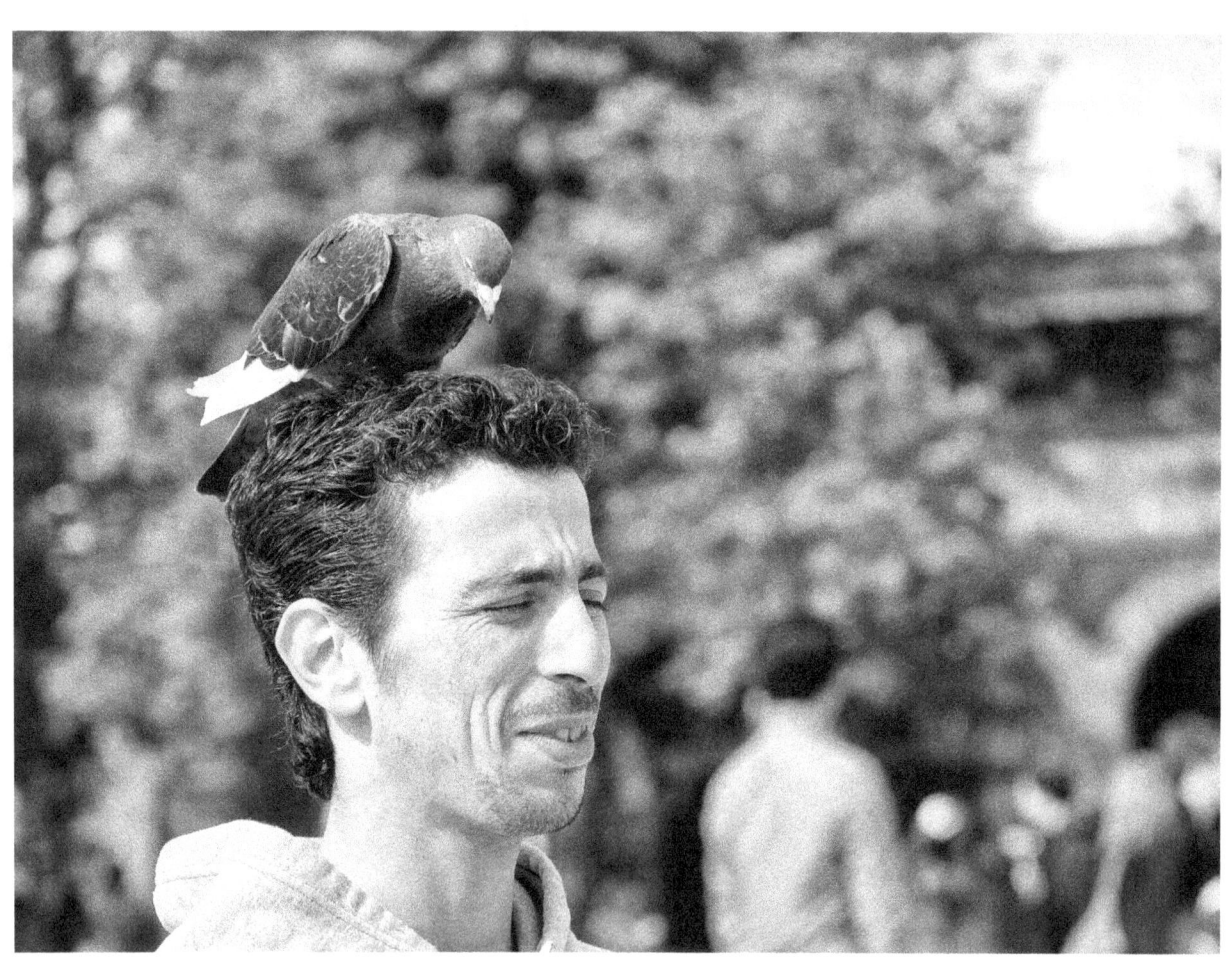

One euro, please, 2012

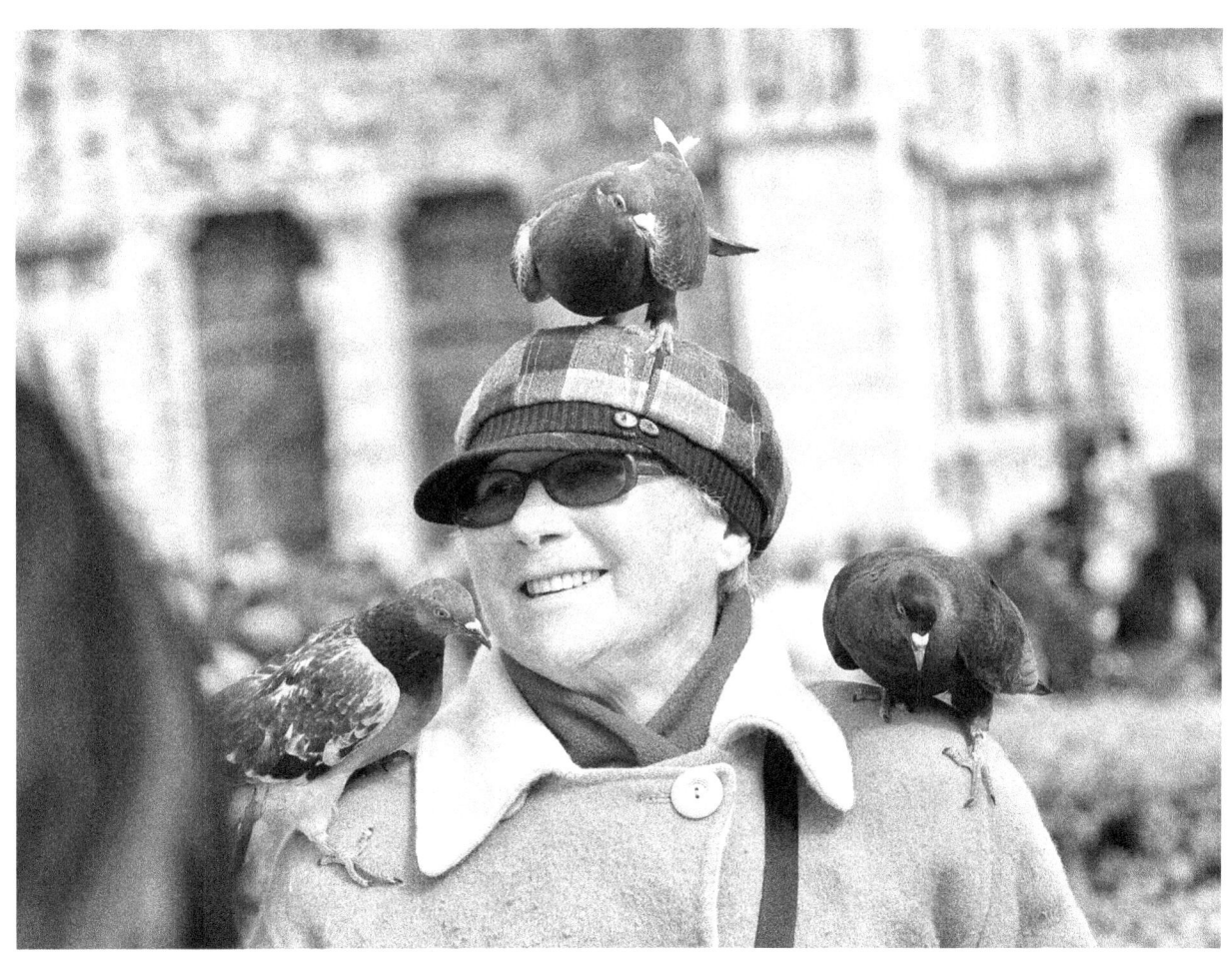

Lord of birds, 2012

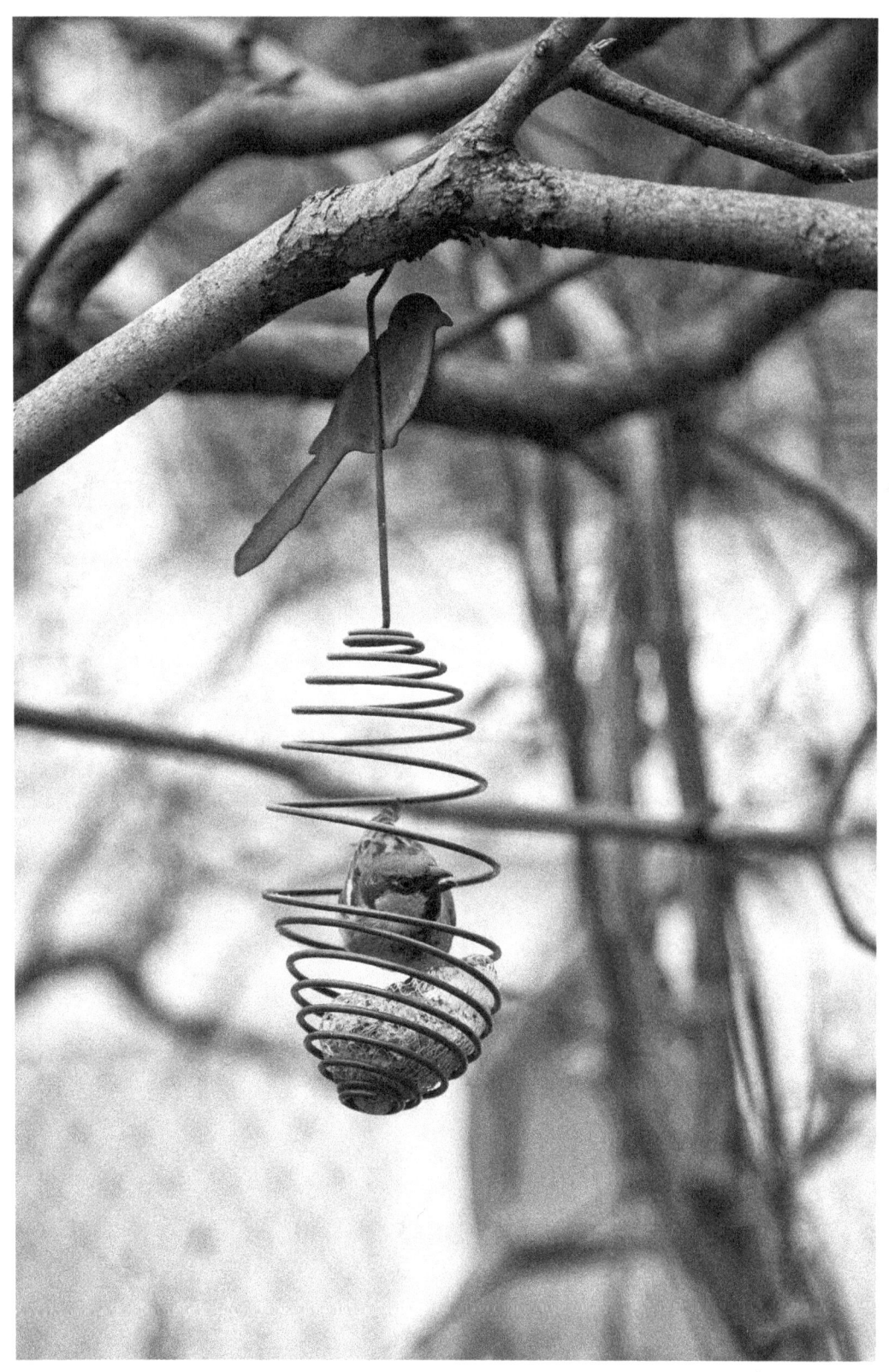

Spiral, 2016

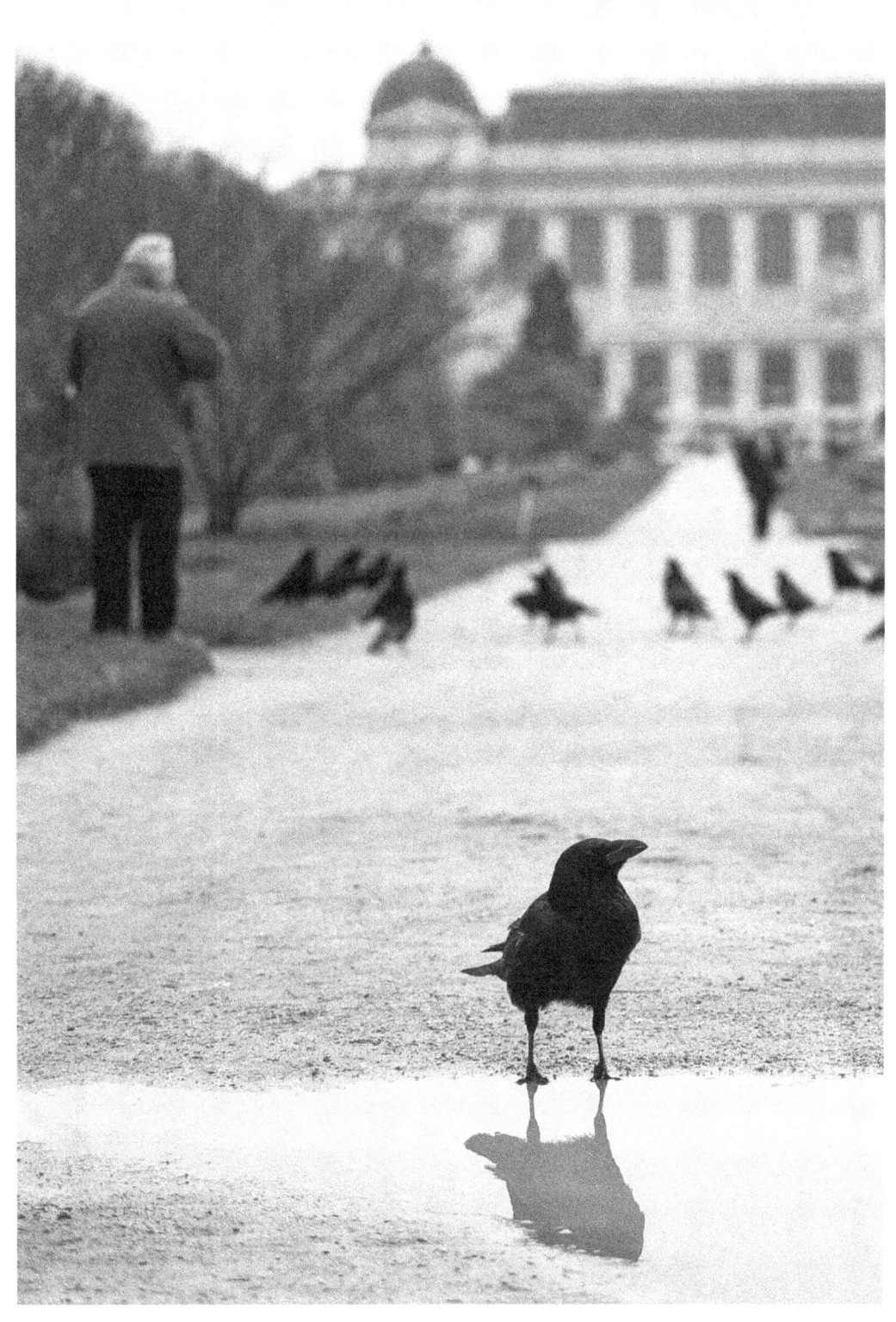

Gentleman, 2016

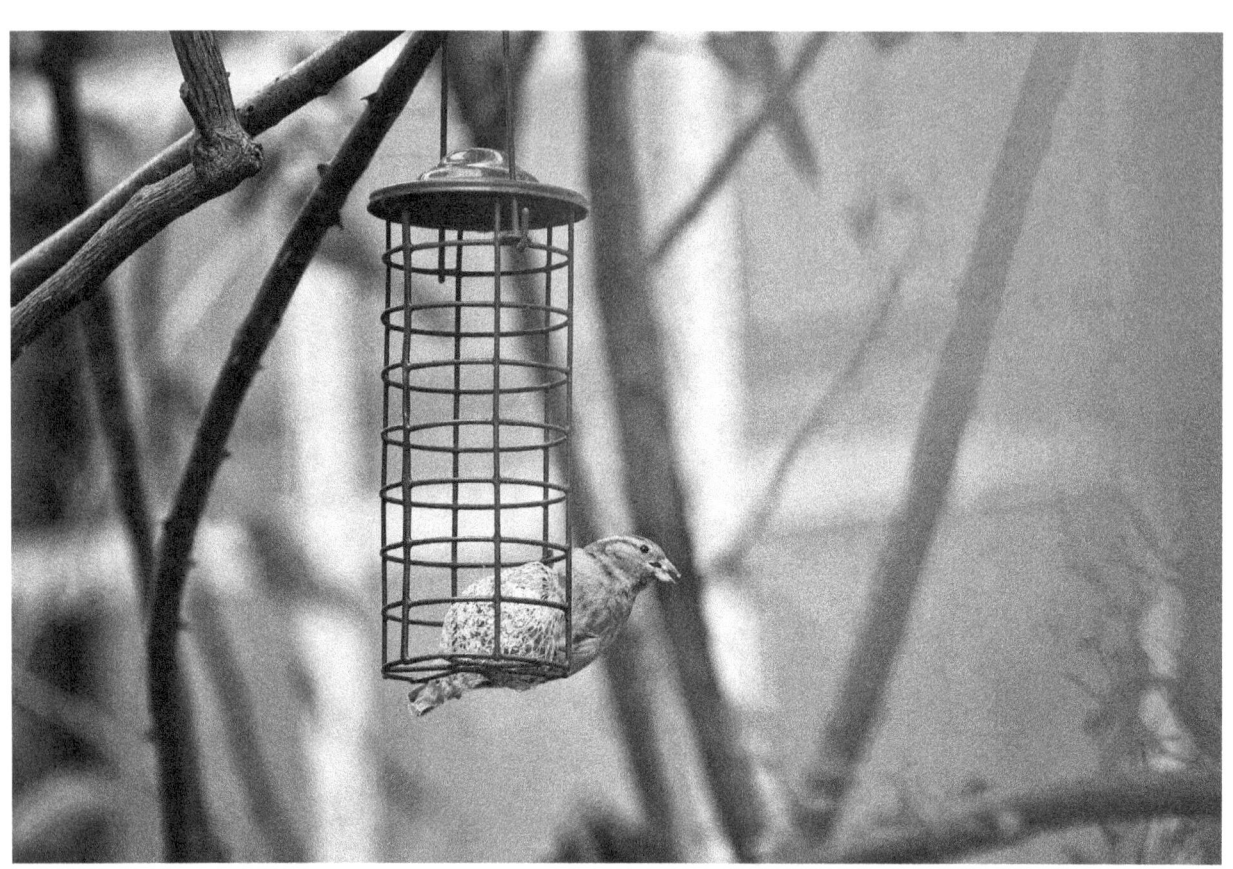

Little bird in the Museum of Romantics garden, 2016

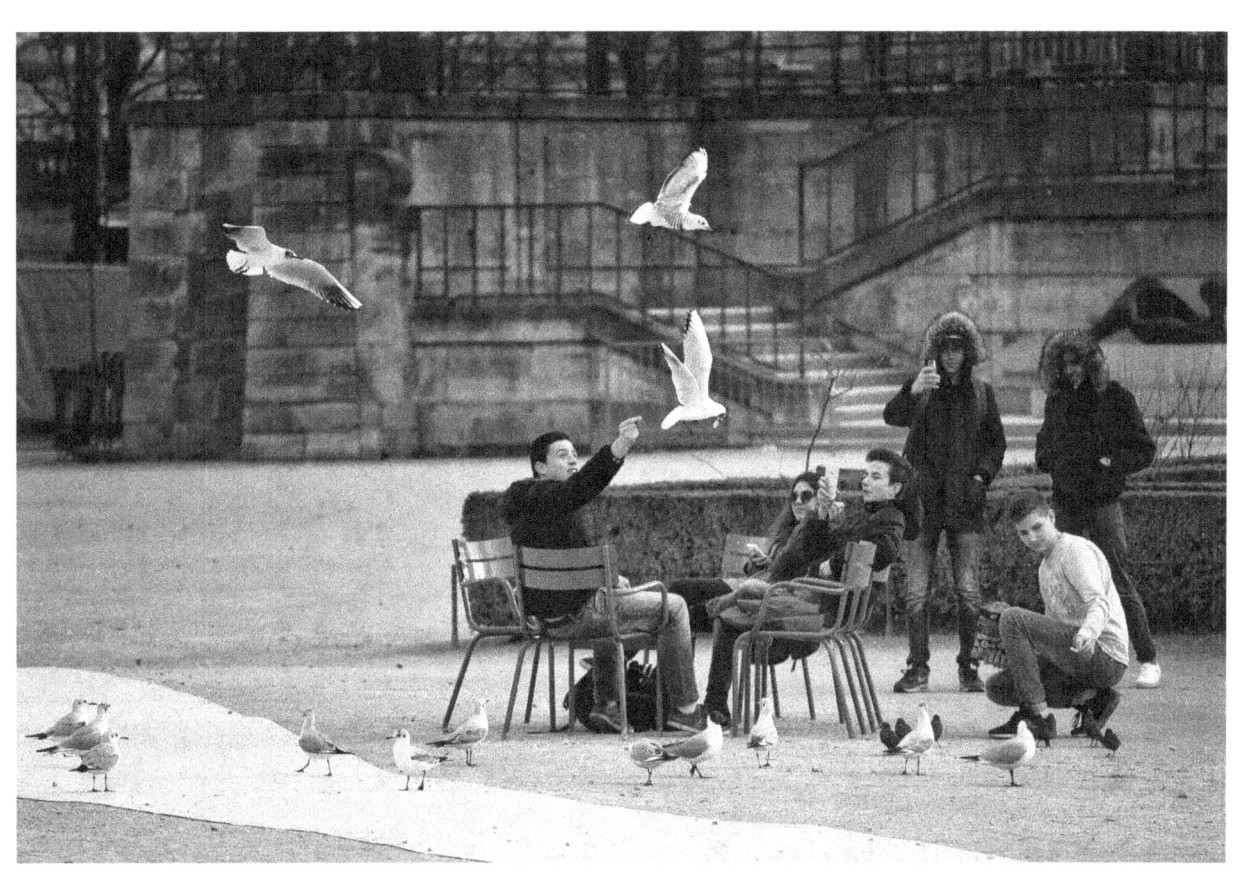

Caught!, 2016

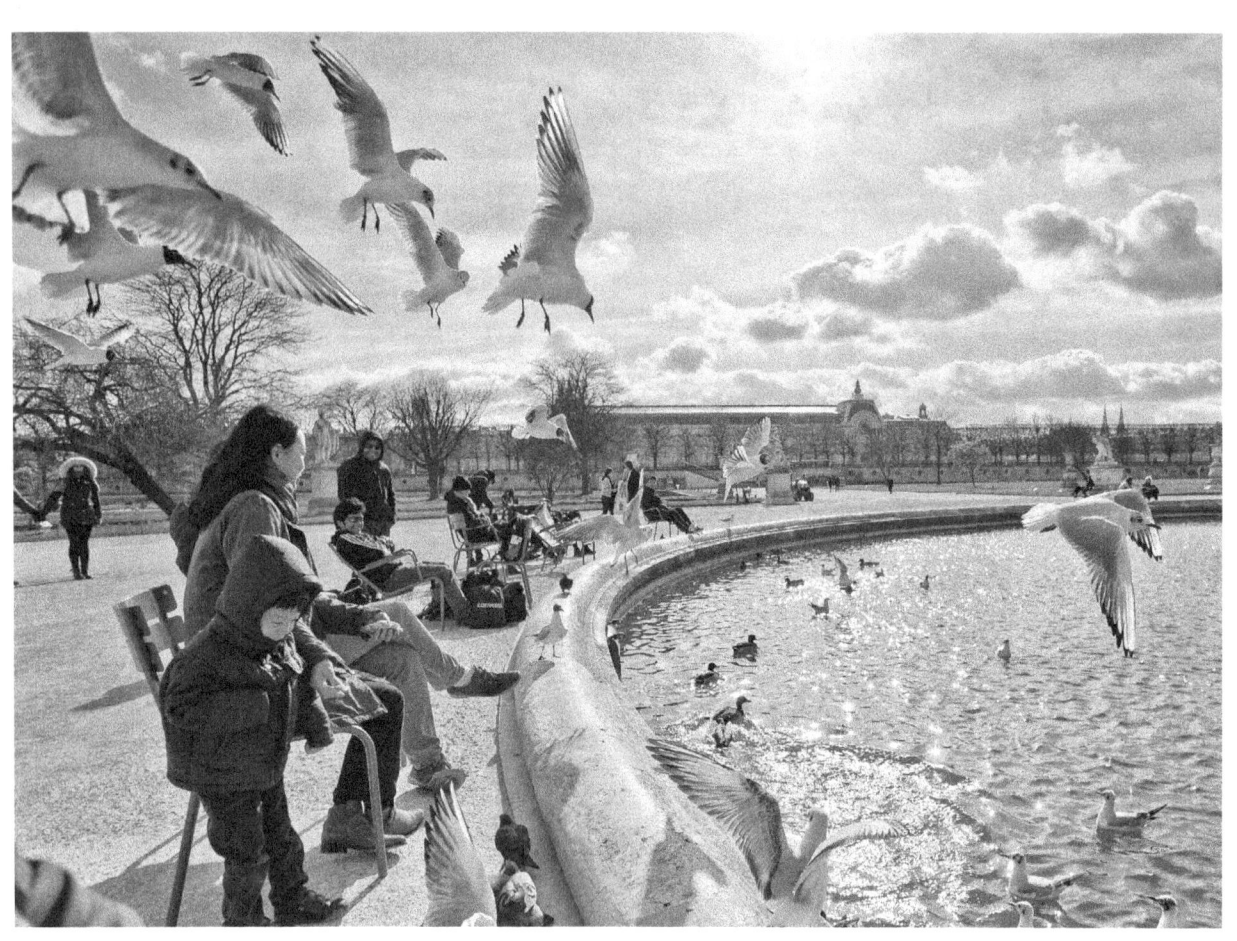

Tuileries Garden, 2016

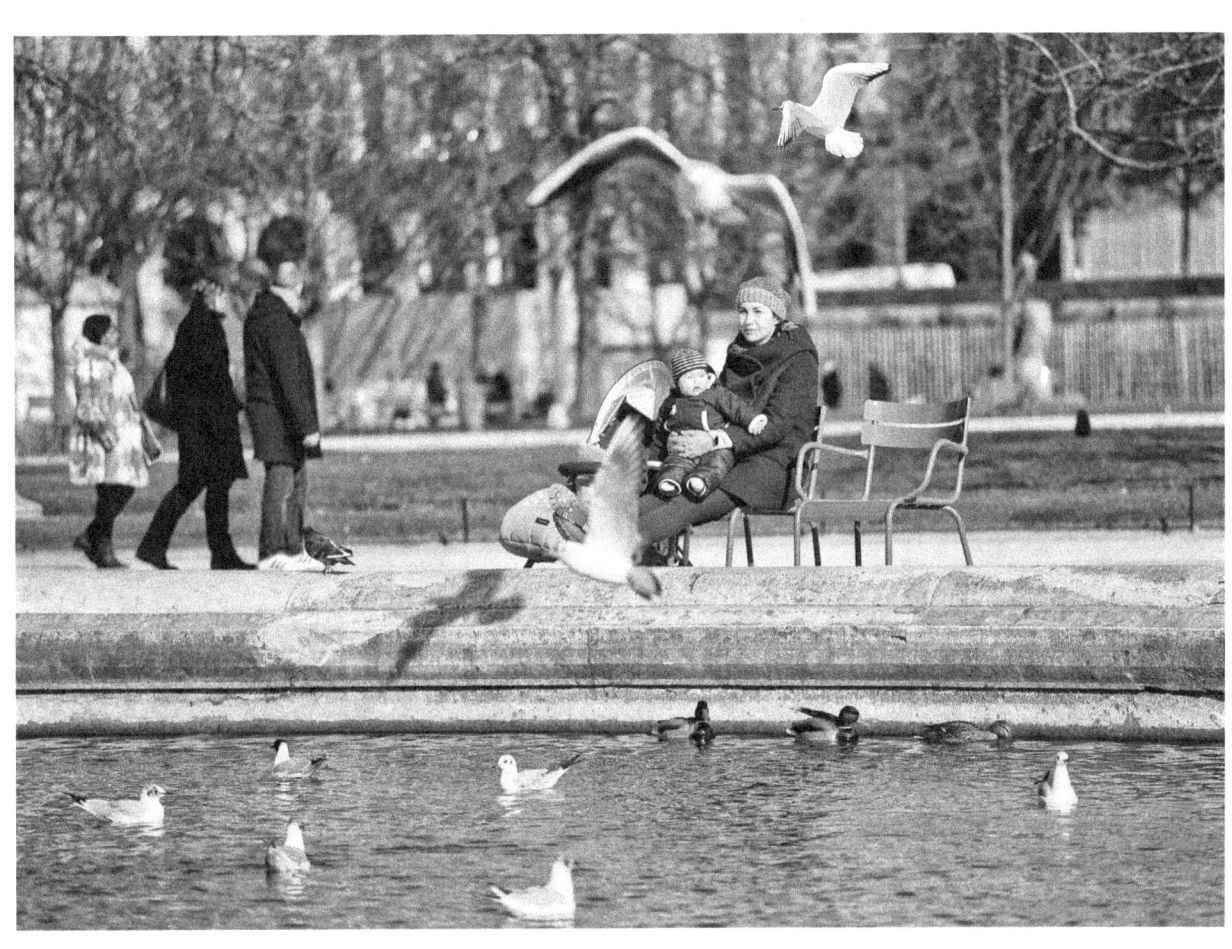

Tuileries Garden 2, 2016

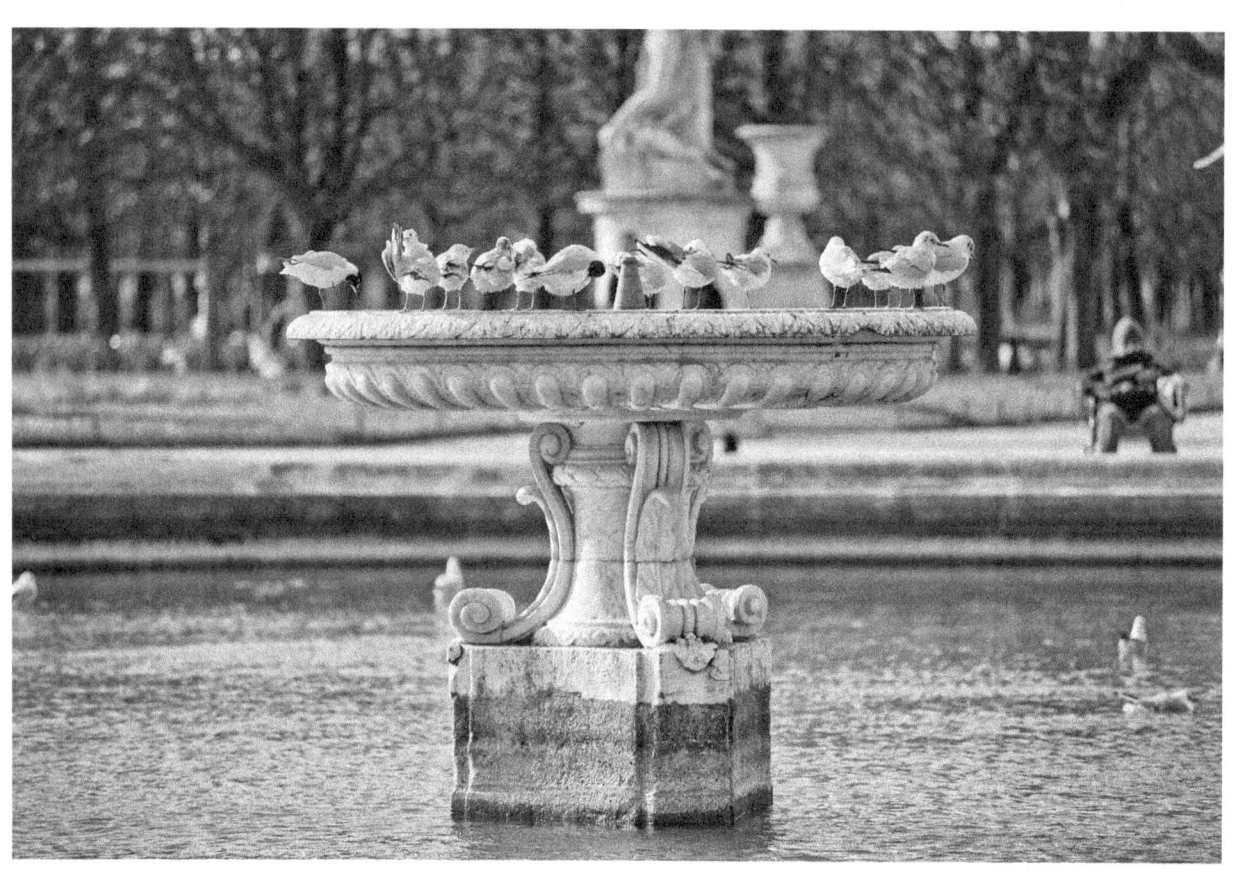

Pedestal, 2016

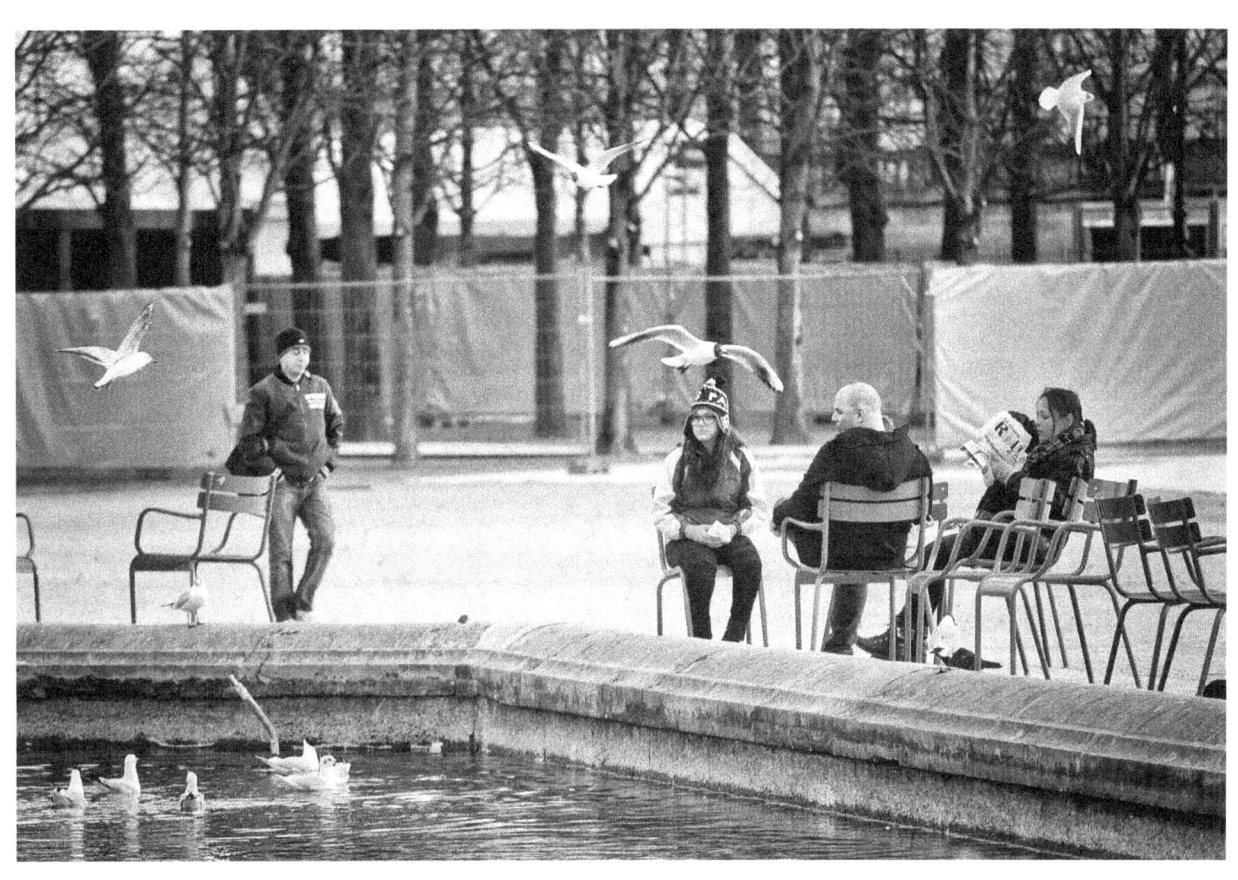

Seagulls, 2016

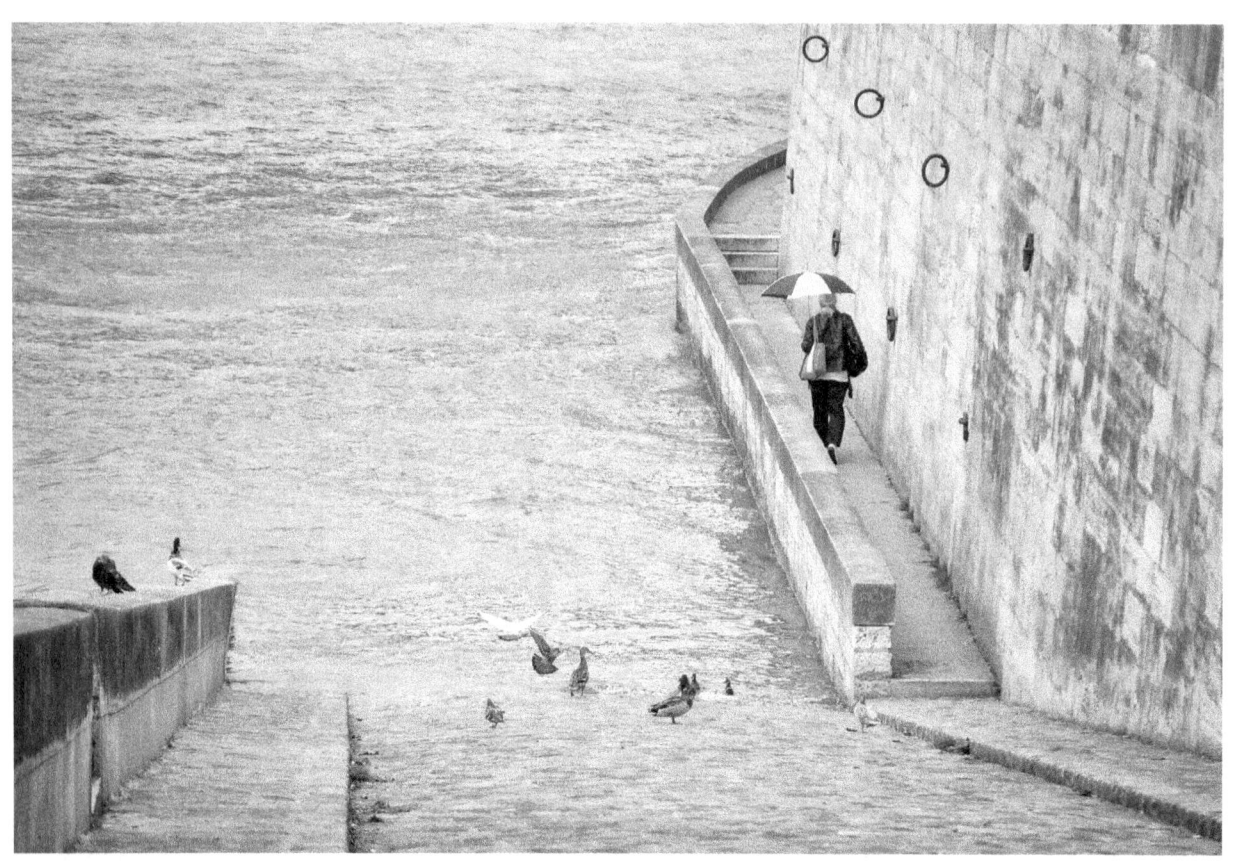

Swimming time, 2012

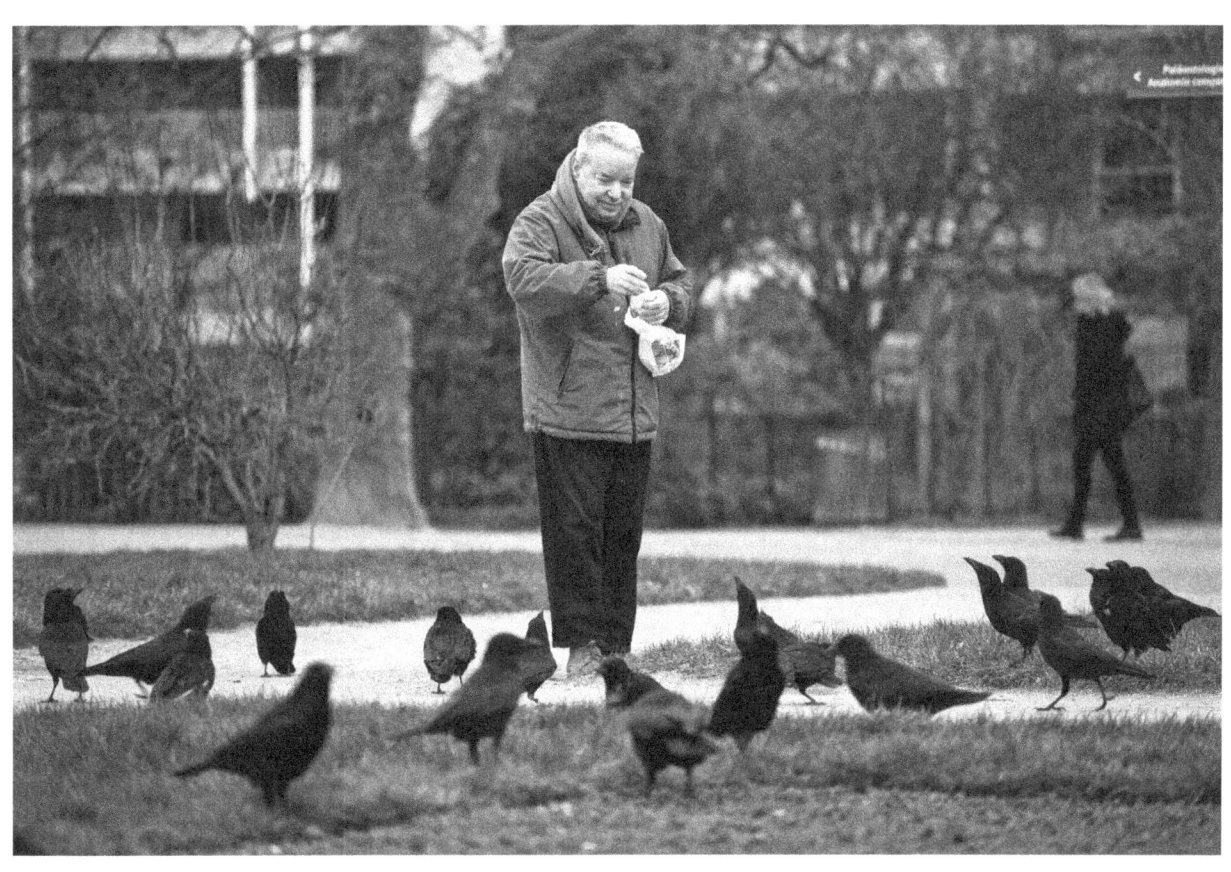

Hello, my friends, 2016

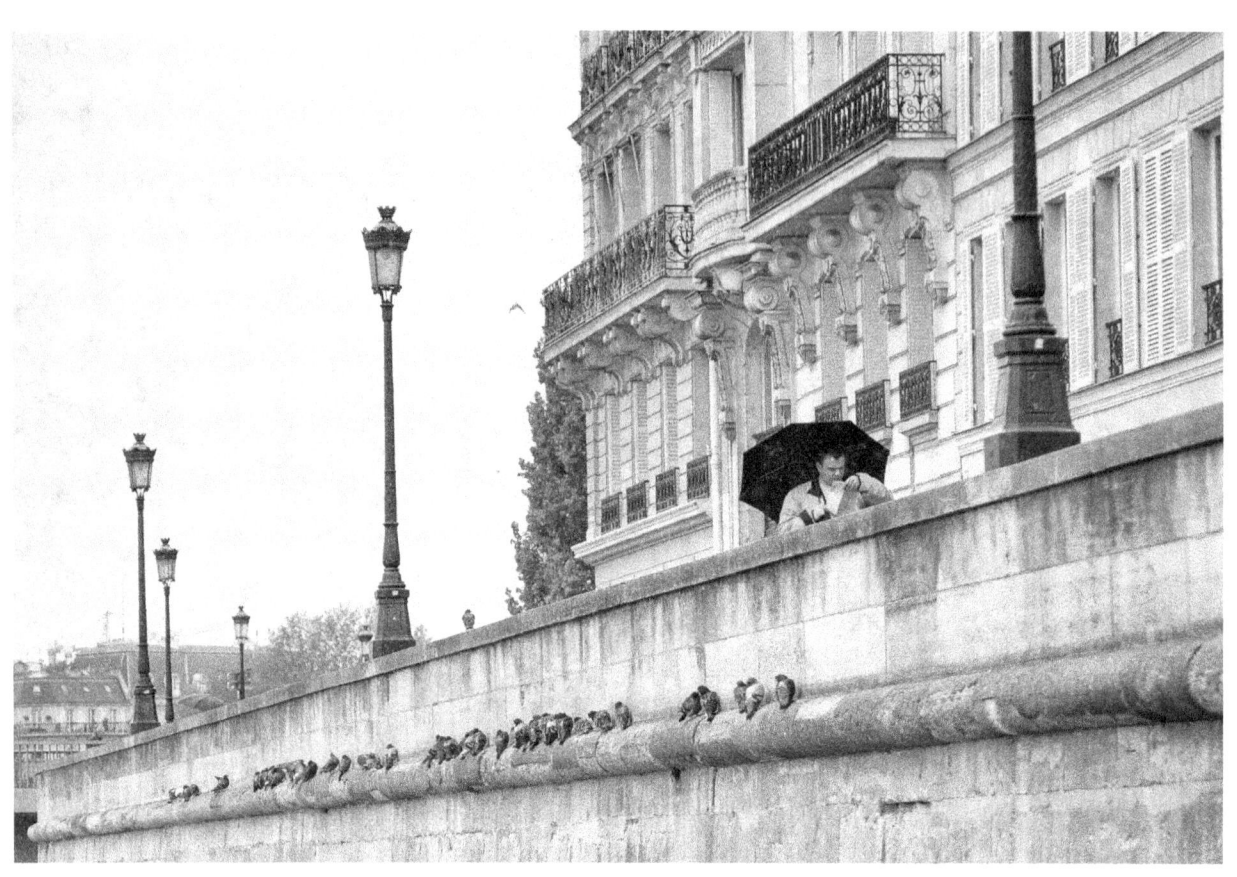

Rainy day, 2012

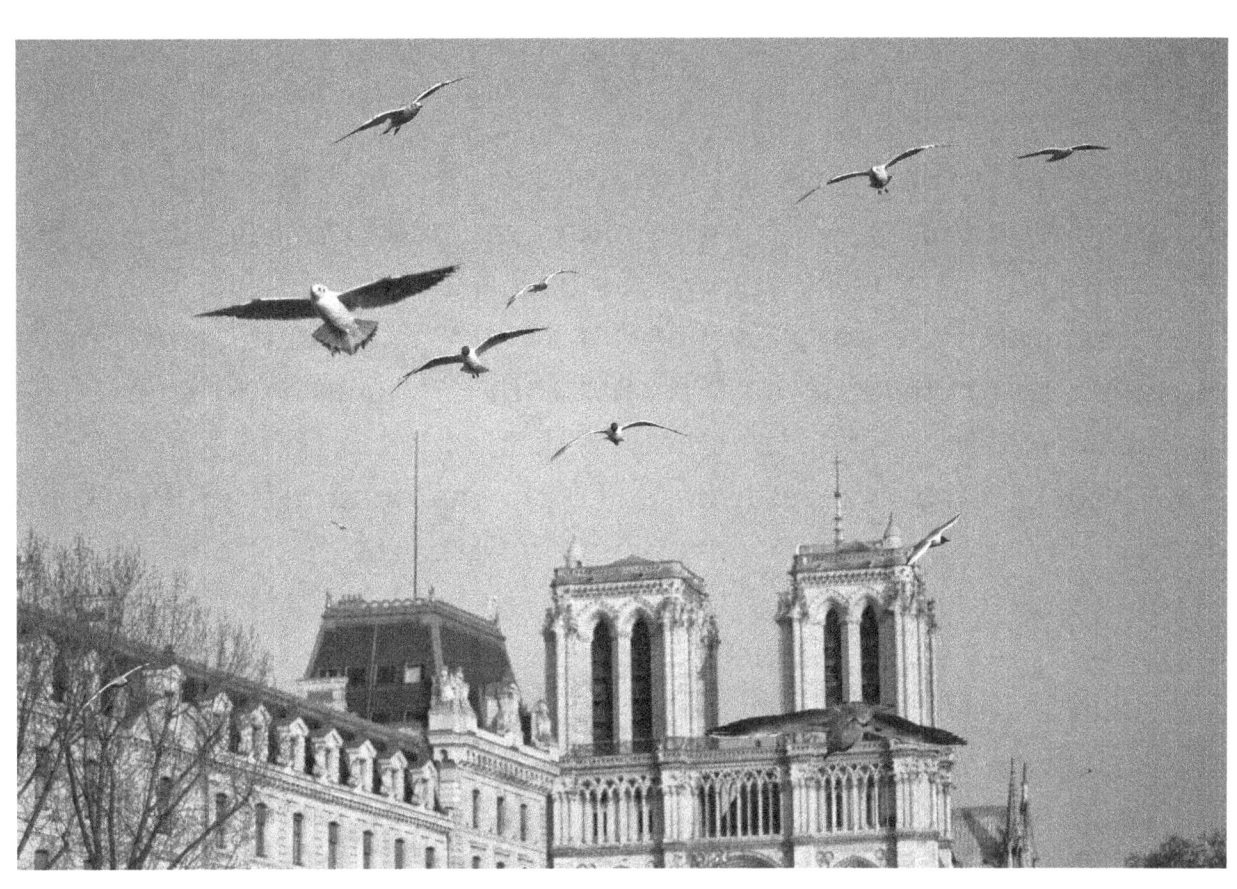

Flying over Notre-Dame, 2016

CHESS

Chess in Paris has a long and rich history. François-André Danican Philidor, a well-known chess theorist, the founder of the modern style of playing chess, was living in Paris in the 18th century. Famous Café de la Régence in Paris was an important European center of chess in the 18th and 19th centuries. All the strongest chess masters of the time played there.

World Chess Federation (FIDE) was founded in Paris in 1924. Nowadays, large tournaments with the participation of strongest grandmasters of the world are held in Paris, for example, one of the stages of the Grand Chess Tour.

Fans of chess in Paris like to play in the fresh air in parks and gardens. There is no chess battleground more legendary, or for that matter picturesque, than the Jardin du Luxembourg. Any day of the year, come rain, hail, or shine, a band of faithful players and spectators will be gathered around its numerous tables – which are free to use and open to everyone – and, in the actual event of inclement weather, under its wrought iron pavilion. Tournaments are regularly organized and the locals are usually happy to be challenged by newcomers.

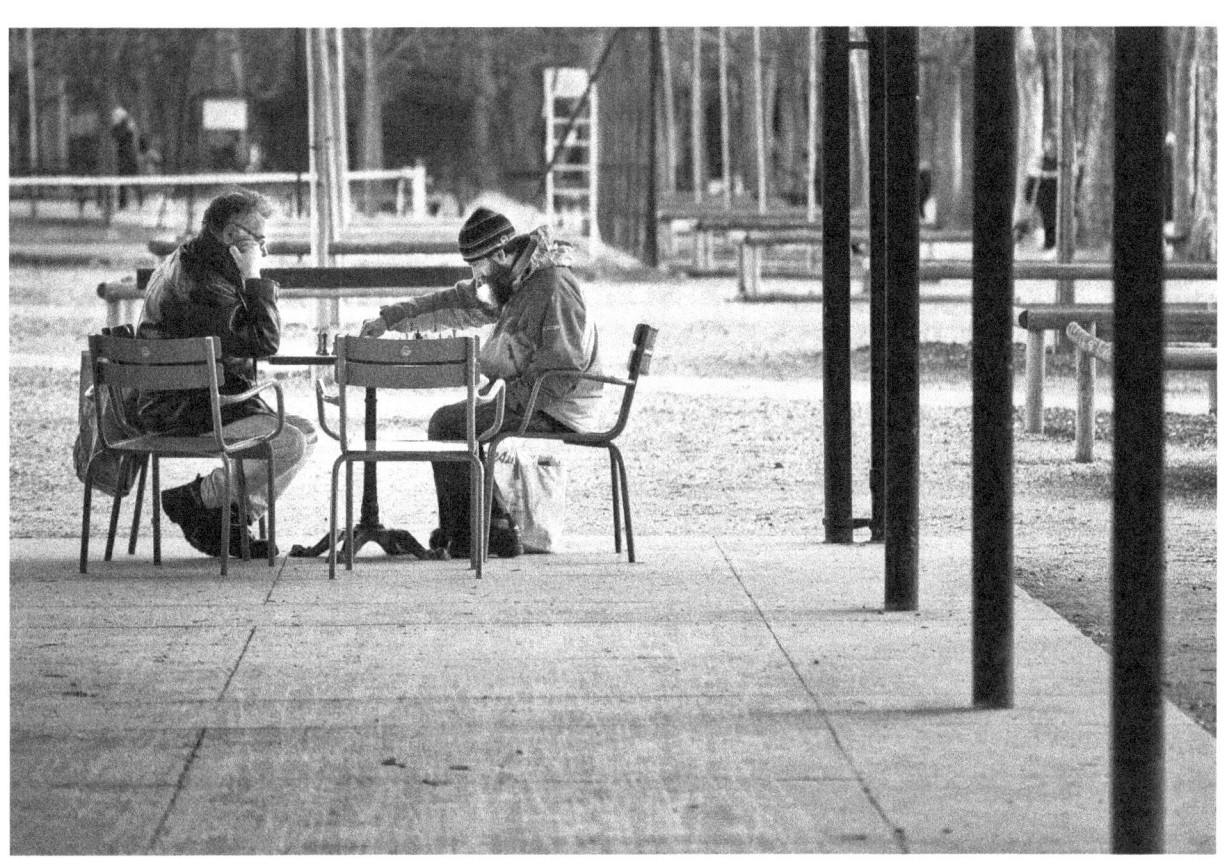

Strained fight, 2016

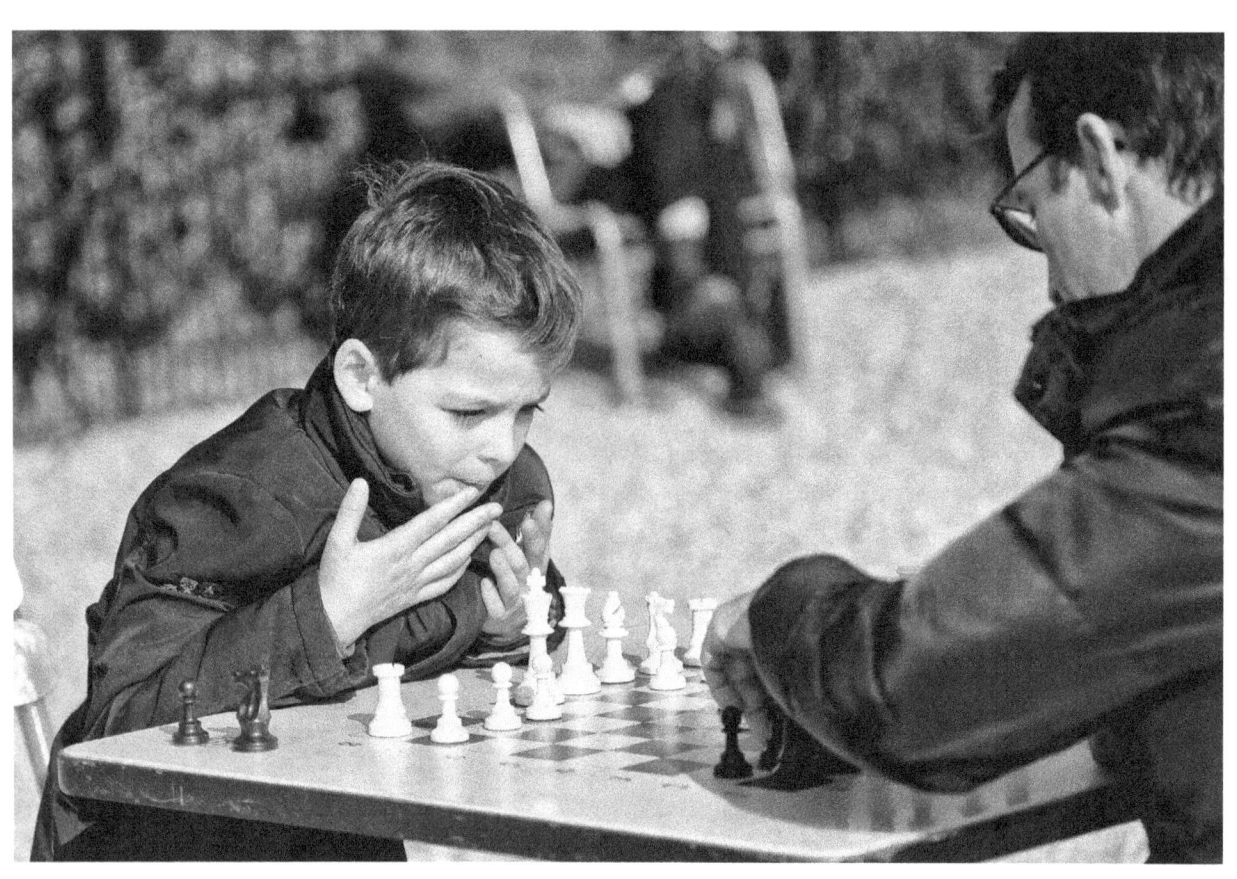

New generation, 2016

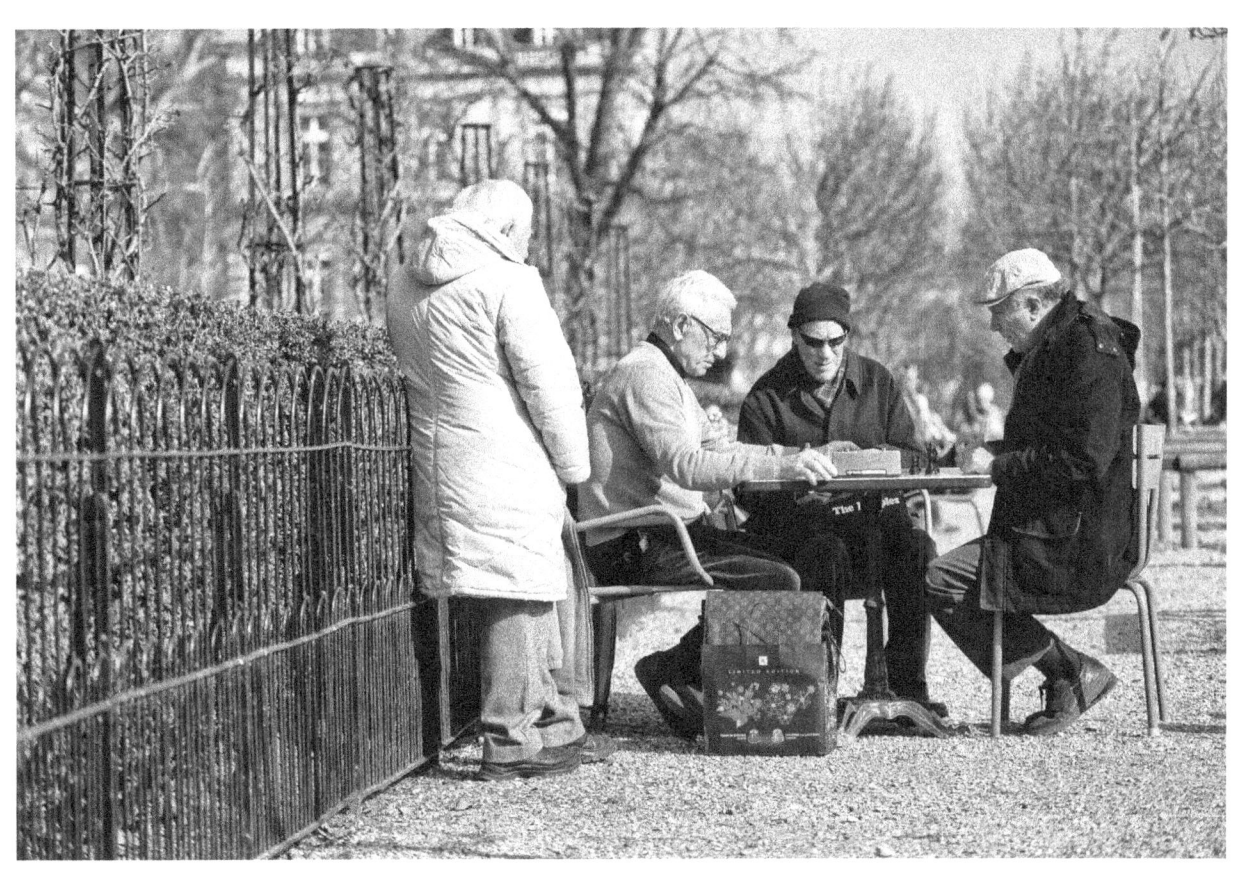

Experienced players, 2016

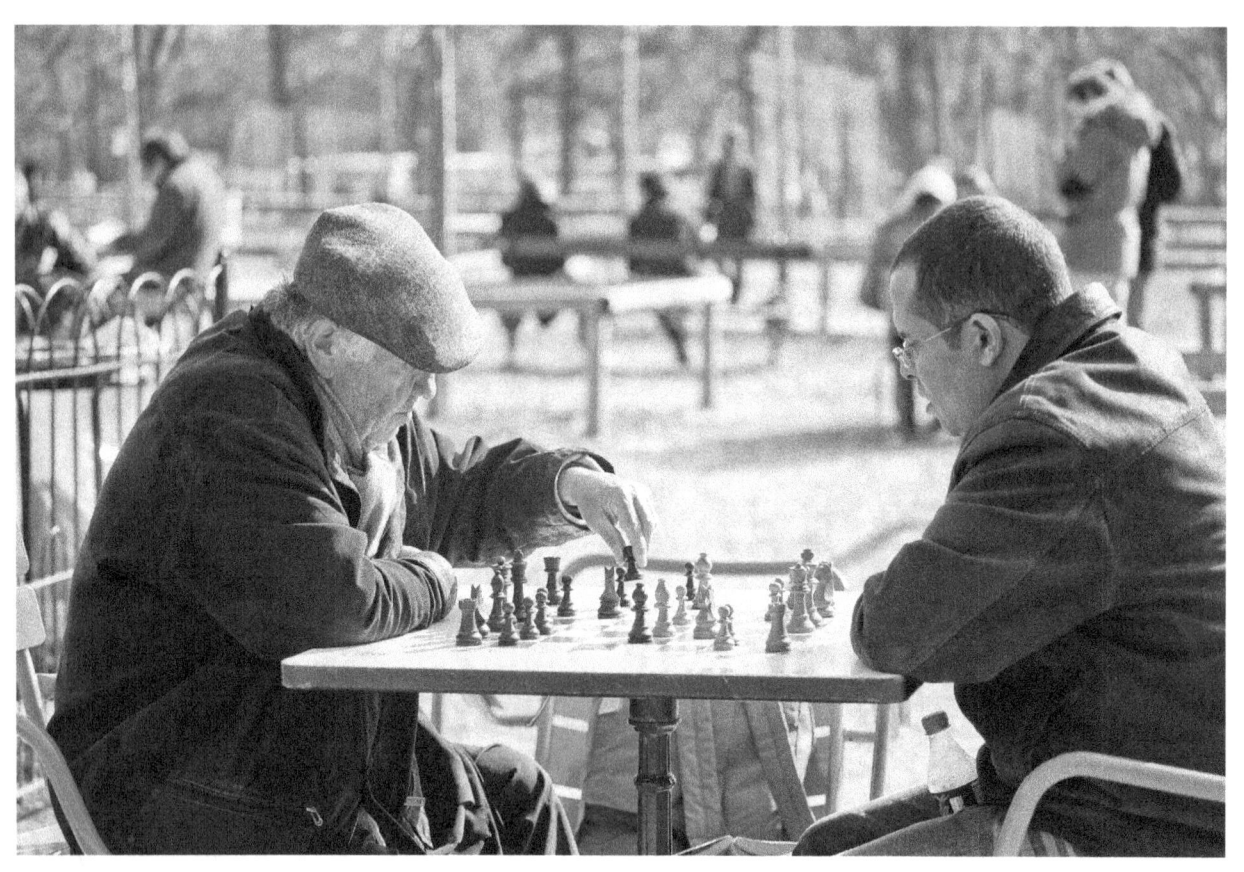

Pawn move, 2016

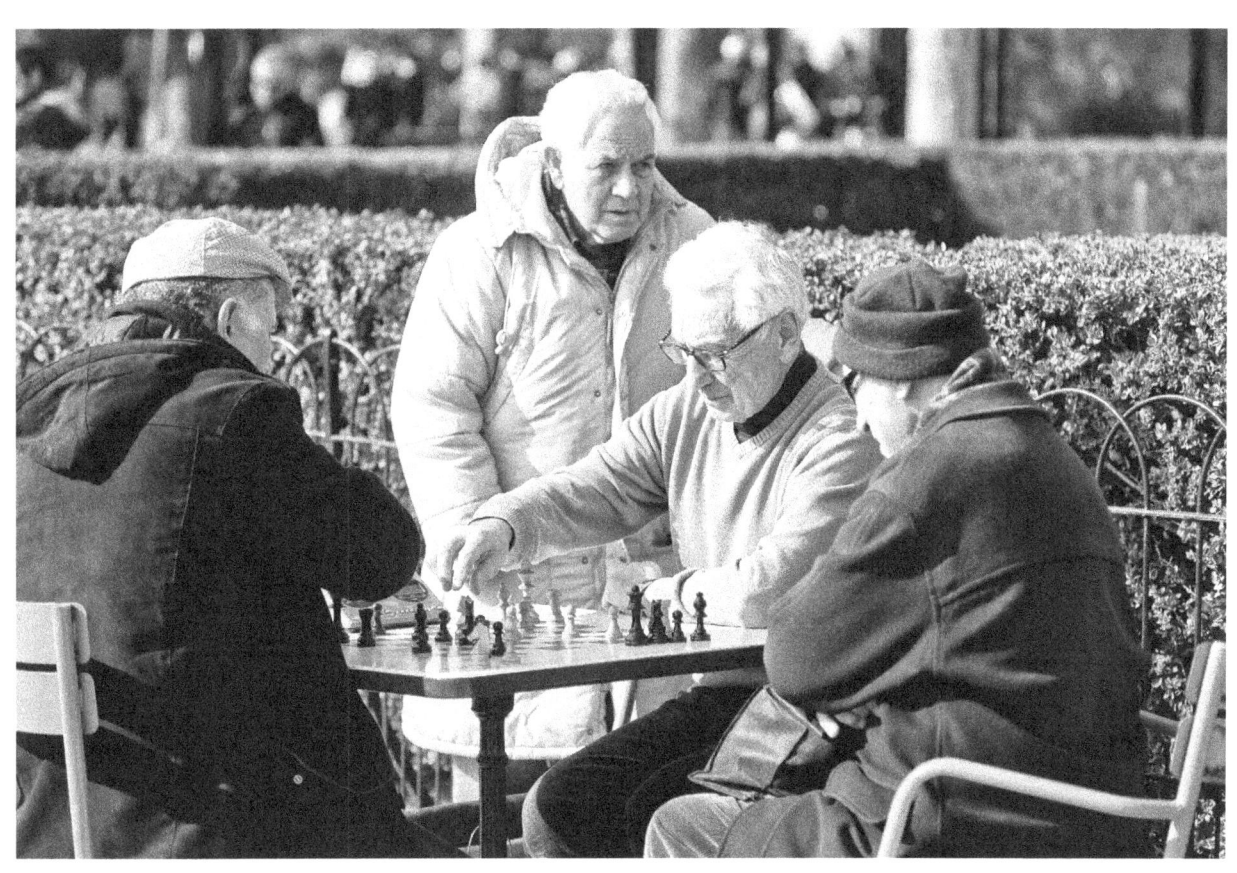

I'll take it, 2016

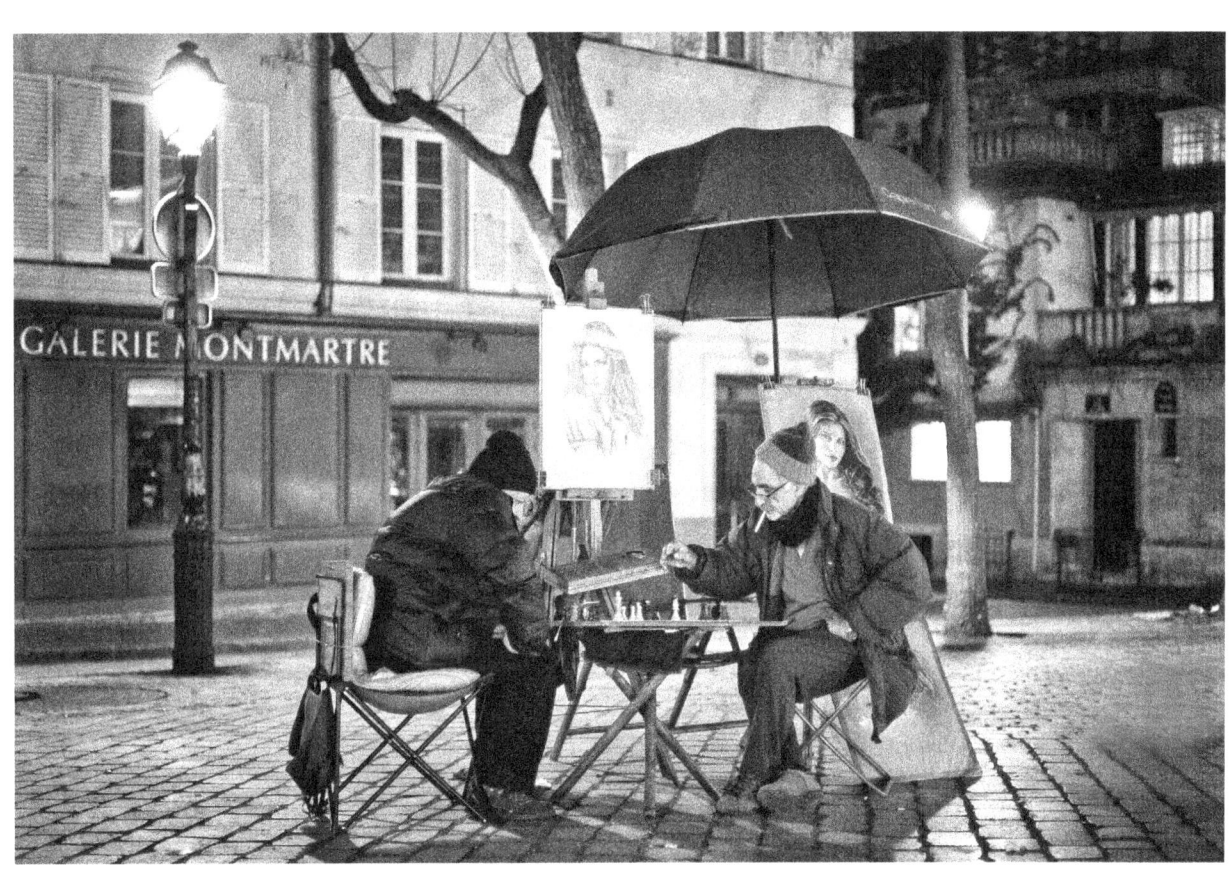

Beautiful spectators, 2016

CYCLISTS

Paris is one of cycling's success stories – for such a huge city, it has much to offer in terms of cycling. But Paris wasn't always so bicycle friendly. After prolonged demonstrations, the number of participants of which grew from hundreds to tens of thousands, city authorities of Paris decided to reduce the space occupied by cars, replacing it with wider bus-bike lanes and bike paths. Paris has steadily increased its network of bicycle paths since the late 1990s. As of 2015 there is 700 km of cycling routes in Paris, including bike paths and bus lanes that had been widened for use by bike riders.

And, of course, everyone knows about the famous Tour de France, the finish of which is held in Paris every summer.

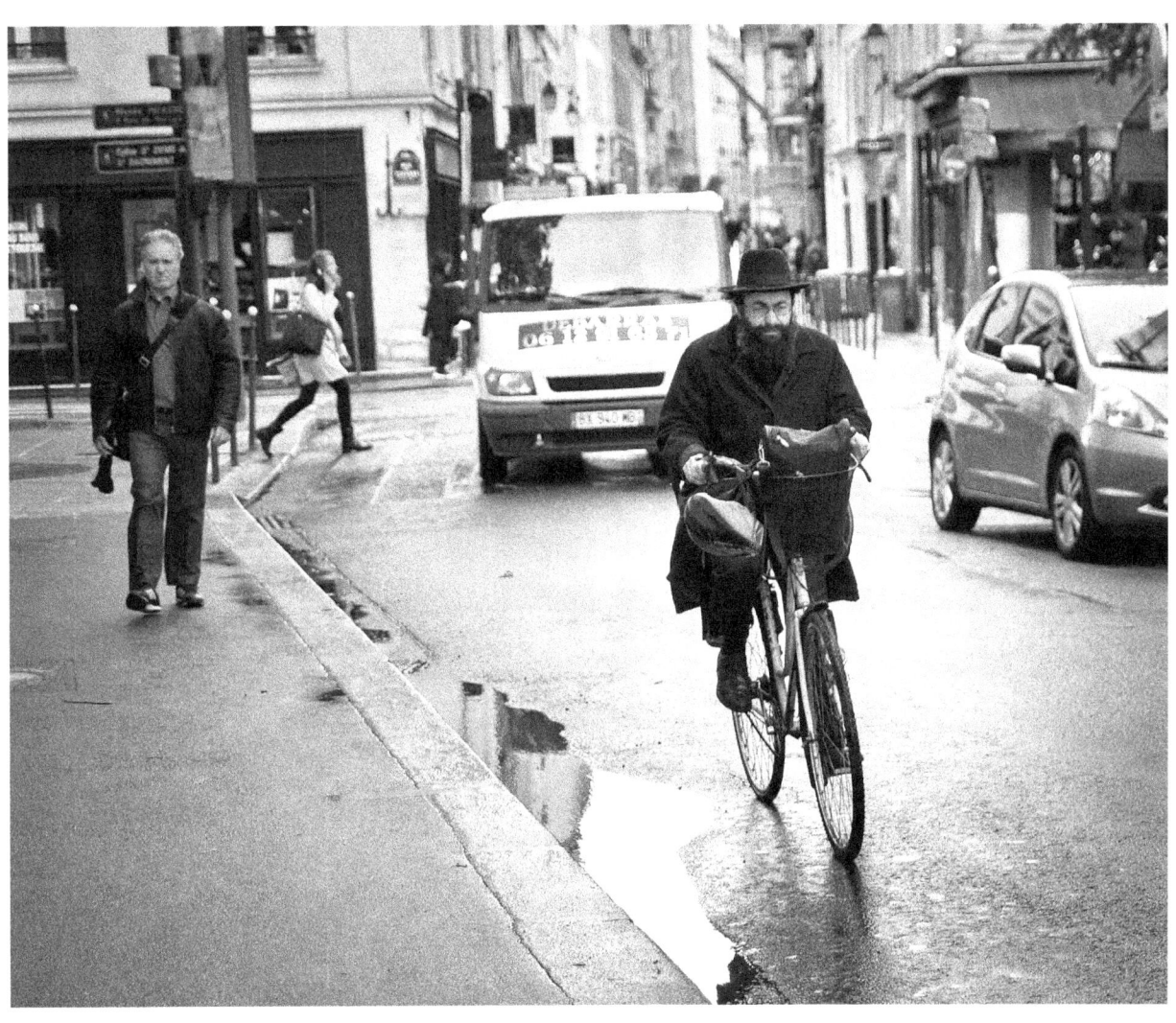

I'm not hurrying, 2012

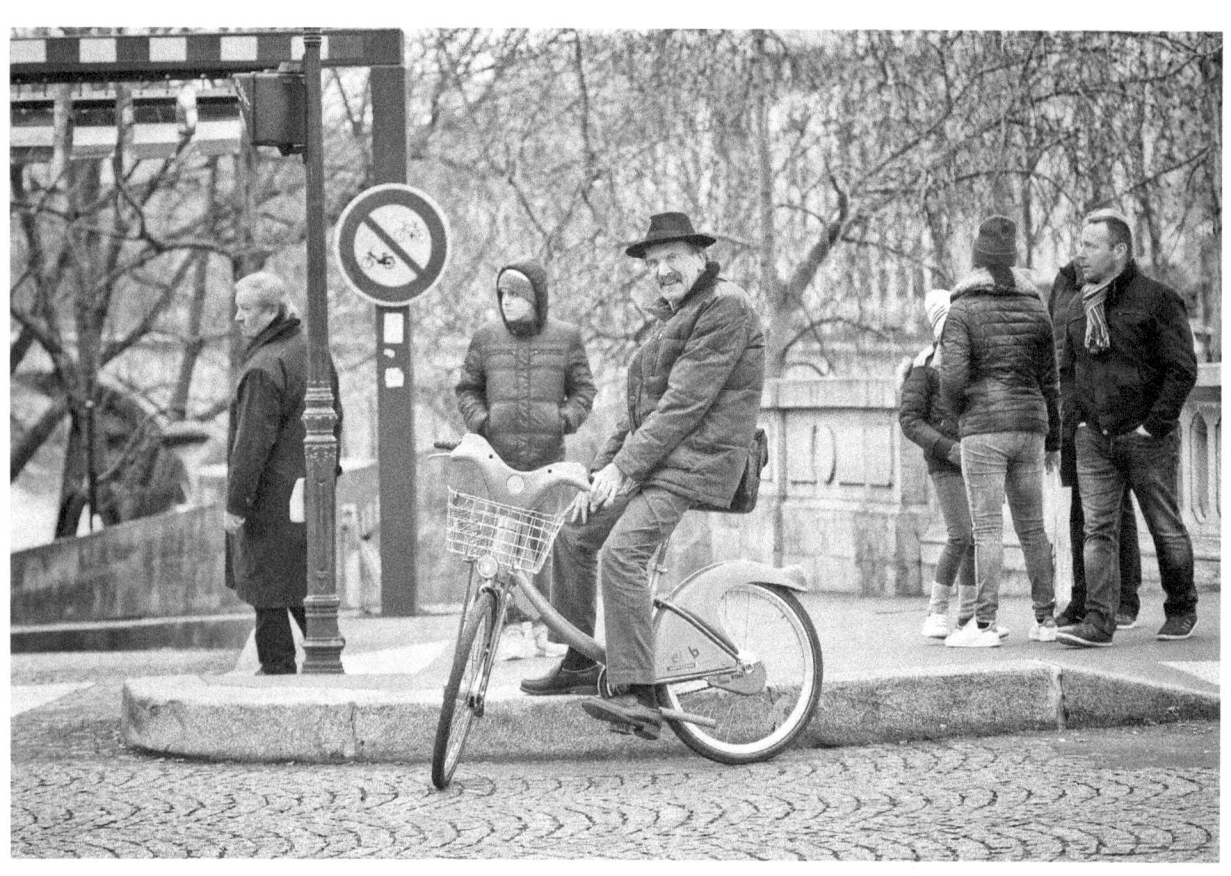

Waiting for traffic light signal, 2016

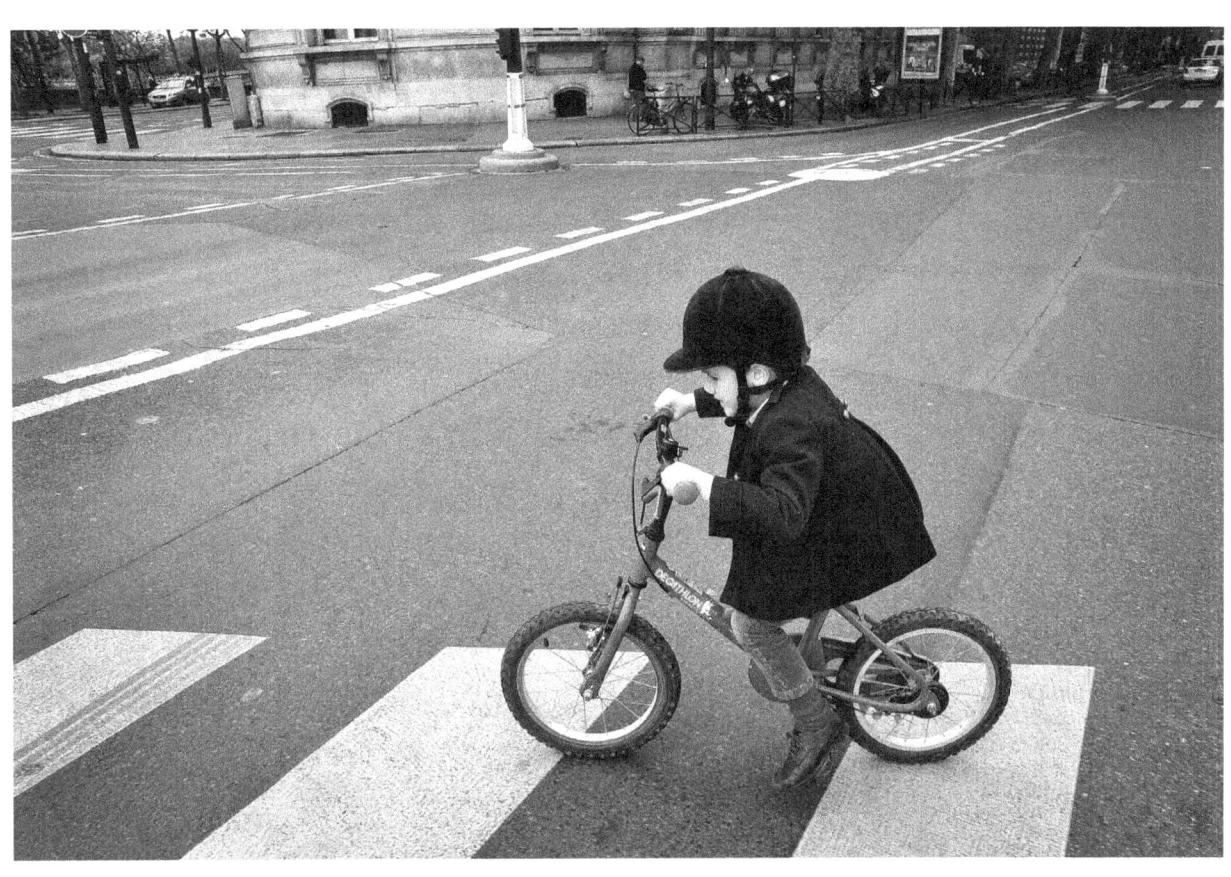

Little gentleman, 2012

PETS

Parisians like dogs and cats. No capital city in the world seems to treat dogs better than Paris. As anyone who has spent some time in Paris will know, dogs have a special place in Parisian society. Most striking is the way that dogs accompany their owners to places usually exclusively reserved for humans, such as restaurants, shops and public transport. Why? One reason might be the small size of people's apartments.

But dogs in Paris appear to have a very sophisticated life. While they are welcomed in bakeries, cafes, shops and bars, most parks have large signs saying "no dogs - even on a leash" - "pas de chien, même tenus en laisse". Fortunately, this is Paris and most rules are not strictly enforced - the standard Parisian attitude seems to be "rules don't apply to me or my dog".

If there are leash laws, they are ignored. You see plenty of well-behaved dogs walking with no leash. Small dogs can be taken on buses, trams, metro and RER. Larger dogs, with the exception of guide dogs, have long been officially banned from the Metro but you still see them all the time.

With cats, everything is a little different, because they walk by themselves...

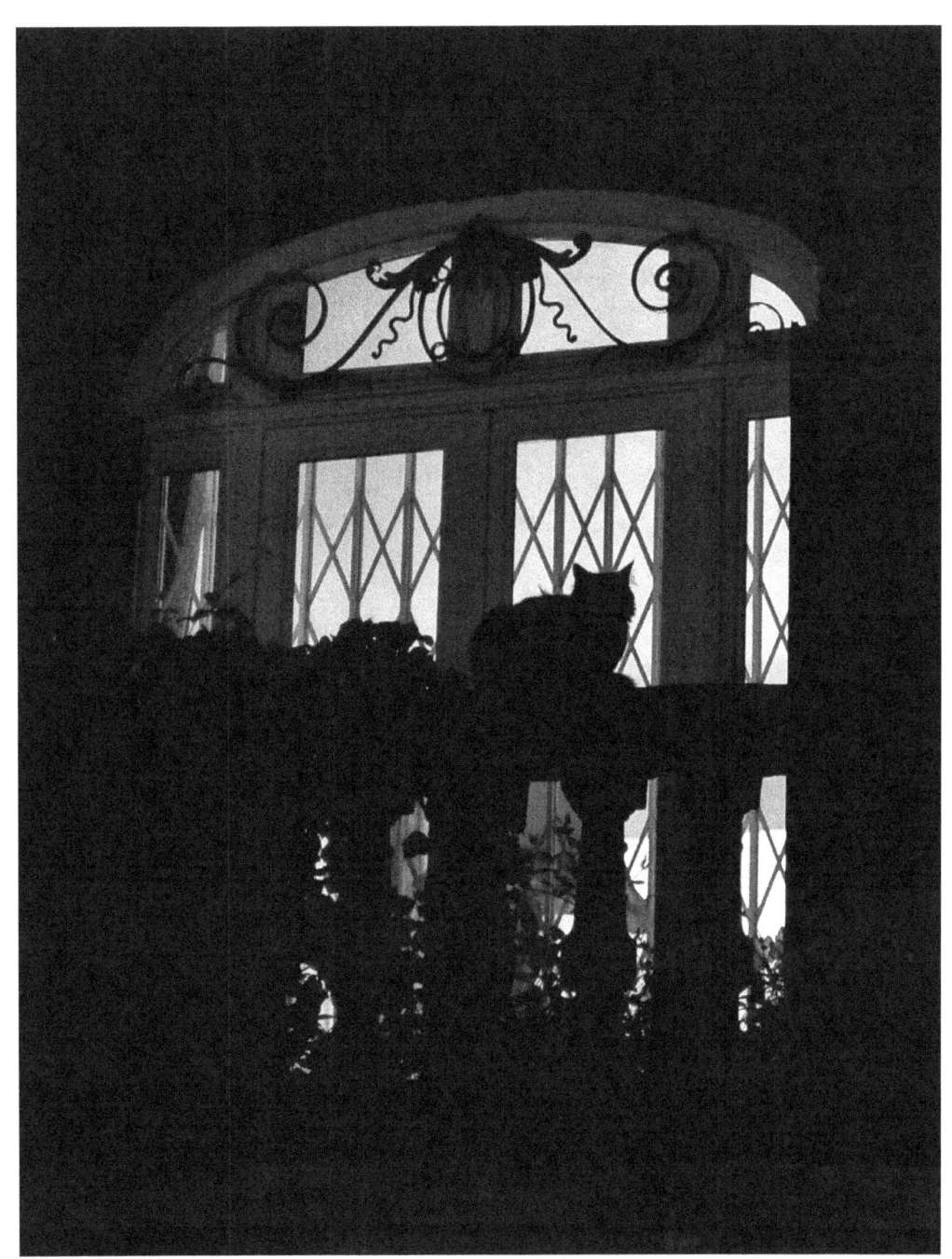

In the window, 2012

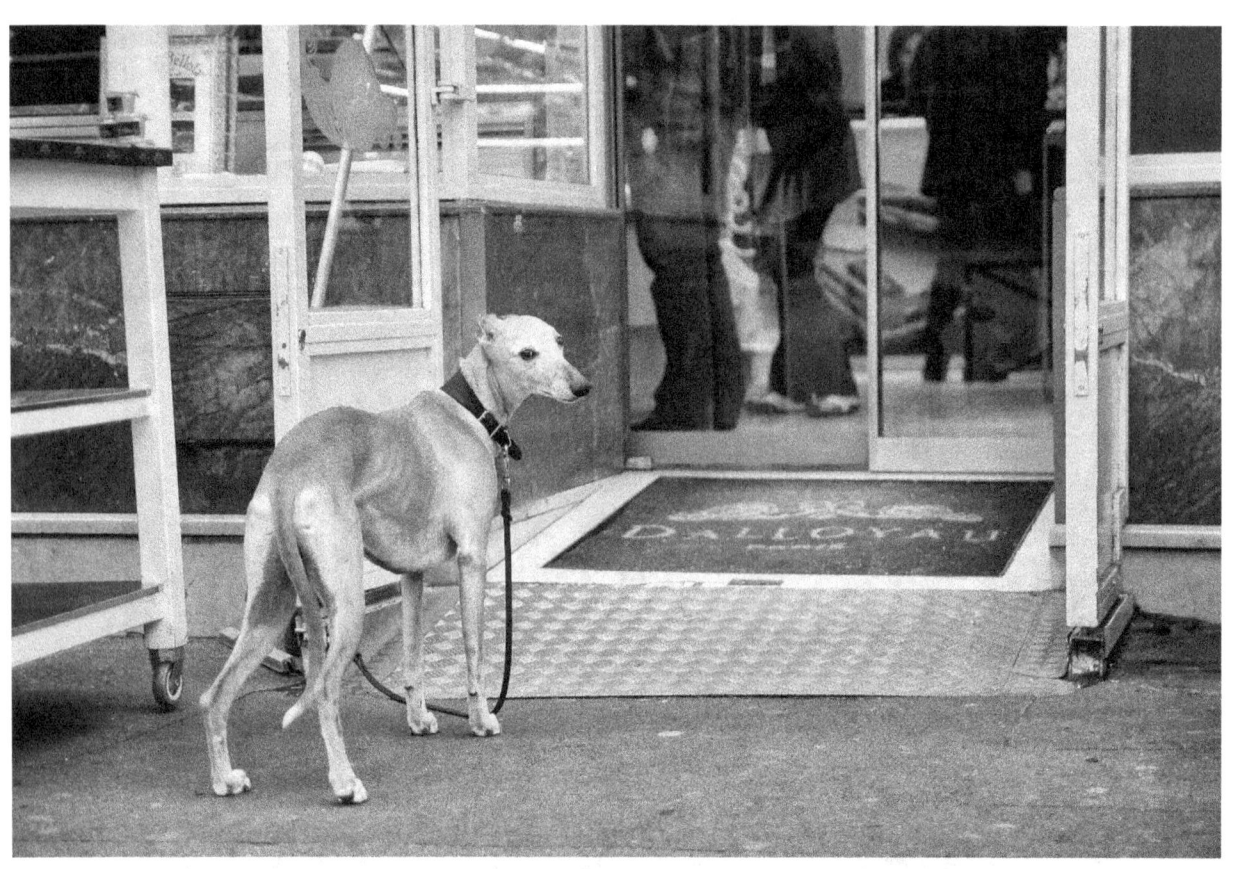

My owner loves sweets, 2012

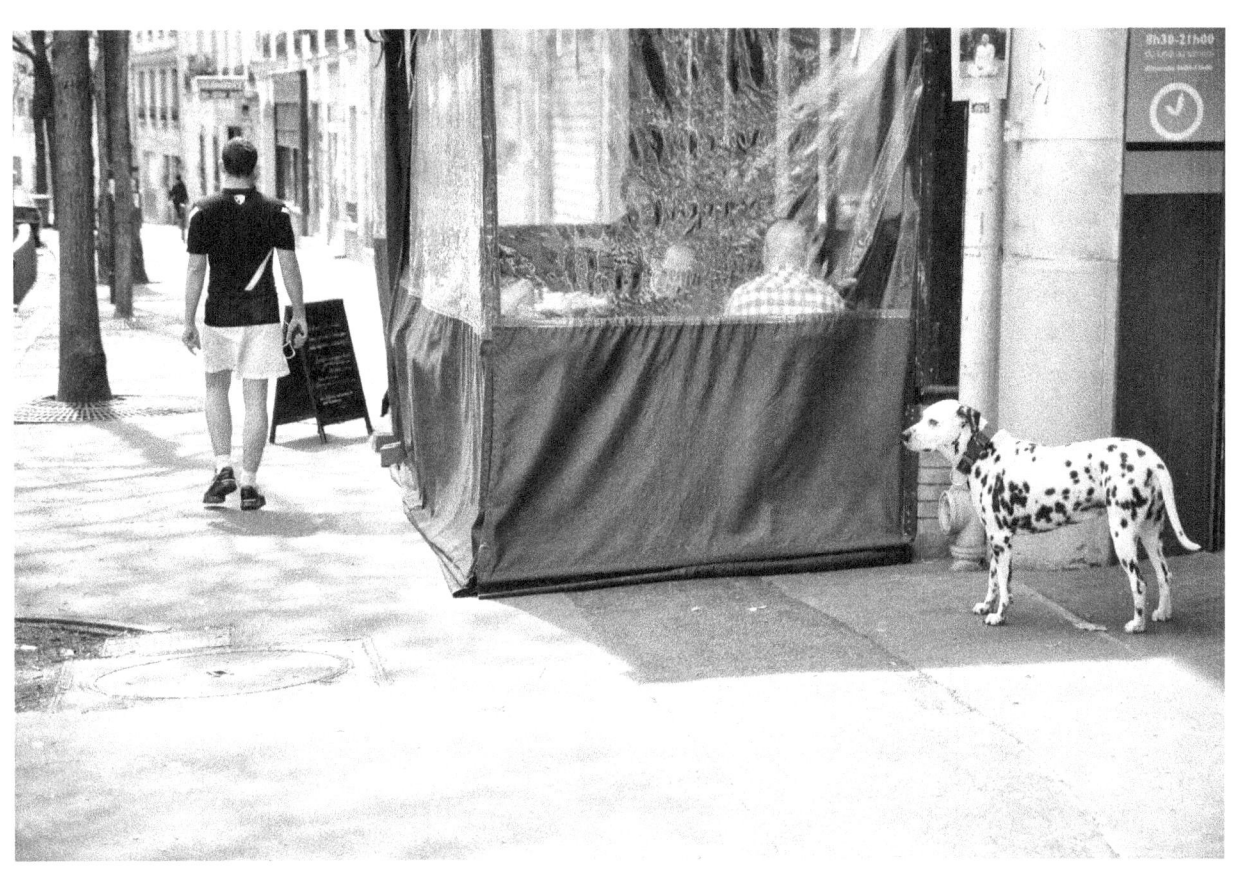

I hope, he will buy something tasty for me, 2012

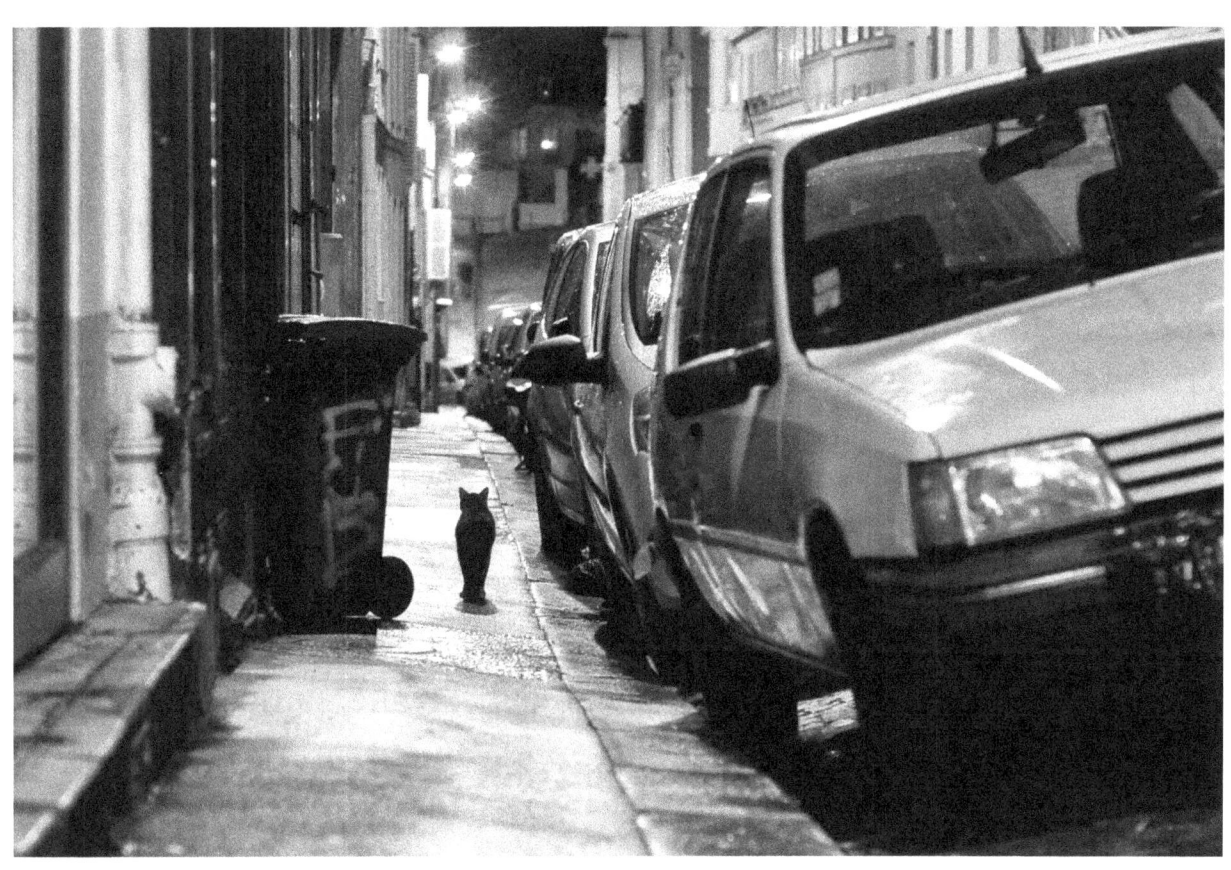

Night walk, 2012

POLICE

Everything is special in Paris, and the police are also special. The most famous and recognizable is probably Police department 36, quai des Orfèvres, often simply referred to as 'The 36' or 'PJ' - home of the Police Judiciaire de Paris. This iconic building is the criminal investigation division of the Police National, responsible for investigating large-scale crimes, drug trafficking, prostitution, racketeering, kidnap, hostage taking, bomb attacks, organized crime and homicides. This is the place of work of the legendary Commissaire Jules Maigret, the hero of 84 novels and 18 stories of Georges Simenon. Sadly, the iconic 36 quai des Orfèvres is no longer deemed to be suitable premises for the Police Judiciaire and new premises in the 17th arrondissement more suitable for modern police work will soon be ready for occupation. Maigret would hate it.

The modern police of Paris can look like formidable knights, can ride a bicycle and horses, or simply smile to passersby with a gun in their hands.

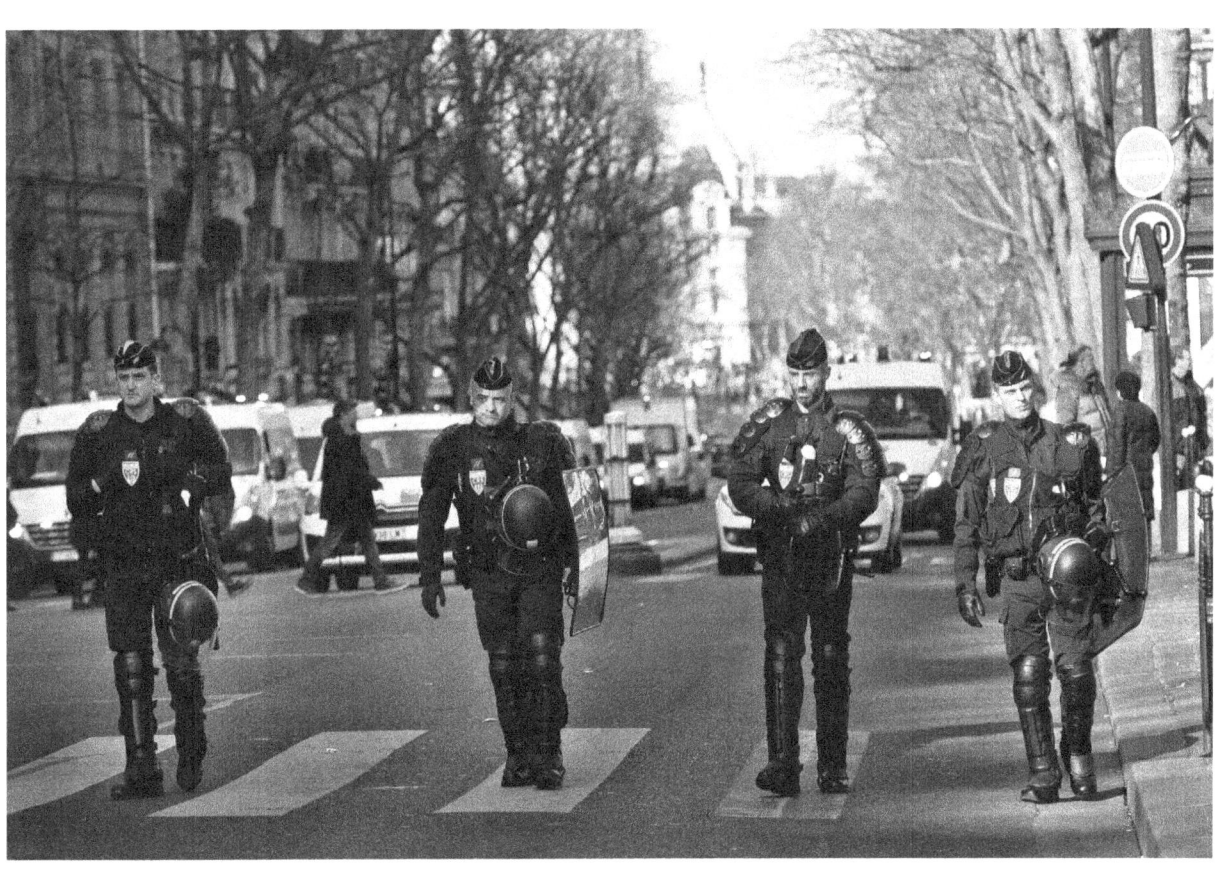

Guardians of the galaxy, 2016

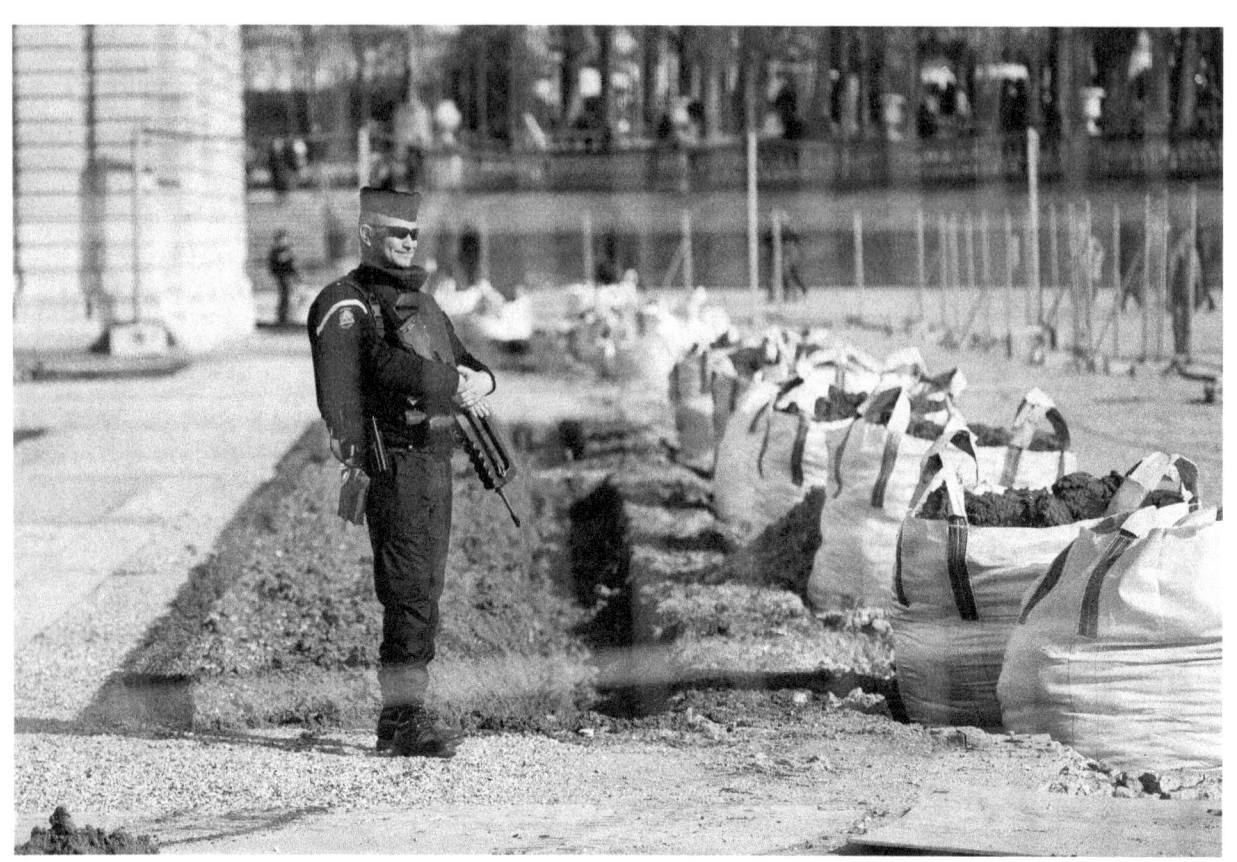

Superhero, 2016

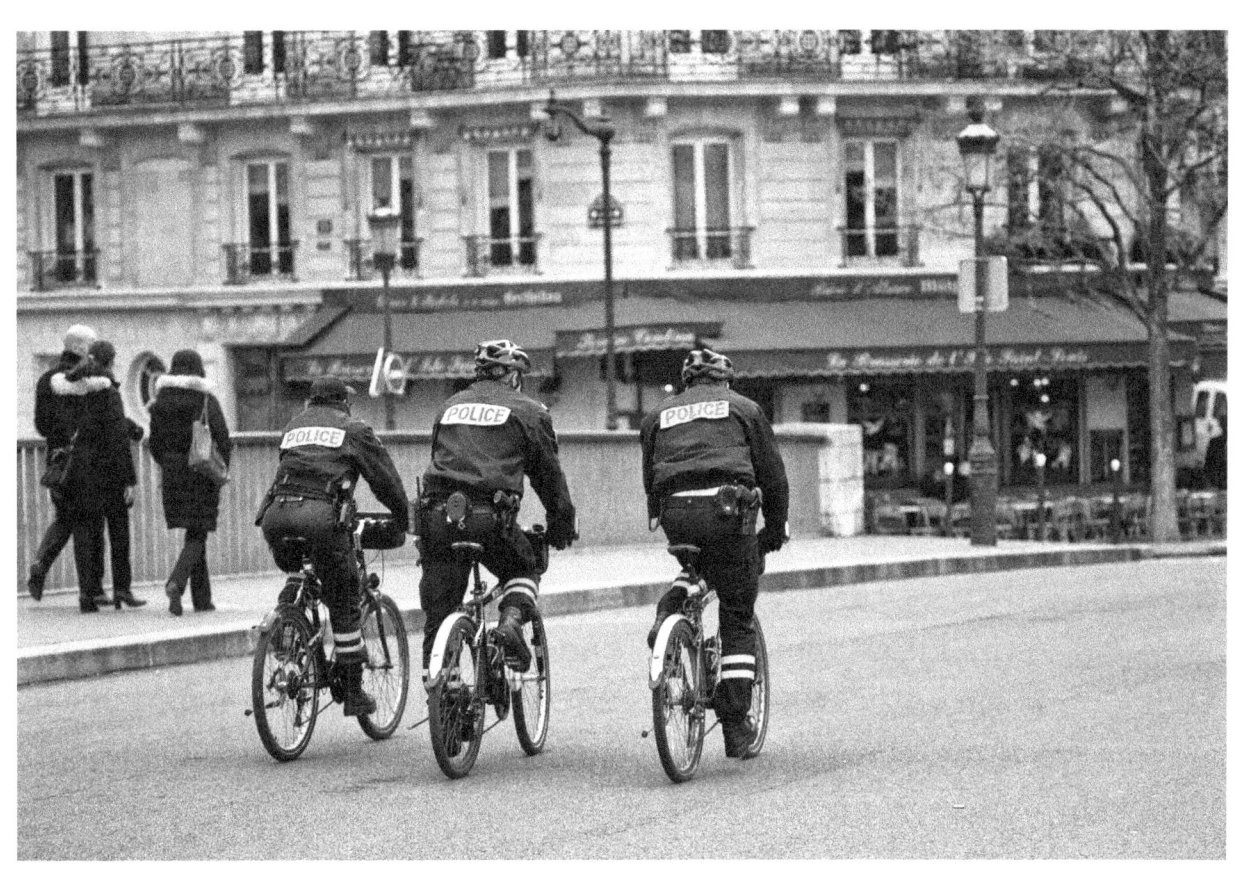

On a mission, 2016

MANIFESTATIONS

Paris has always been the center of political life and advanced political ideas. Demonstrations, or "manifestations" as the French call them, are a way of life in Paris so if you live here you just have to get used to them. Most of the demonstrations in Paris are peaceful. It is only on very rare occasions that any violence occurs. At any demonstration in Paris, the police are present in force, but they always seem to keep a discreet distance and never become visible unless things get hopelessly out of control which happens only very rarely.

Parisians know their rights and know how to fight for them. Strike on large enterprises, in the metro, railways and airports - is a common thing, workers know what they are fighting for, and the leadership must go on concessions.

People take to the streets to express their support for, or opposition against, a wide variety of causes. For the most part, they do it peacefully, enthusiastically and with good humor.

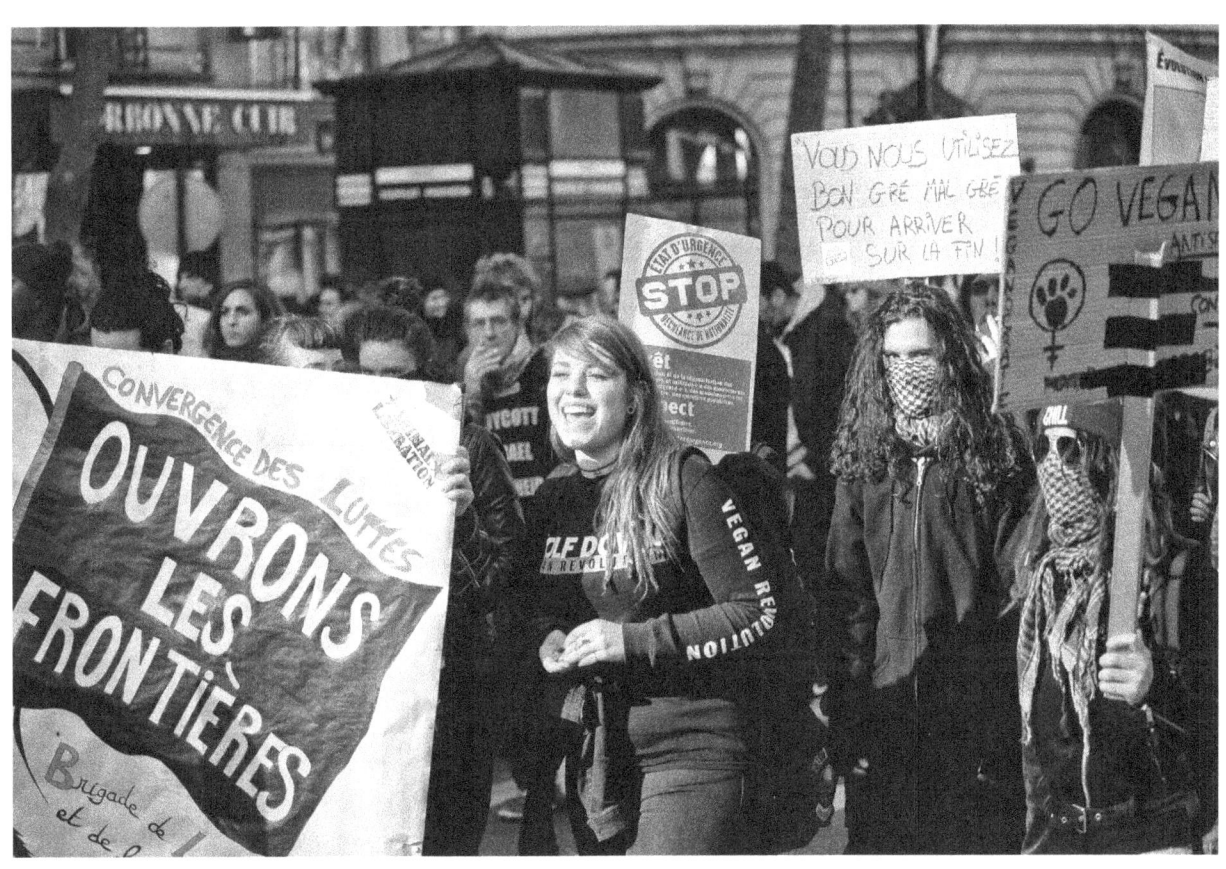

Vegan revolution, 2016

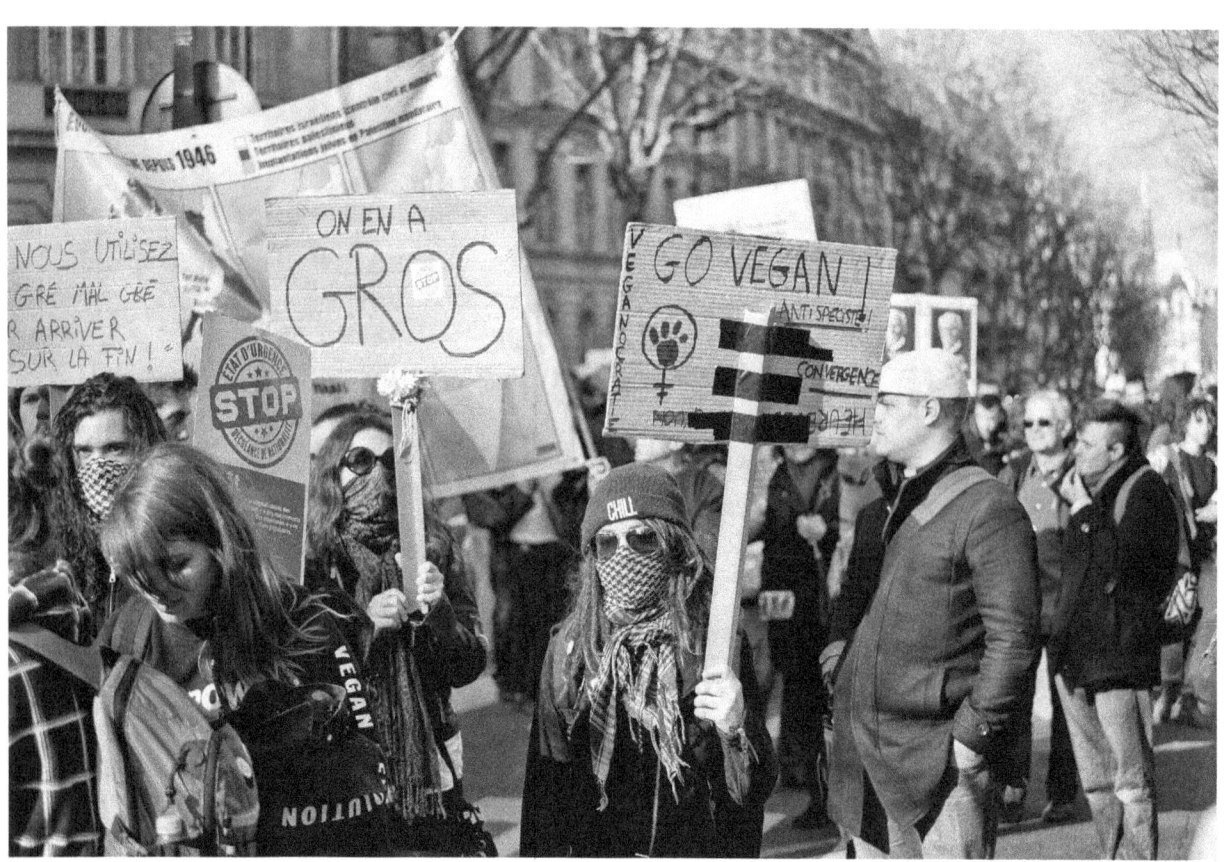

Go vegan!, 2016

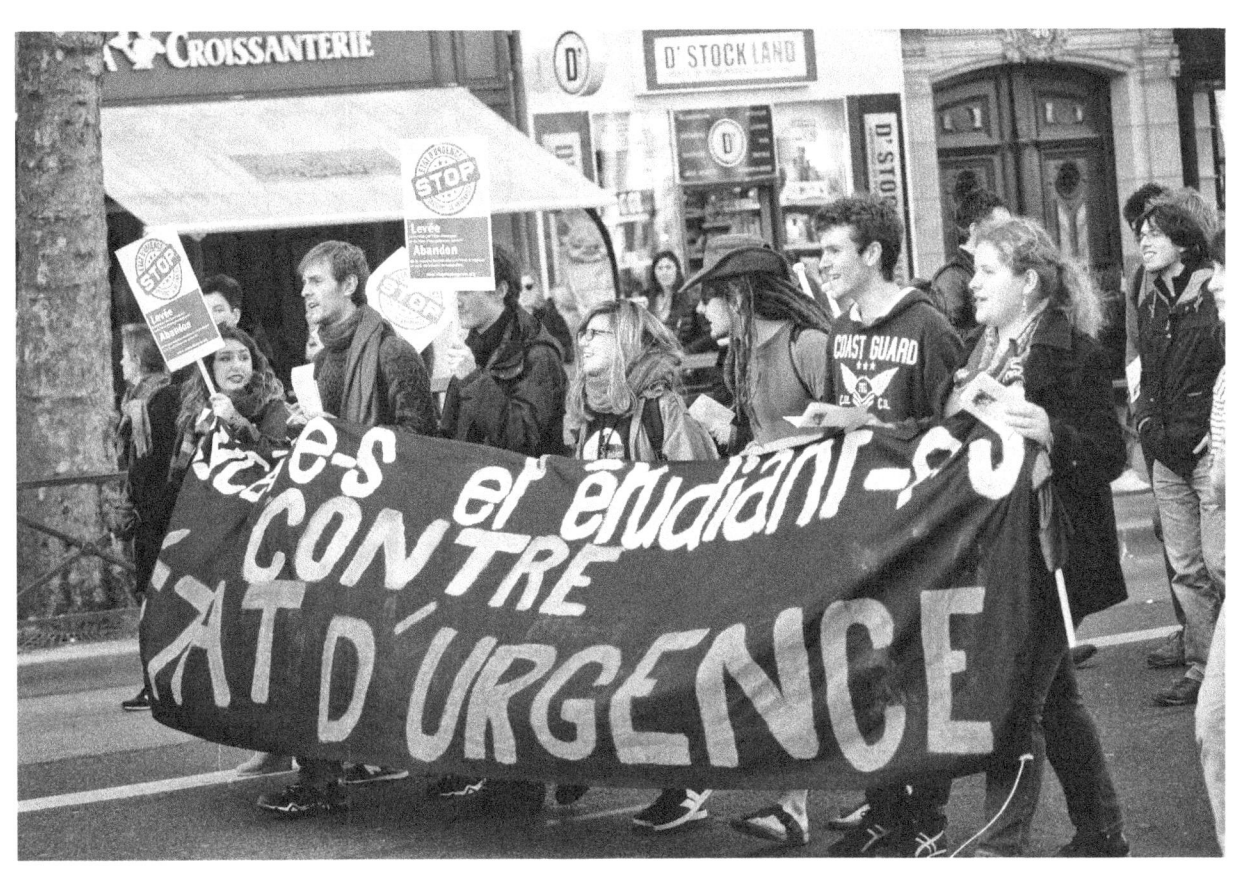

Emergency state, 2016

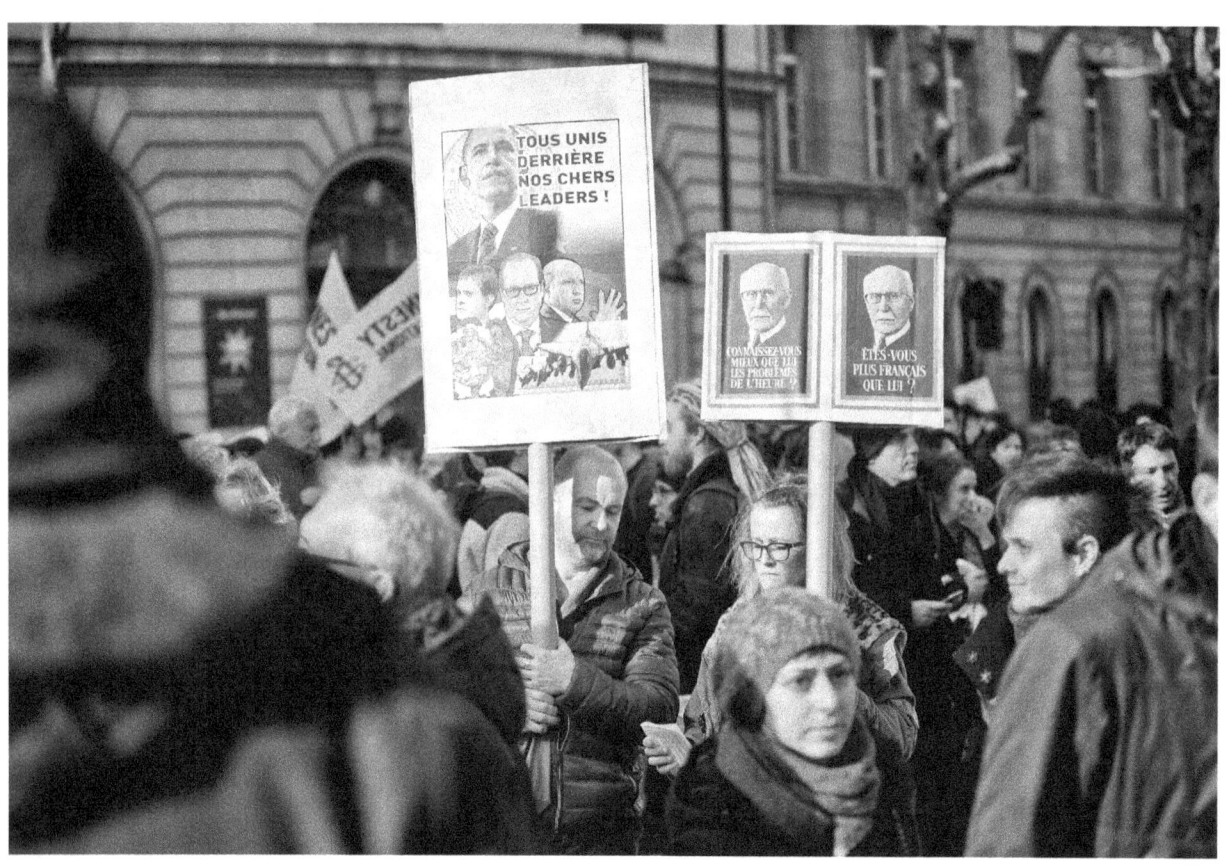

Problems of the present, 2016

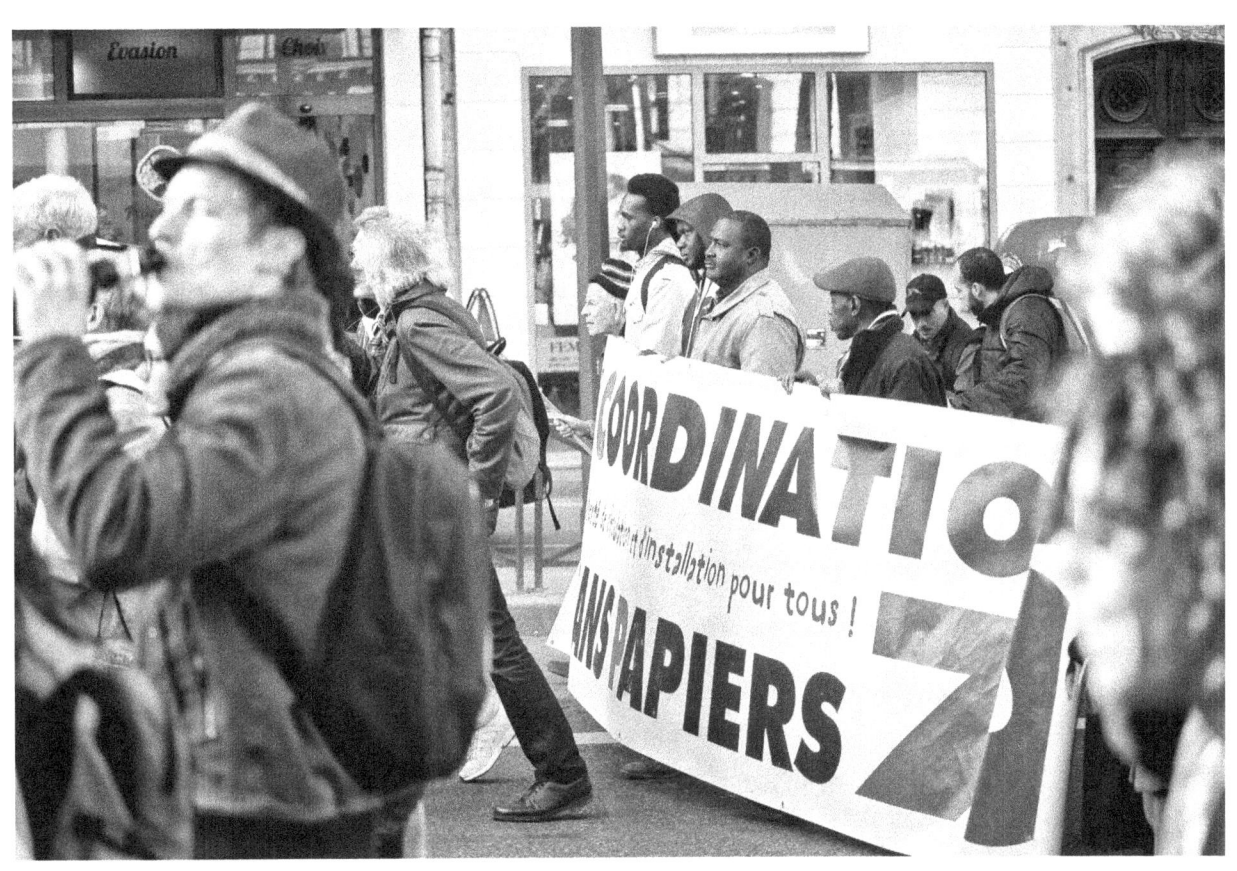

Unity, 2016

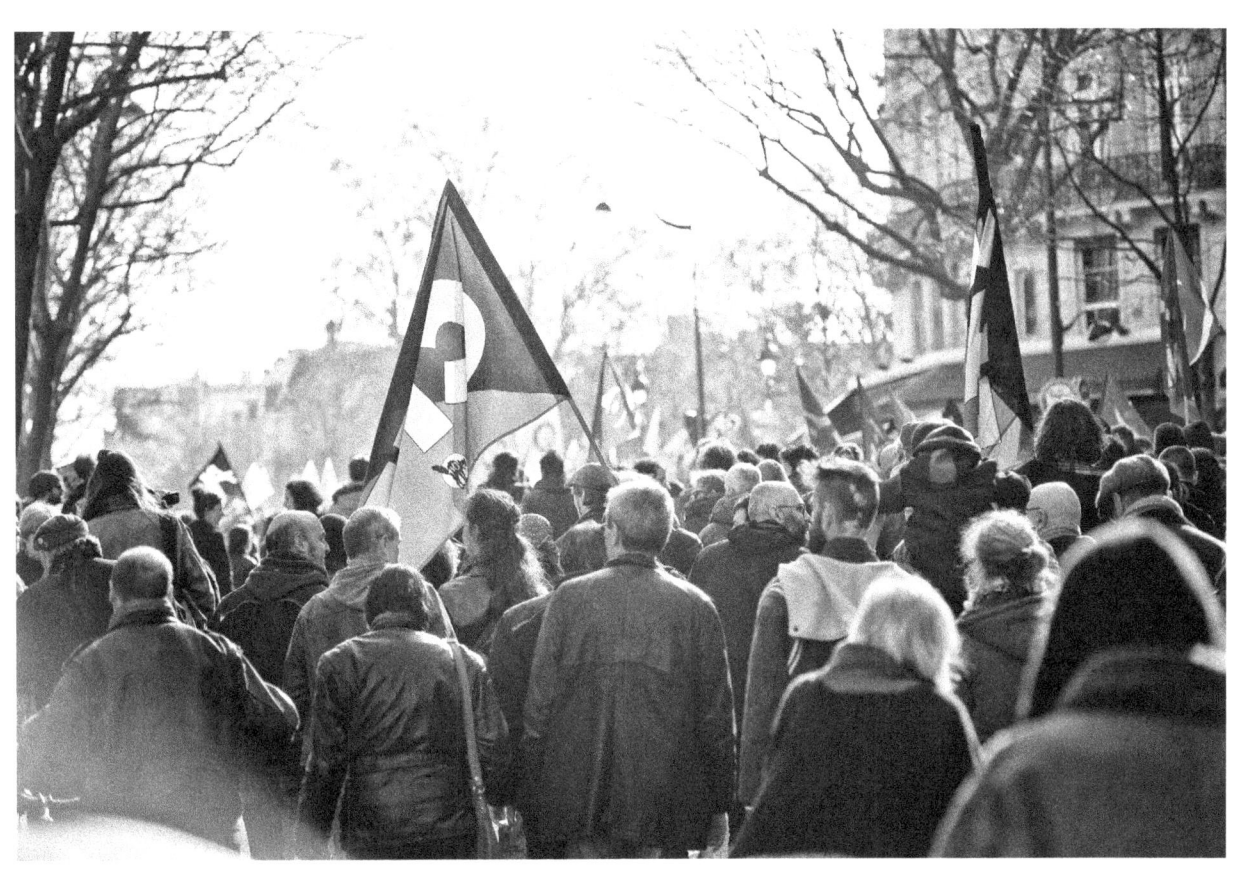

Manifestation, 2016

PARADES

Parisians like parades, probably long beautiful boulevards and avenues are contributing to this. To some extent, they were designed in this way, especially for parades. Every participant of the parade overflows with pride for Paris and France, thousand-year history and personal contribution to it. Patriotism is a pronounced feature of the French character.

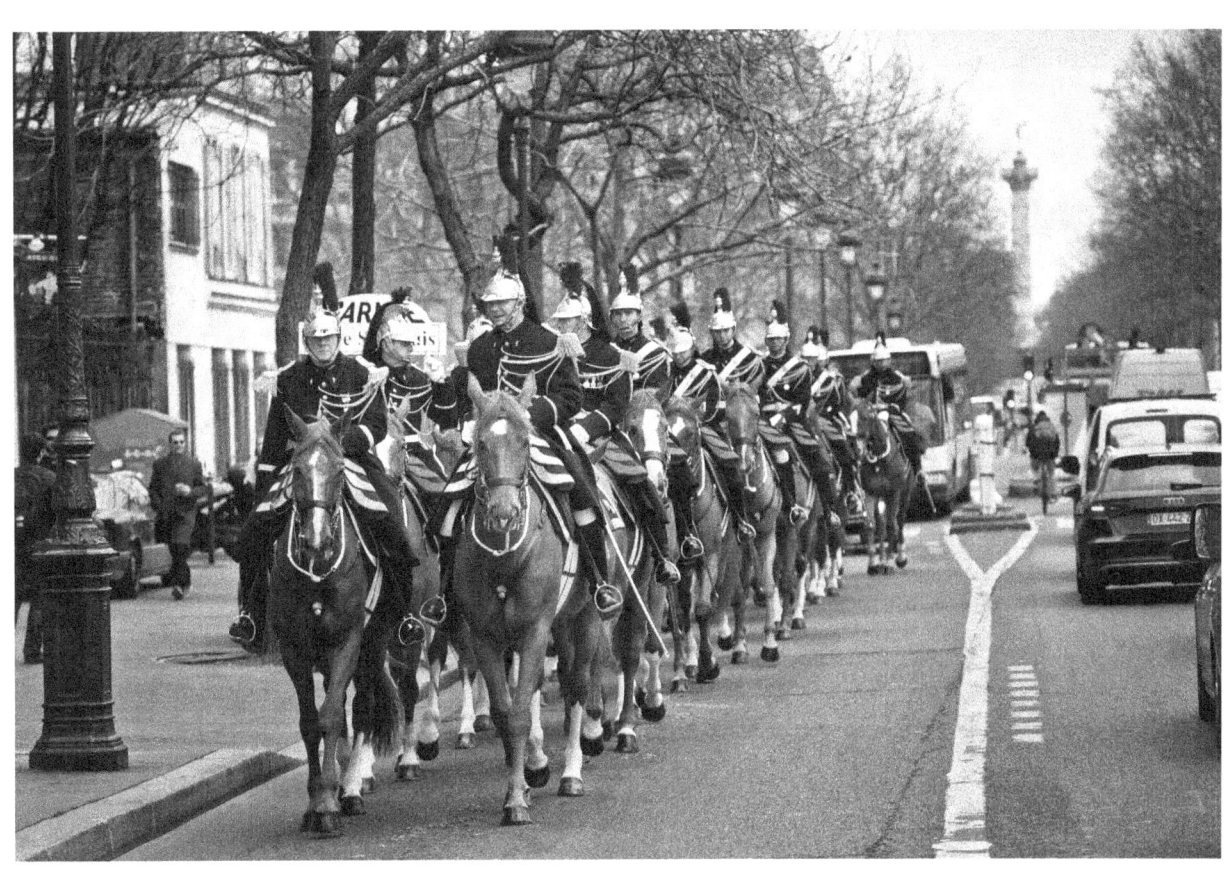

Celebration, 2016

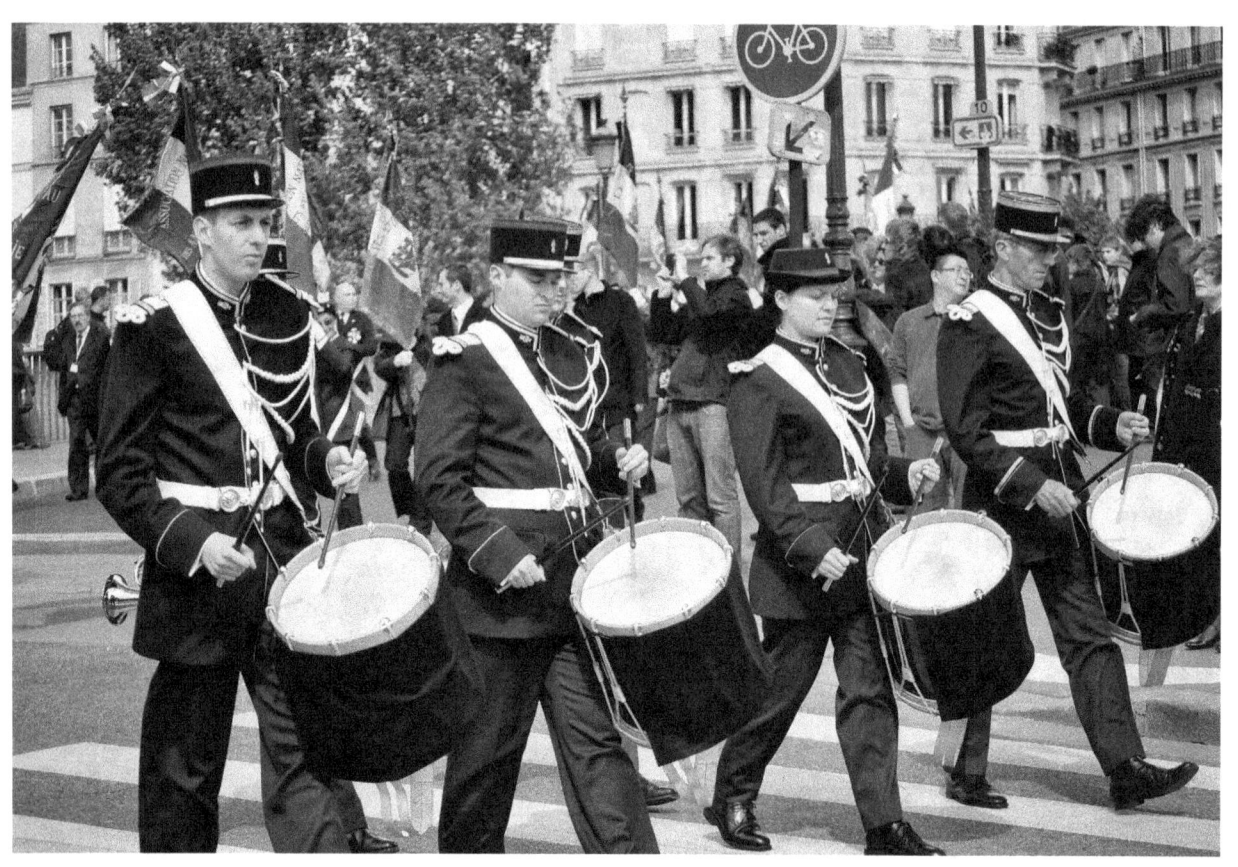

Drummers, 2012

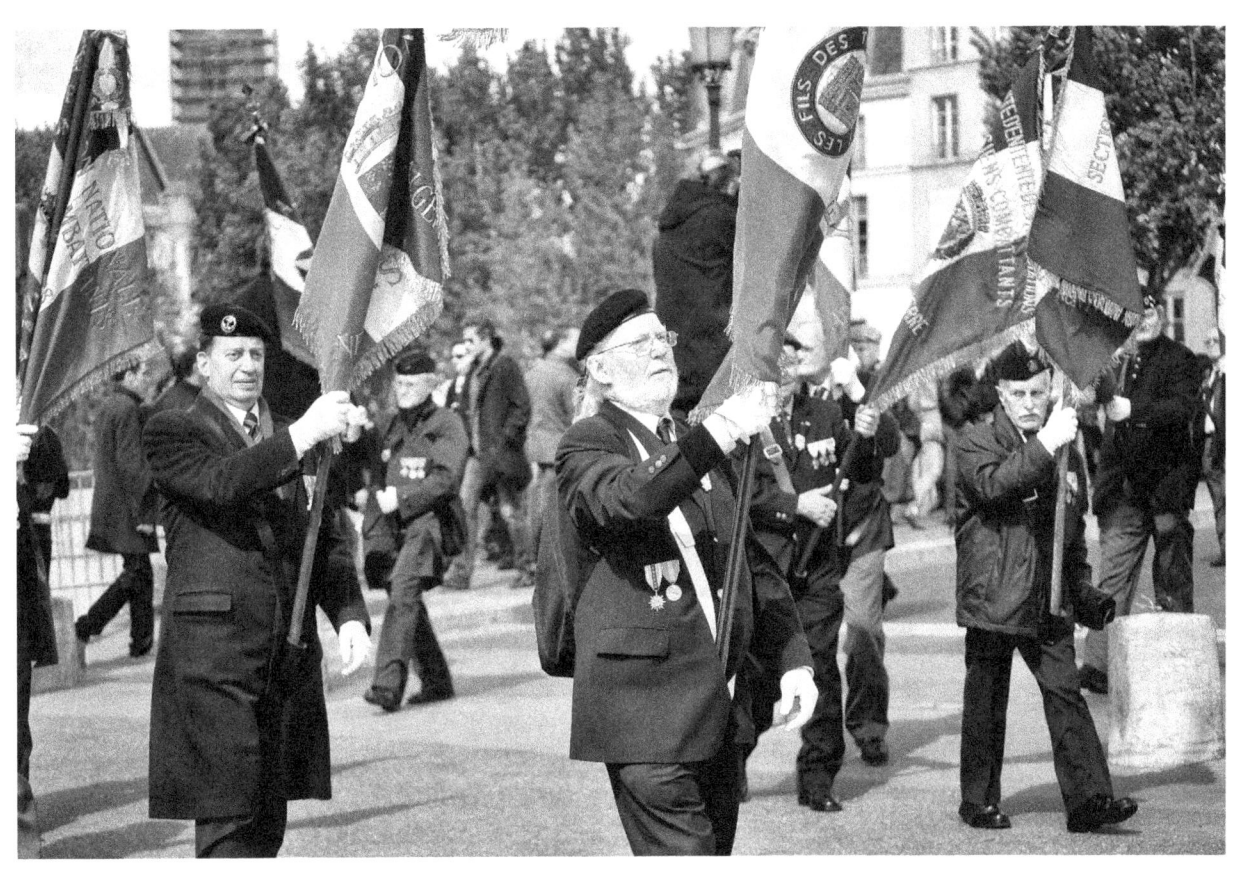

Veterans, 2012

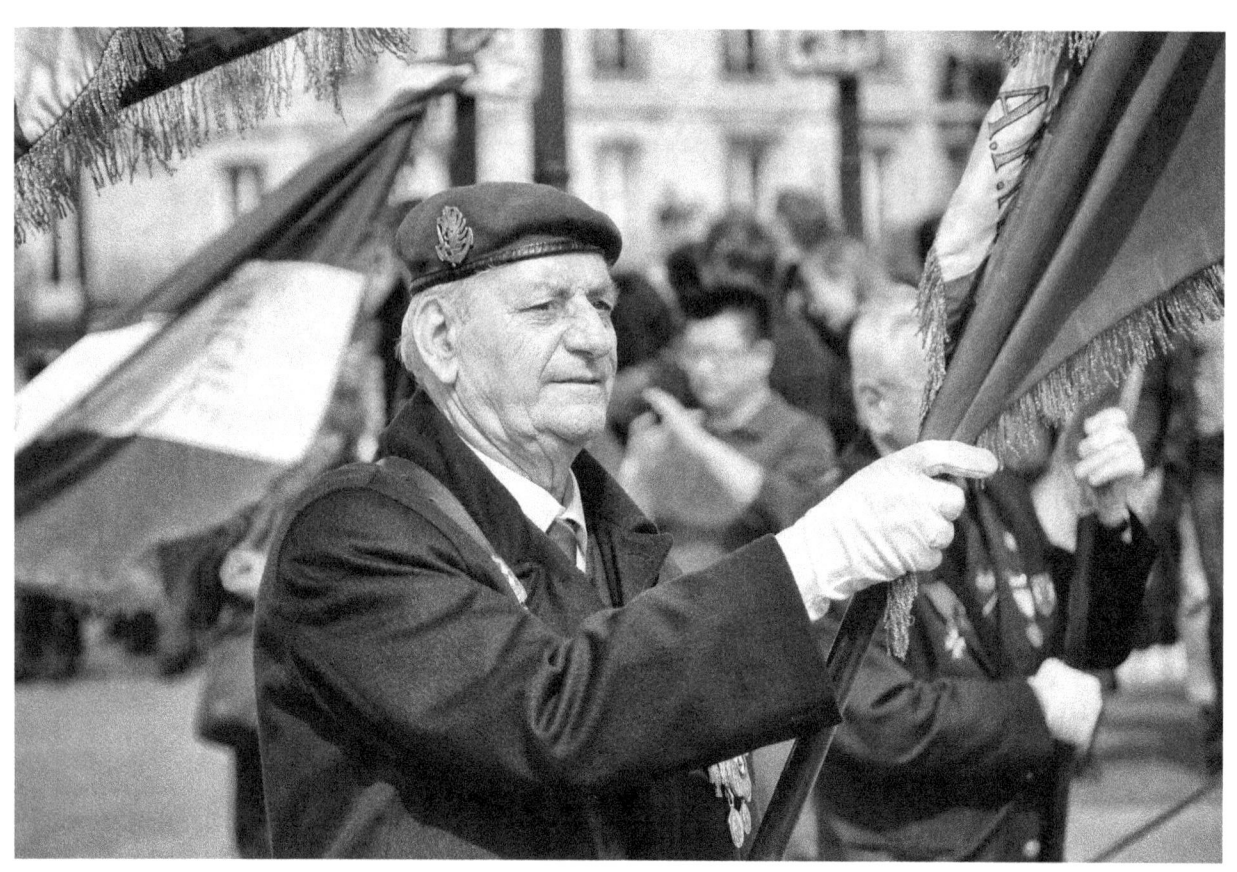

National Pride, 2012

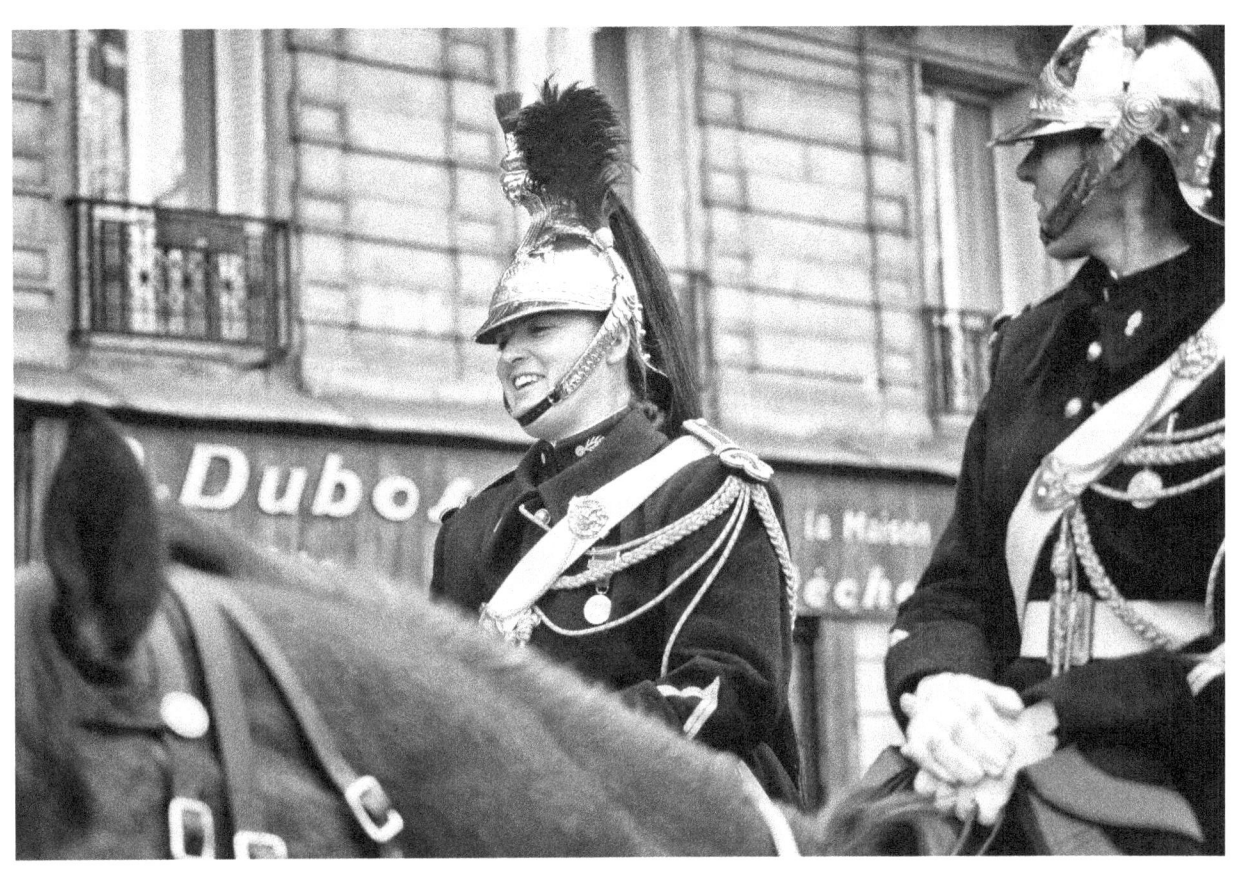

New generation, 2016

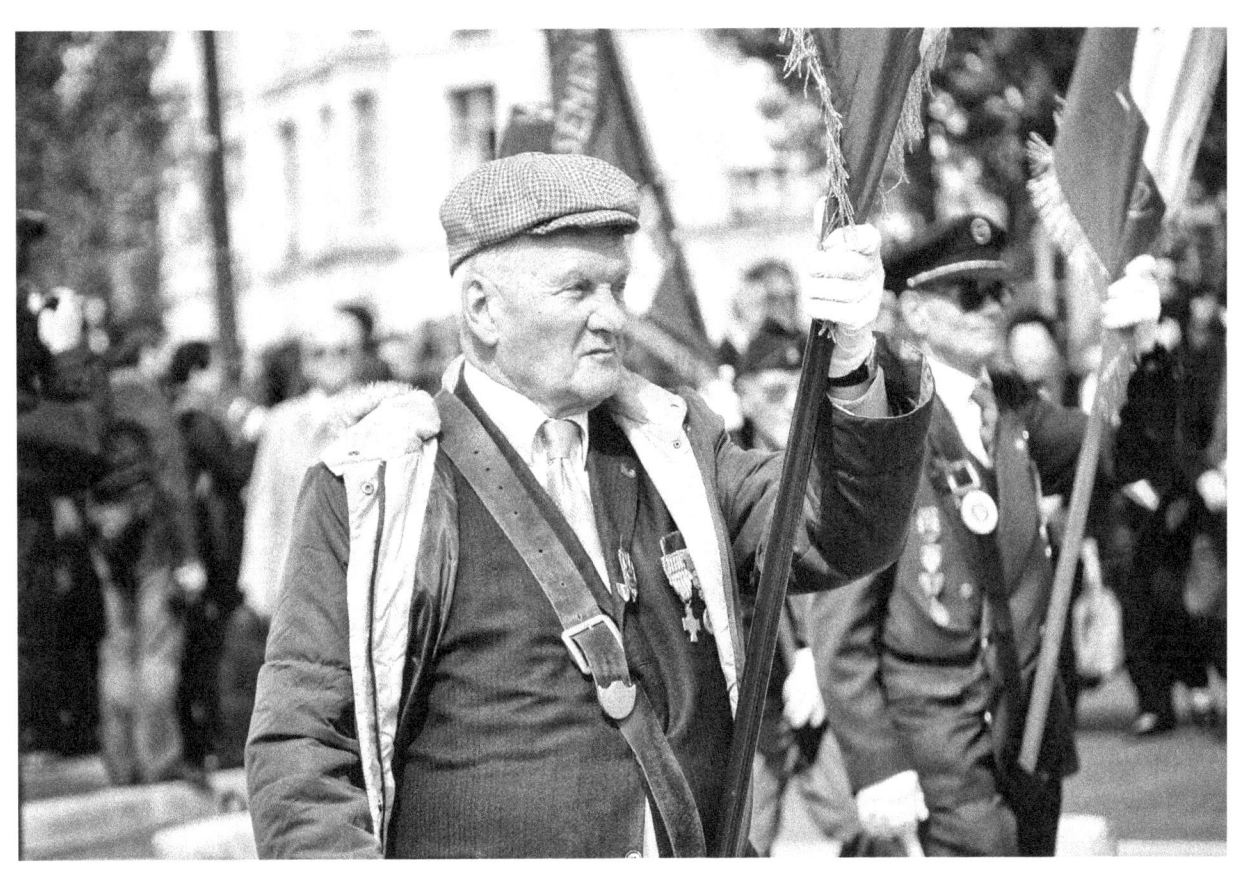

Veteran, 2012

THE PARISIAN LIFE

Photos that are in this section of the book, I couldn't take to any other. They show the life of Parisians from different sides, something that is often impossible to describe in words. Parisians enjoy their life. They aren't stressed out by the hustle and bustle of life. They have figured out a way to combine work and play and do it effortlessly. They have mastered the balance of life by incorporating the pleasurable things into the everyday. Leaving the office for lunch, taking a long walk after work, or having a glass of wine each night—they're living that "joie de vivre" regularly.

But, of course, not everything is so simple and bright. Sometimes you can get on top, and then fall to the very bottom. Our life is full of contrasts.

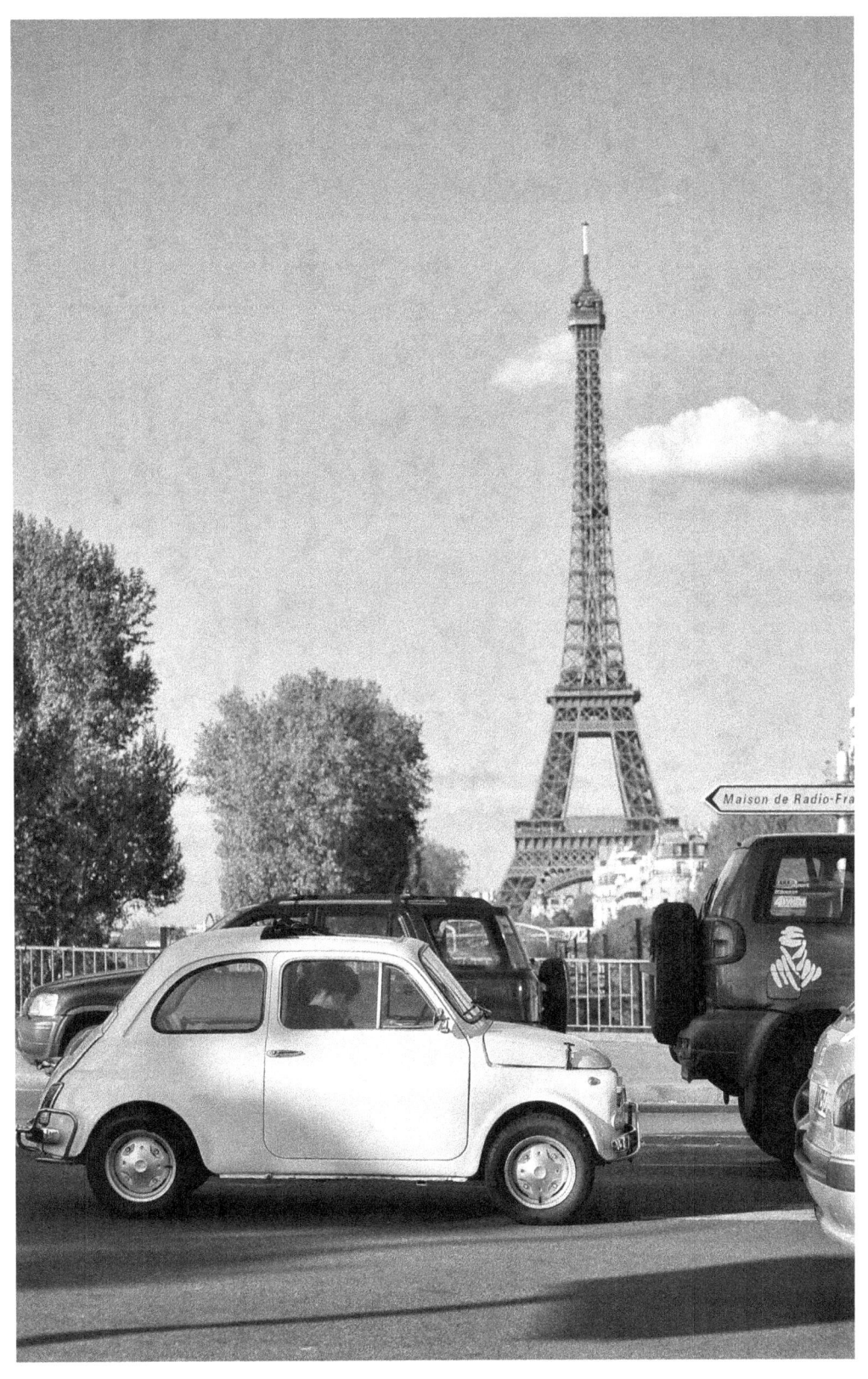

Two icons, 2012

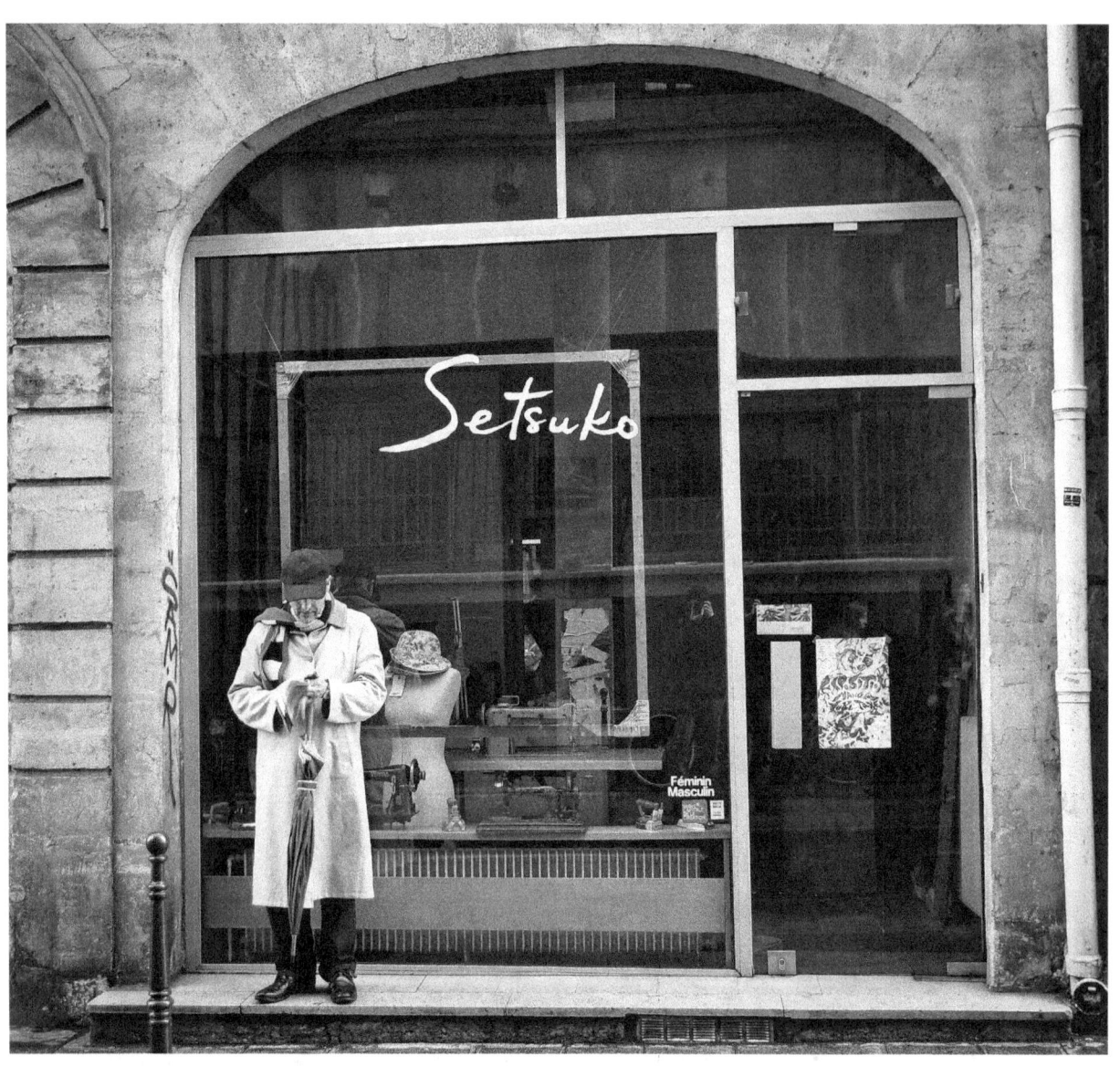

Waiting , 2012

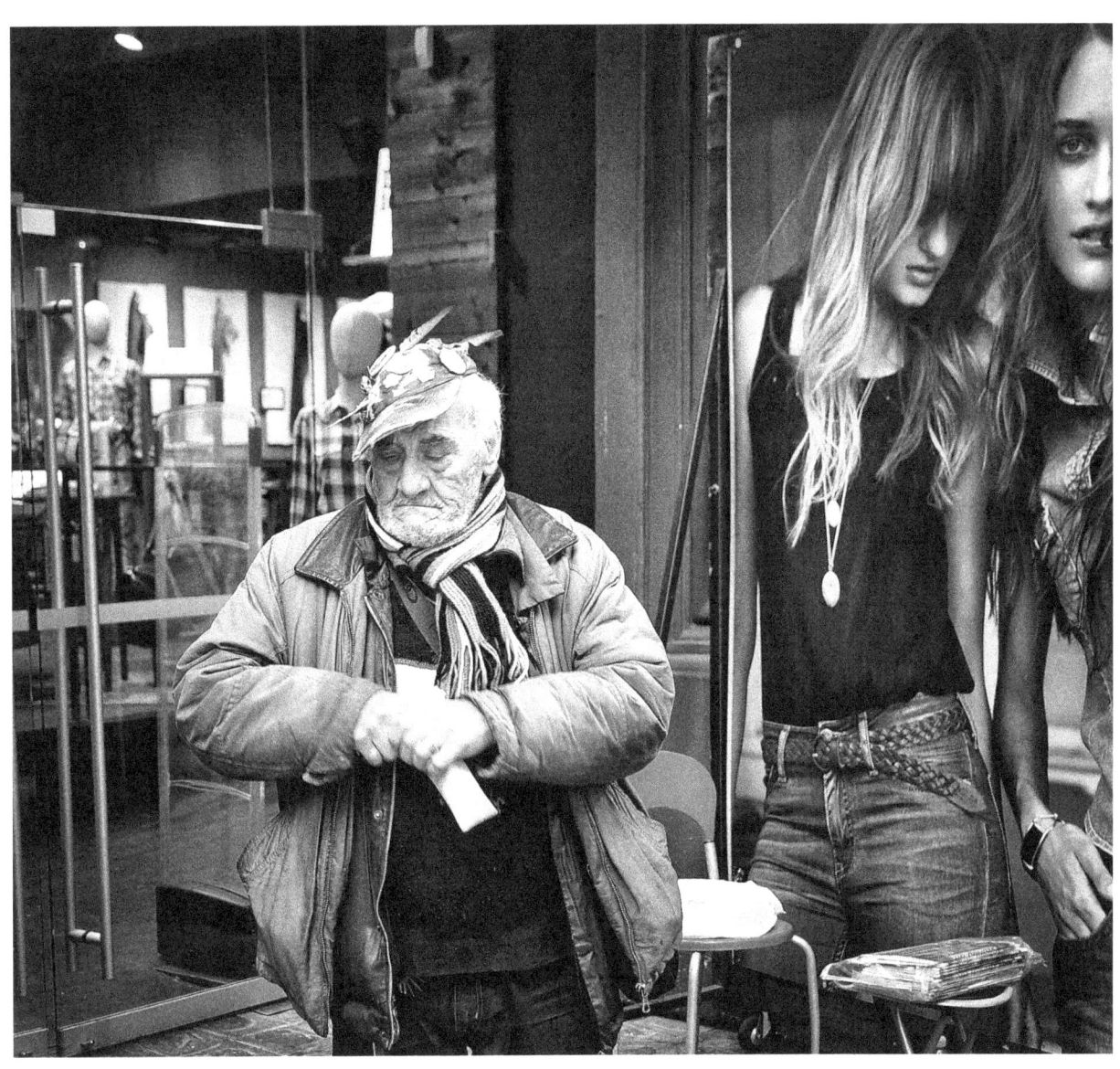

Fashion, 2012

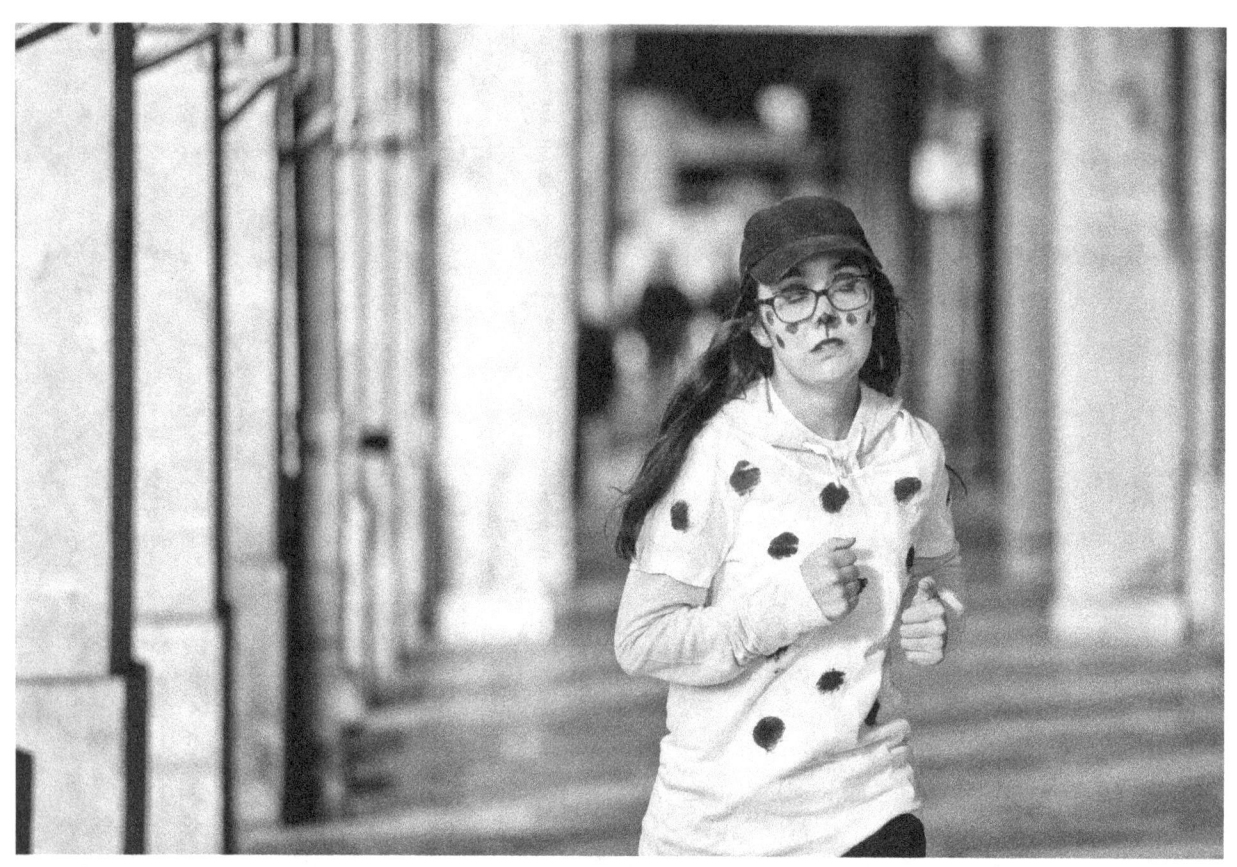

Tired, 2016

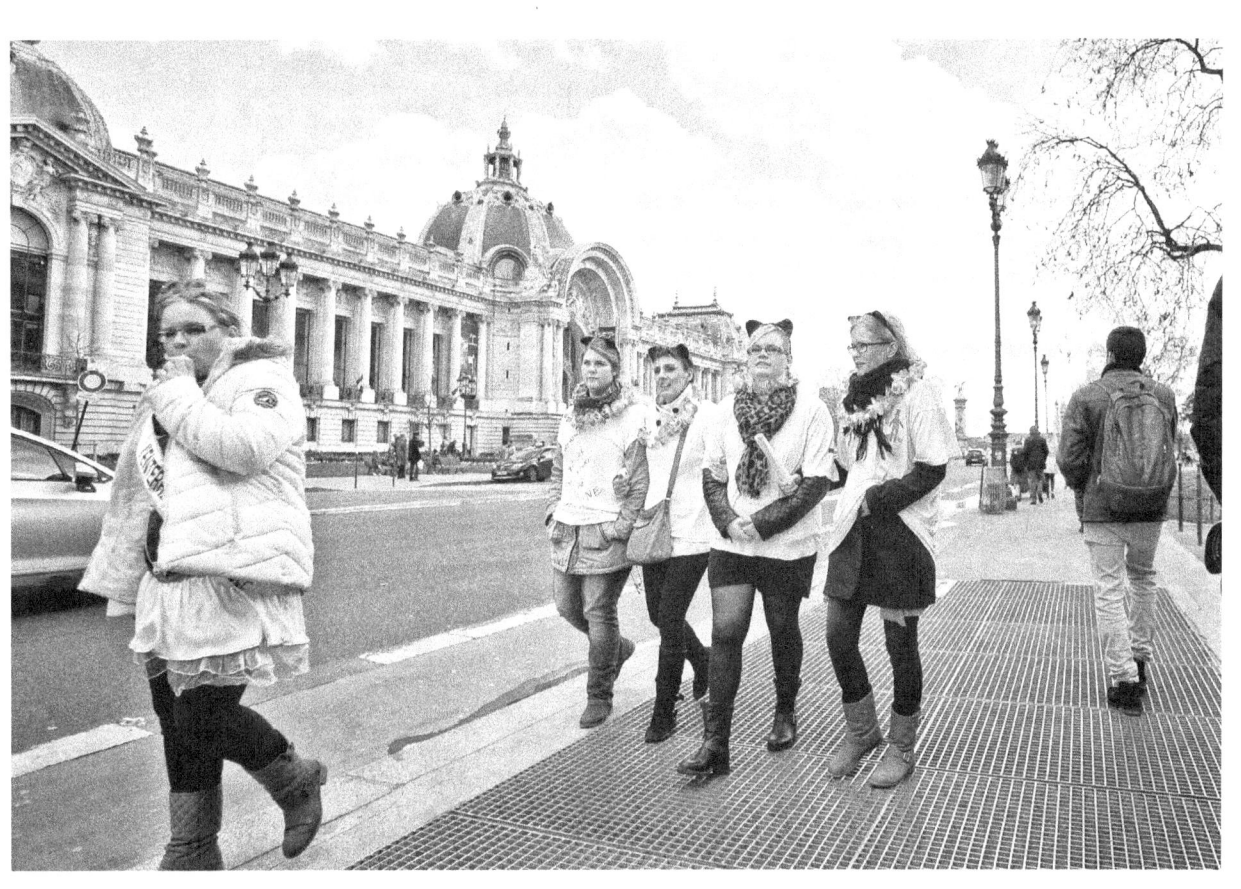

Party hard, 2016

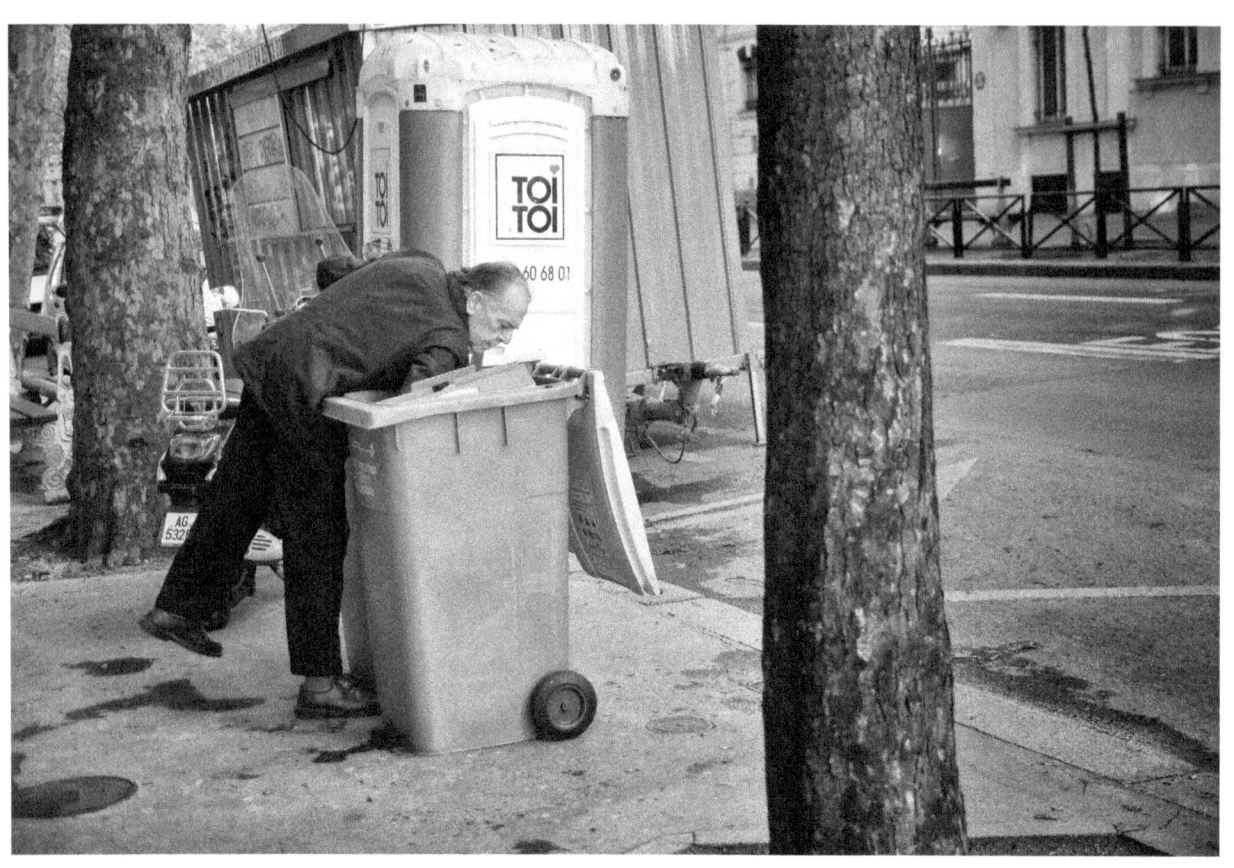

That's life, 2012

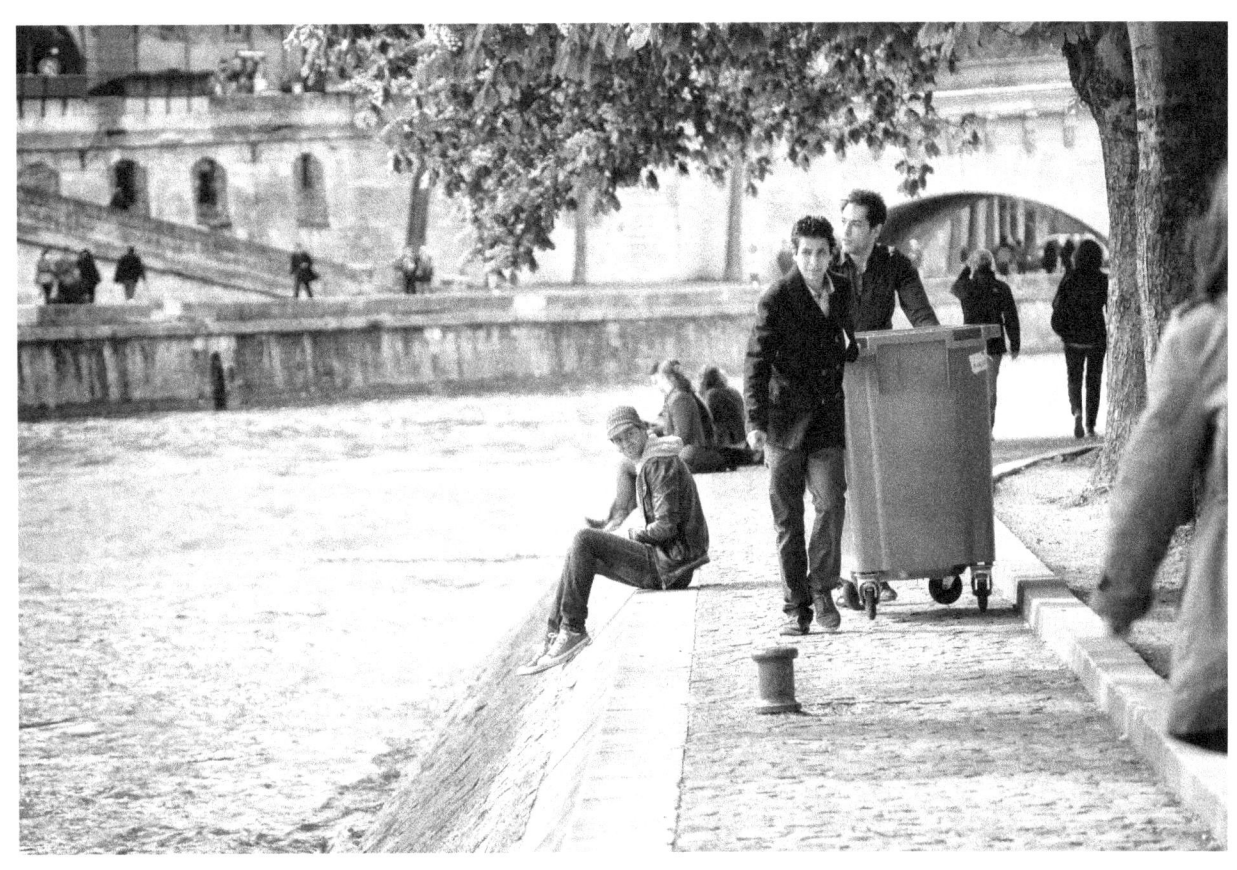

A lot of noise, 2012

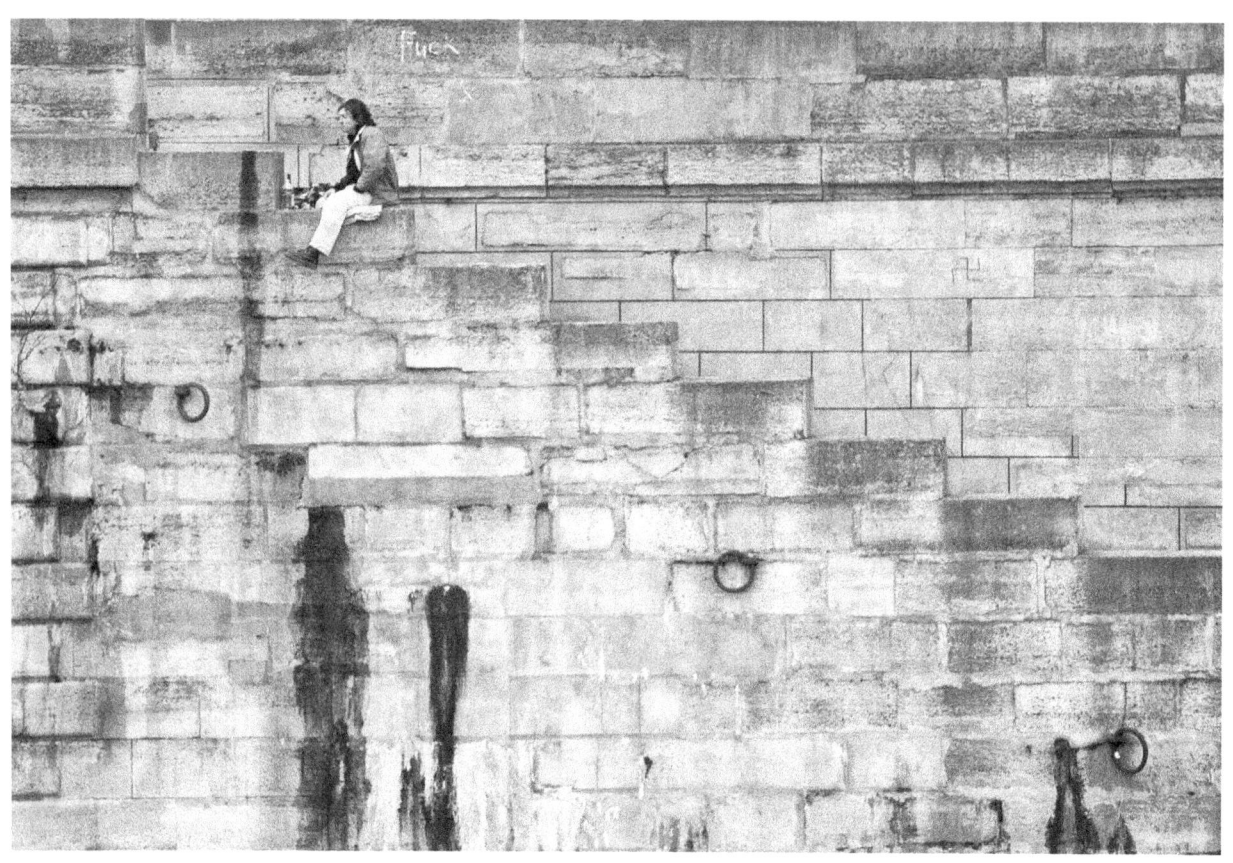

On the top, 2016

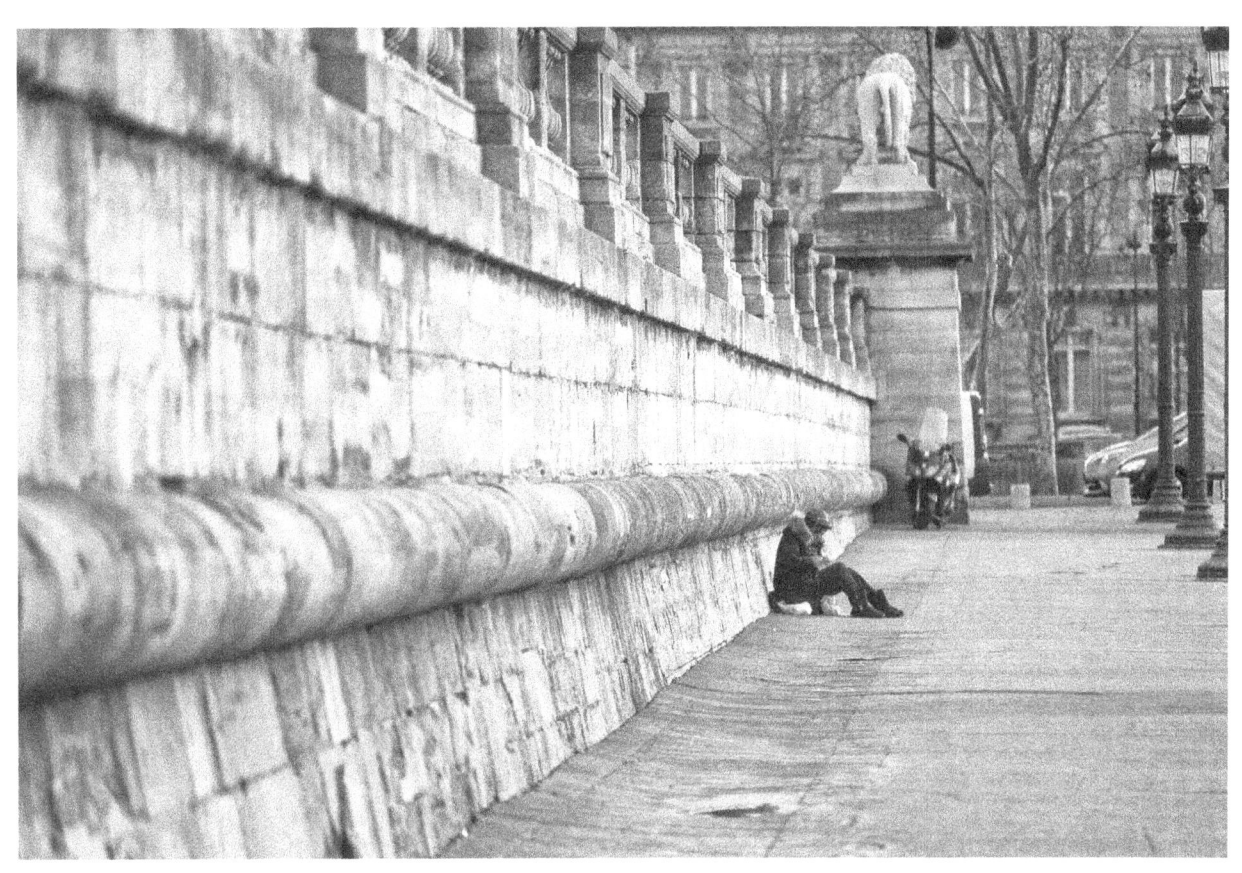

At the bottom, 2016

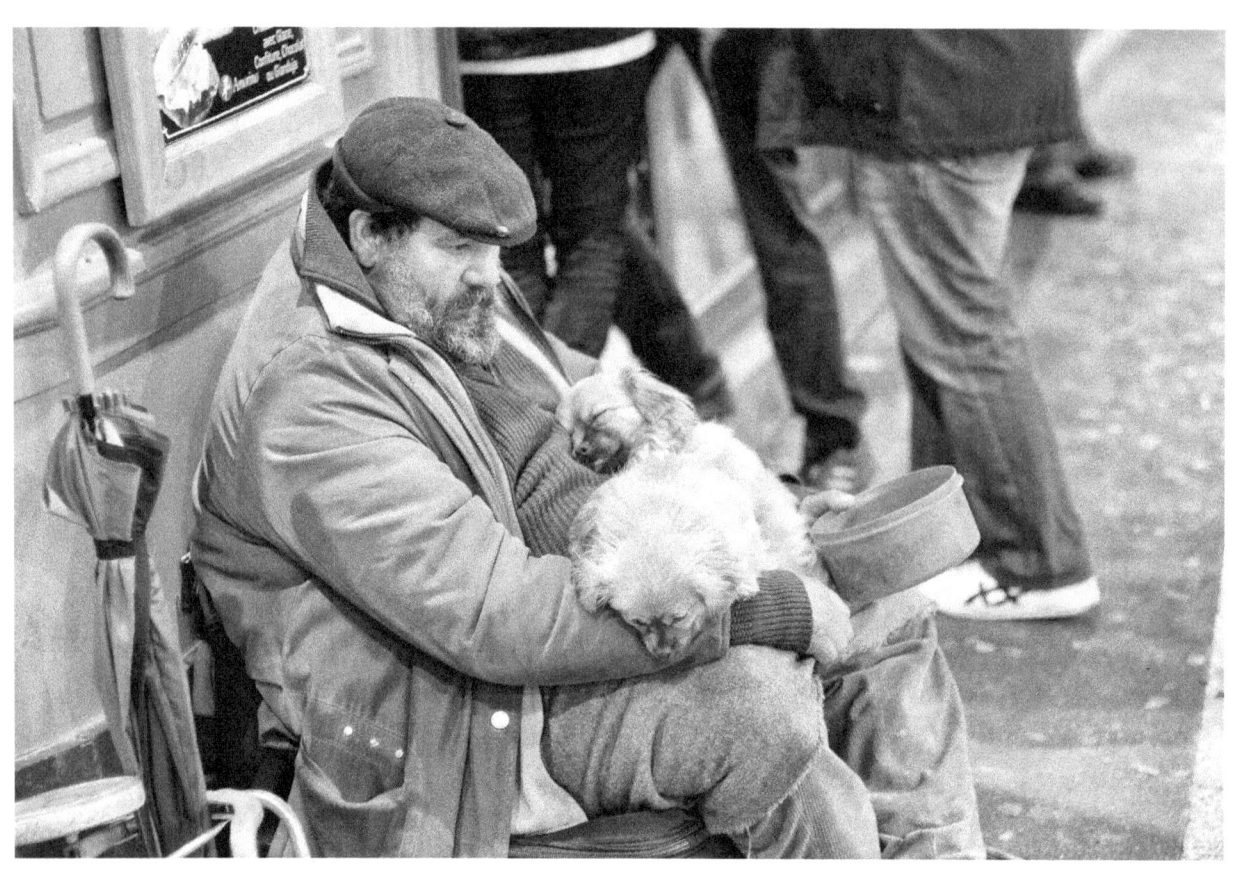

Unsuccessful actor, 2012

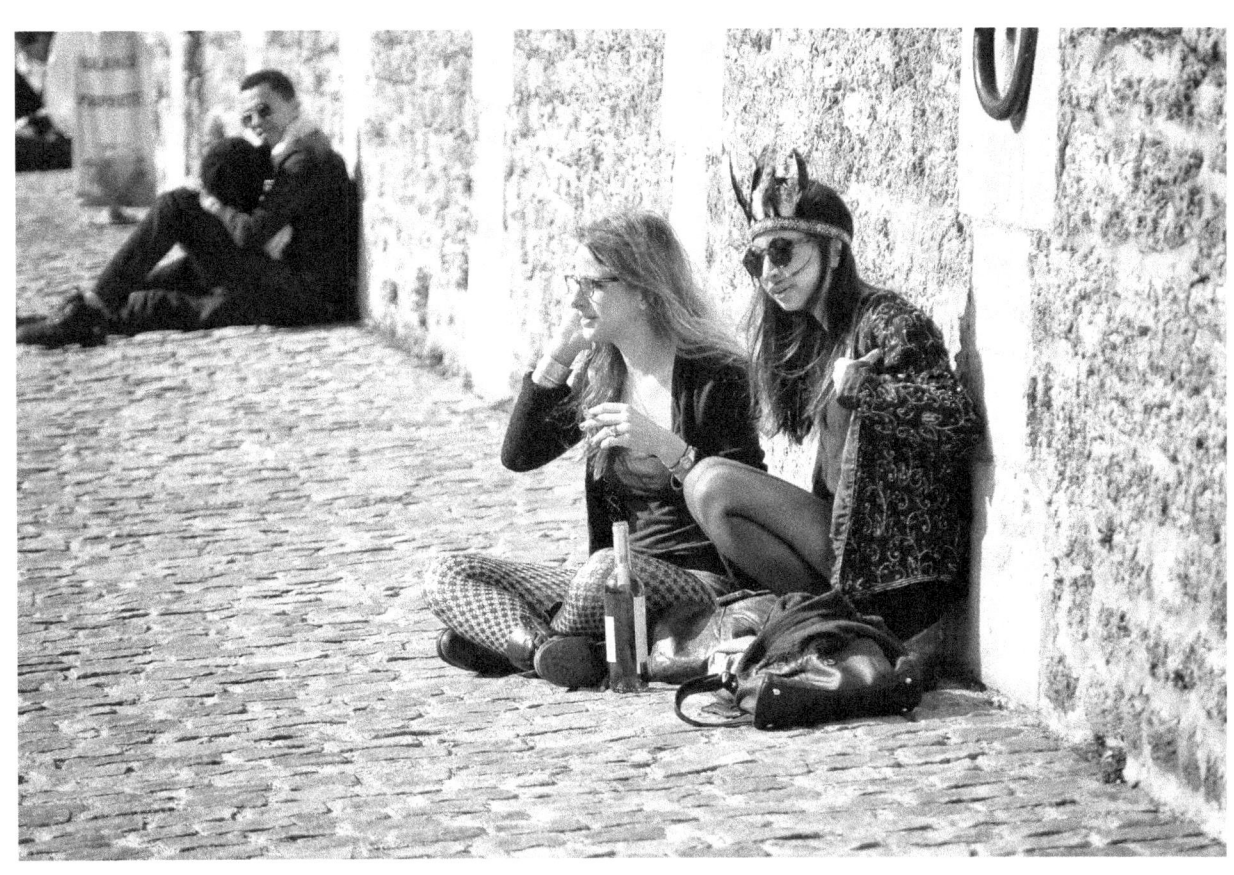

Young and beautiful, 2012

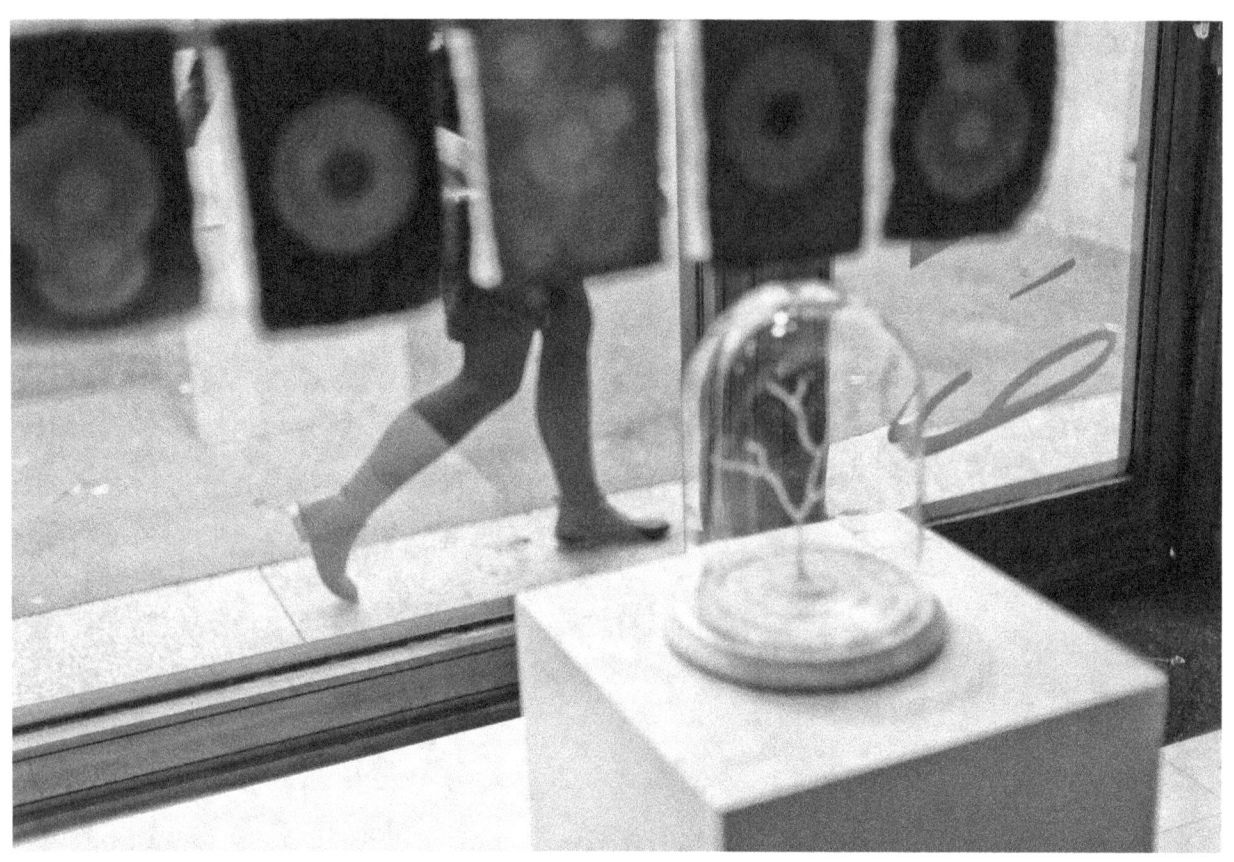

Step, 2016

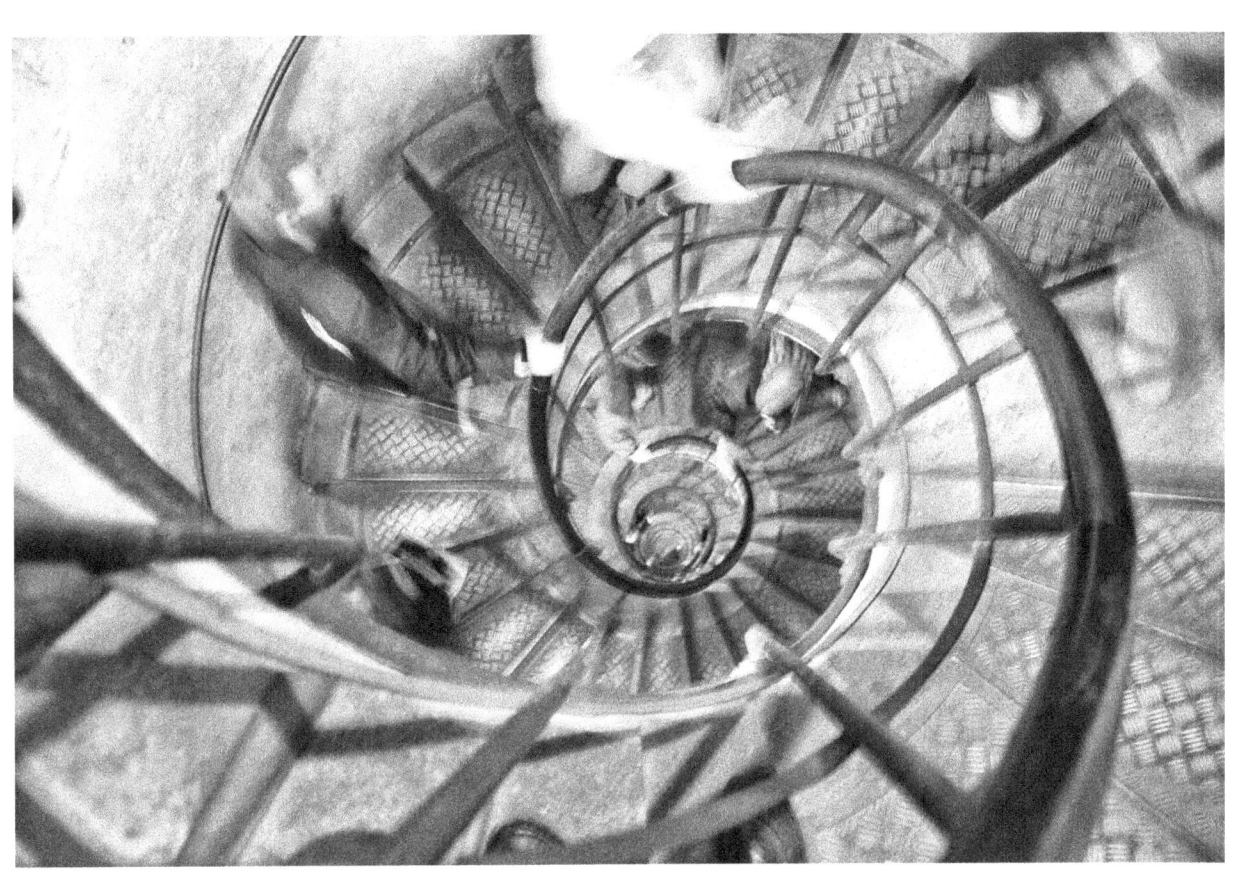

Snail, 2012

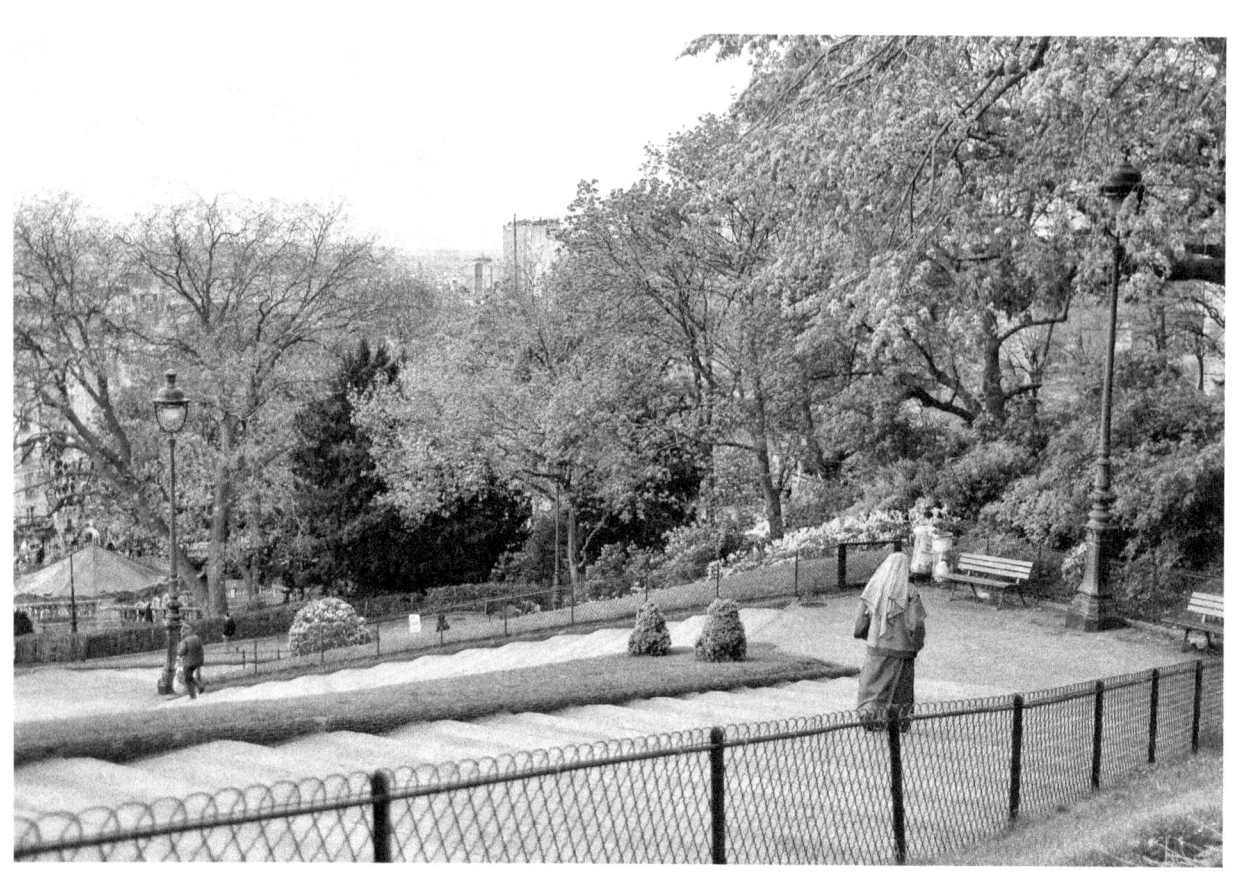

Away from the bustle, 2012

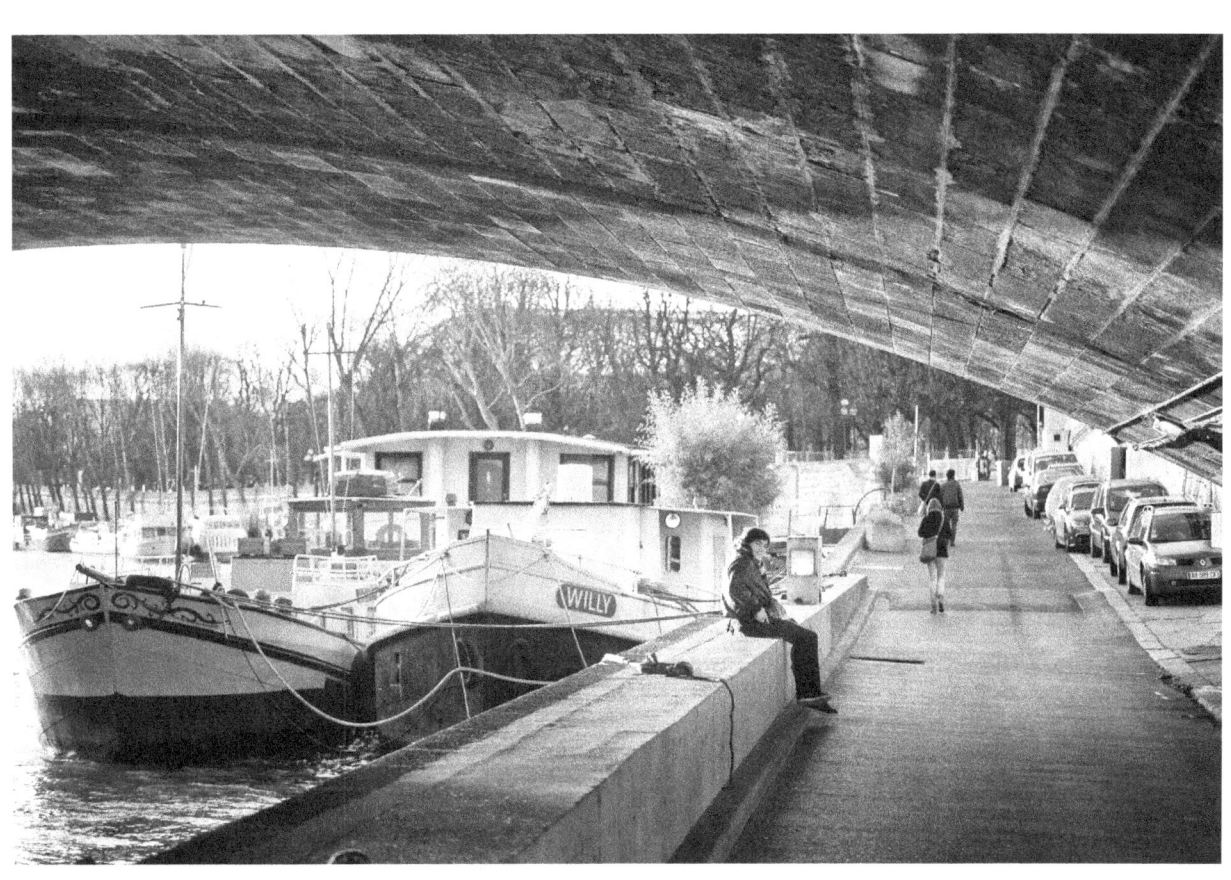

Under the bridge, 2016

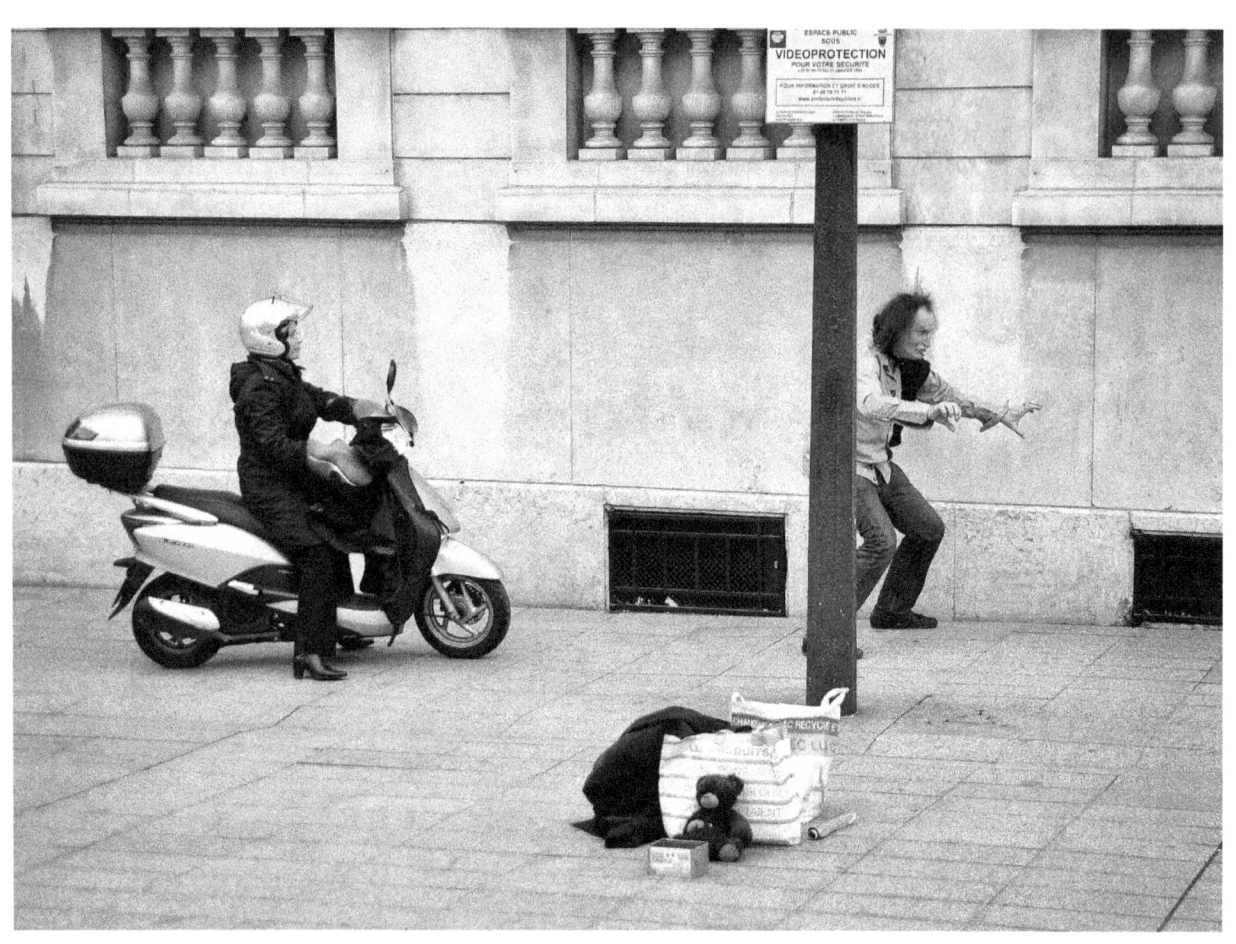

Teddy bear, 2012

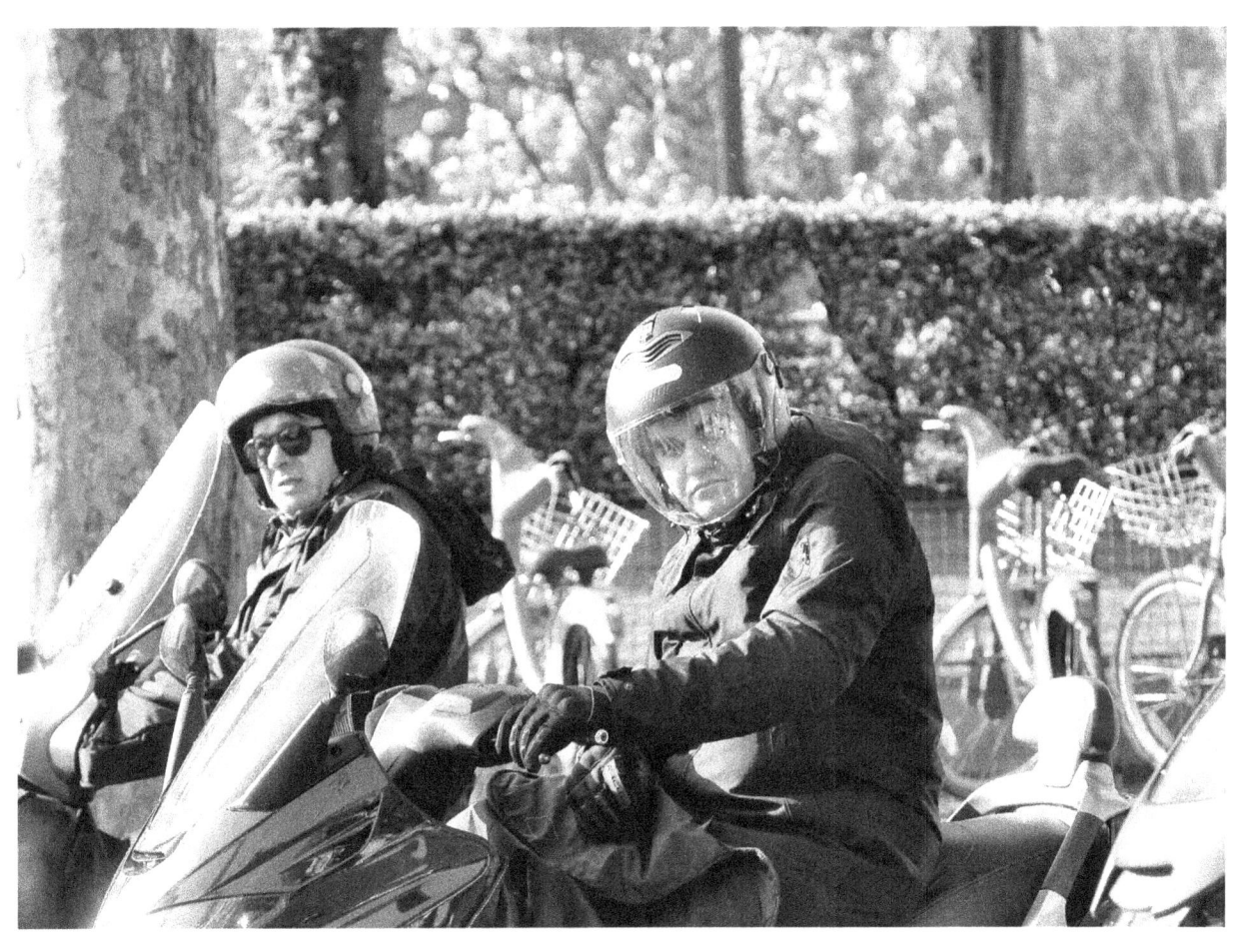

Noise, 2012

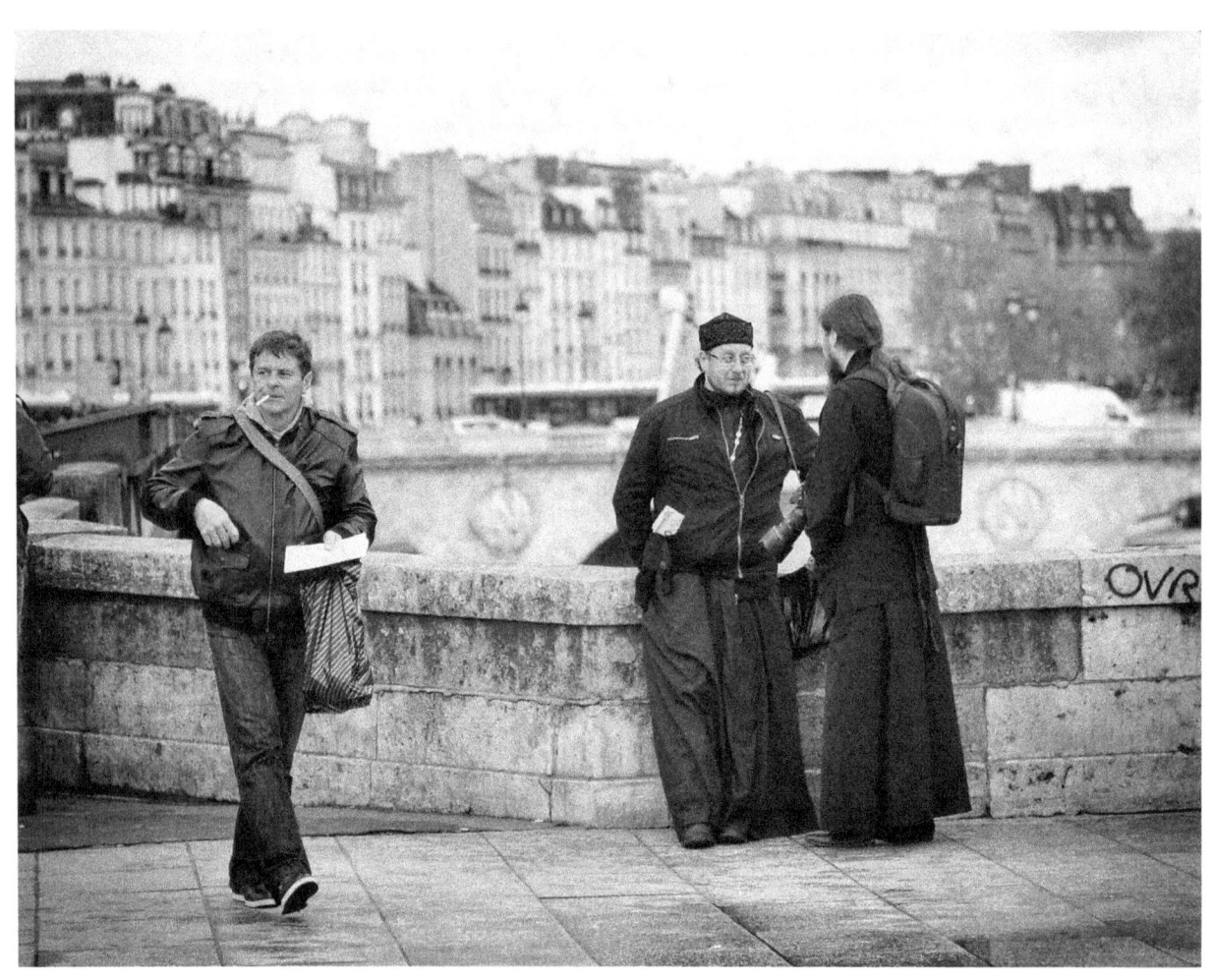

Overheard conversation, 2012

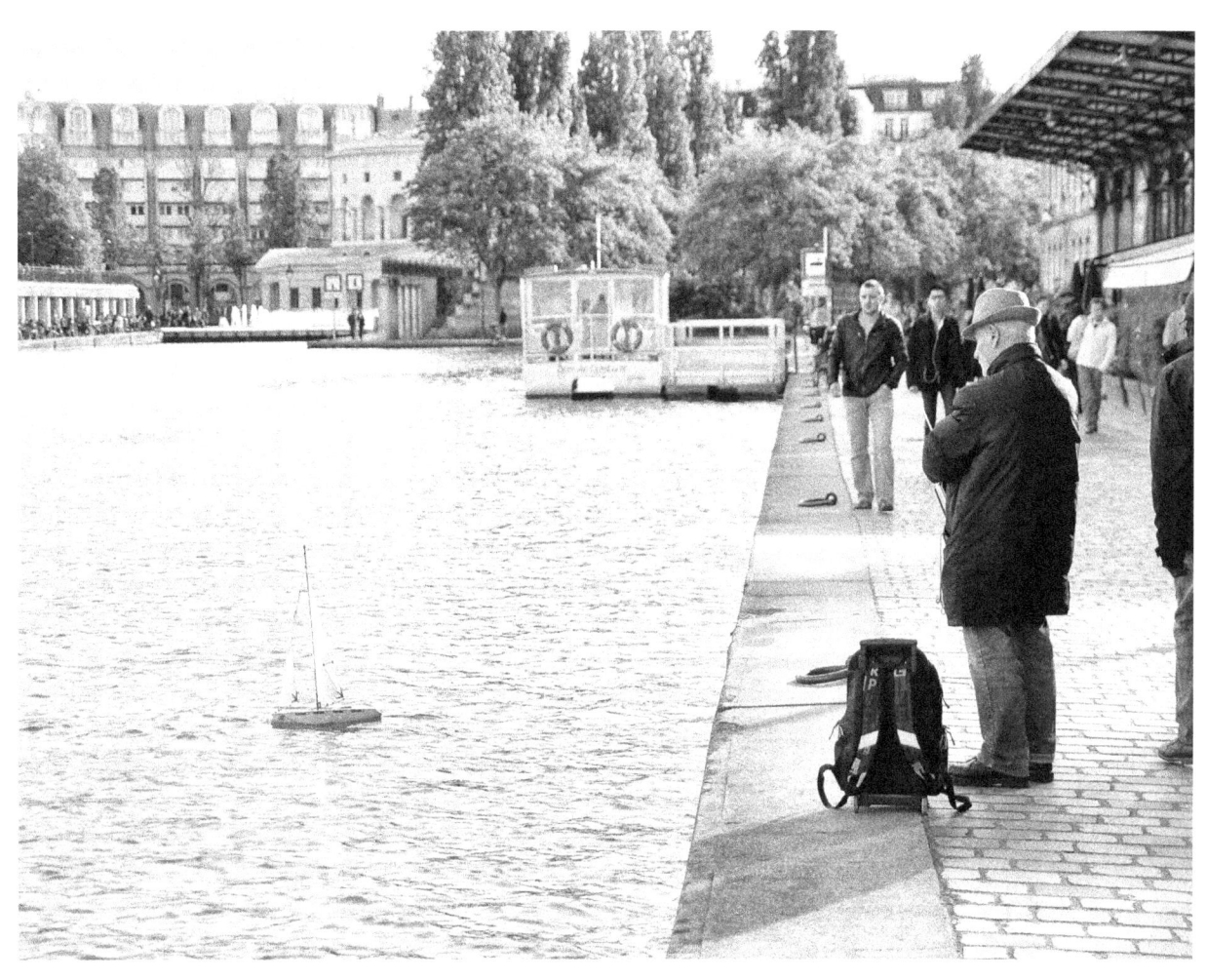

A boat, 2012

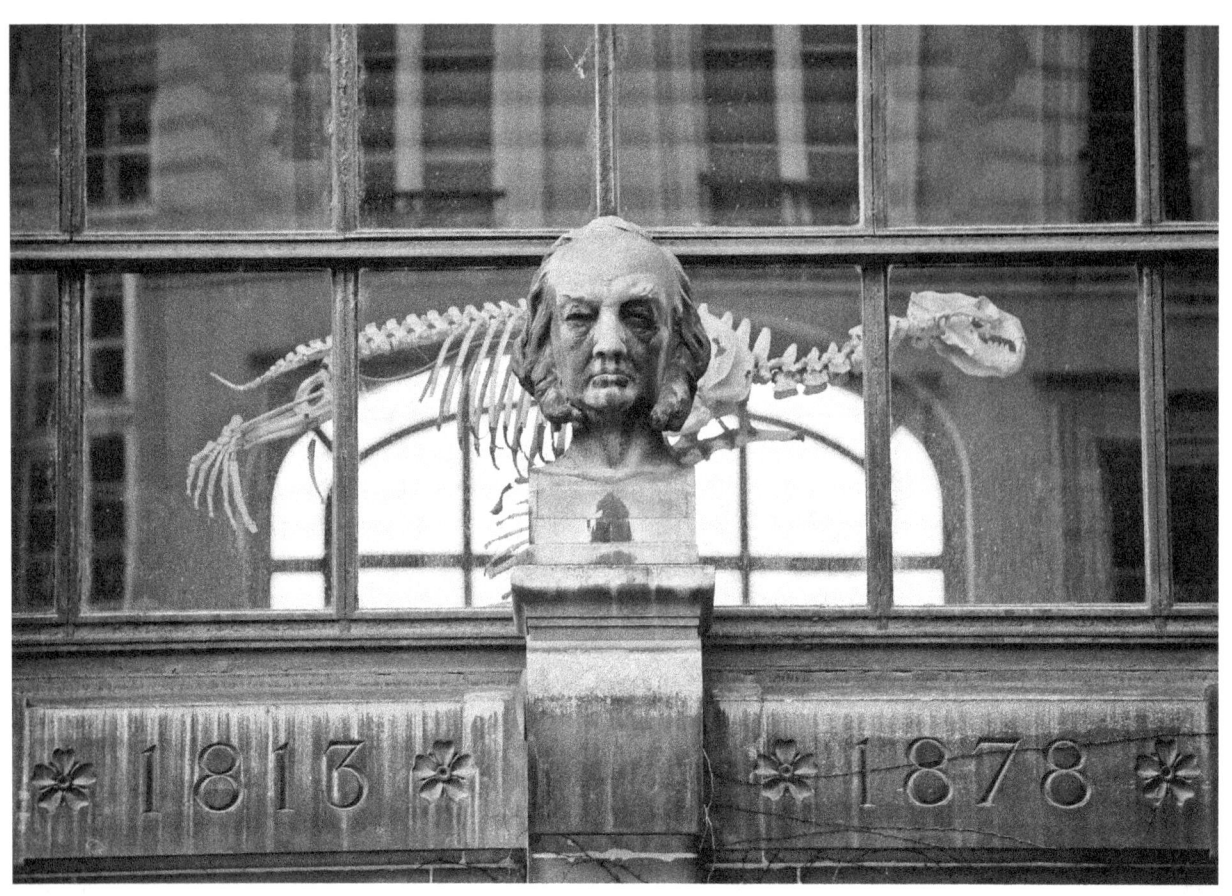

Head in the dinosaur, 2016

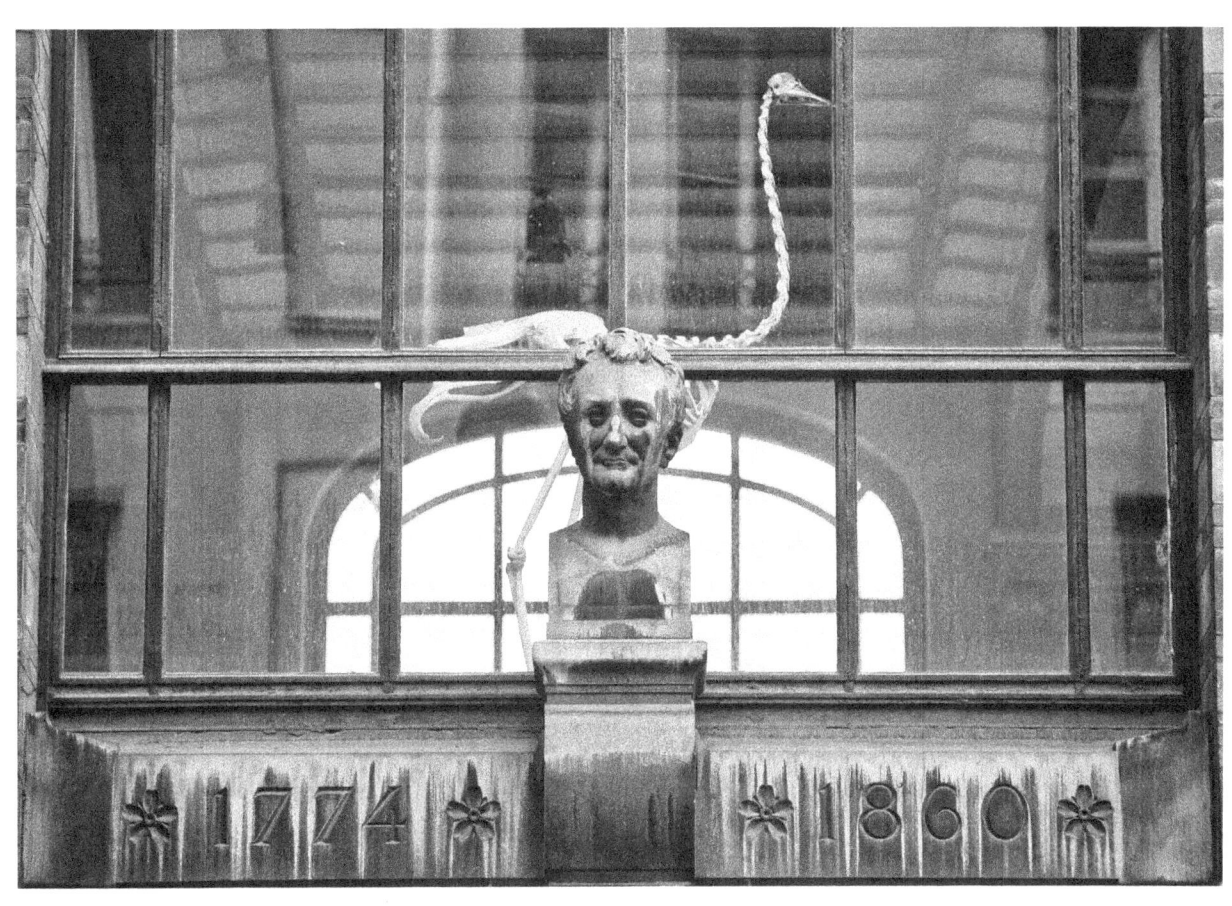

Head in the dinosaur 2, 2016

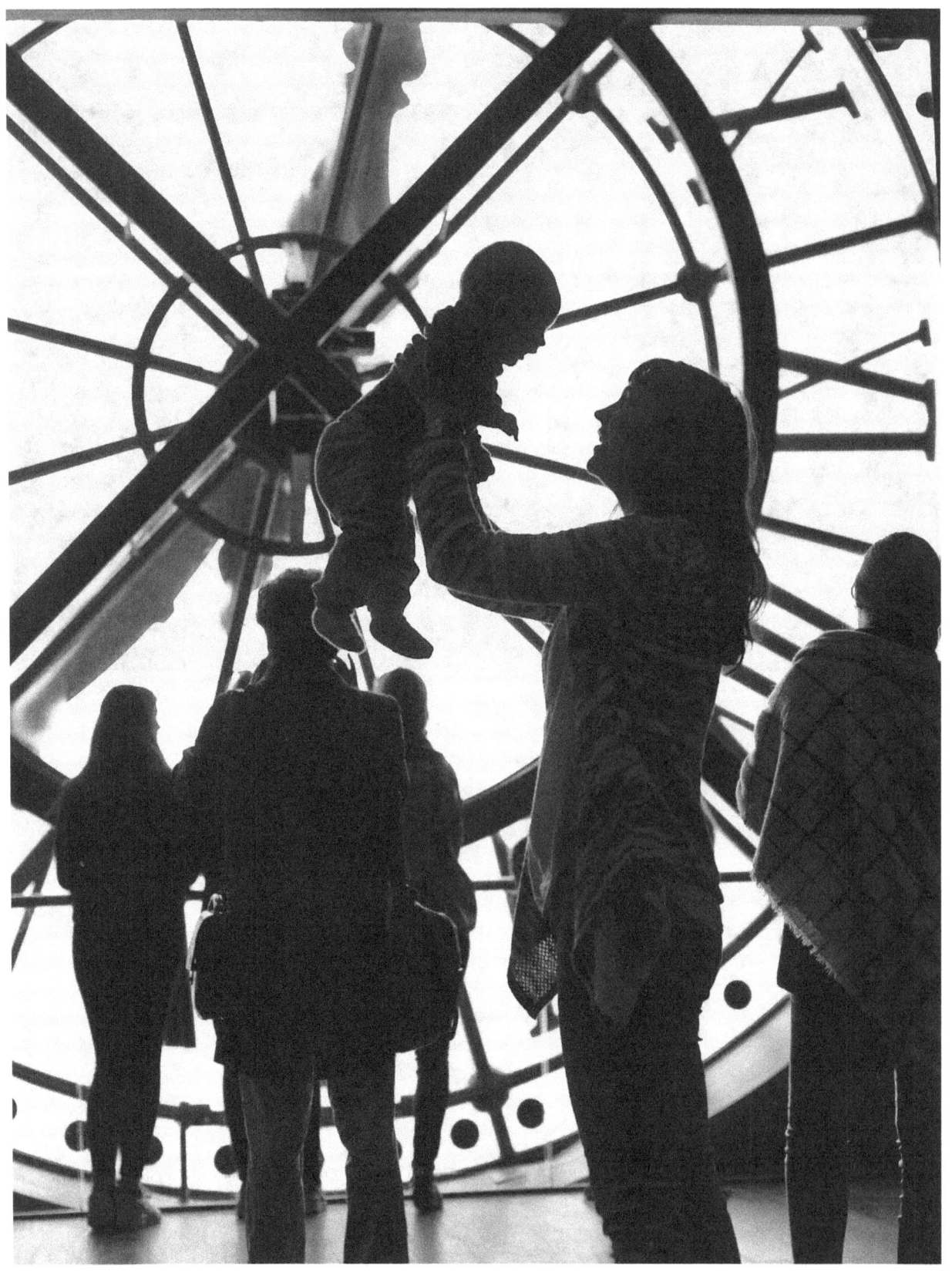

Time, 2016

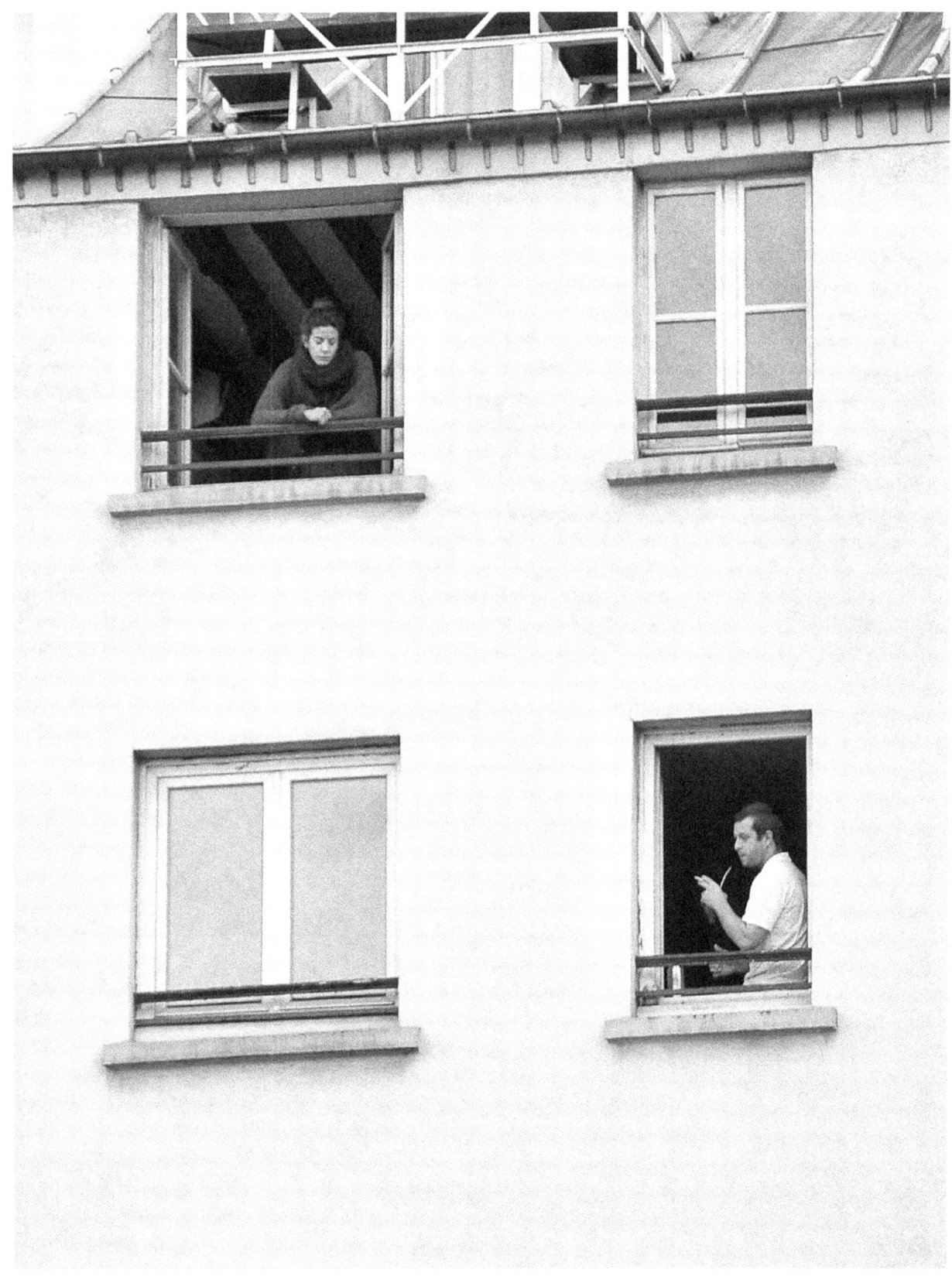

Two, 2012

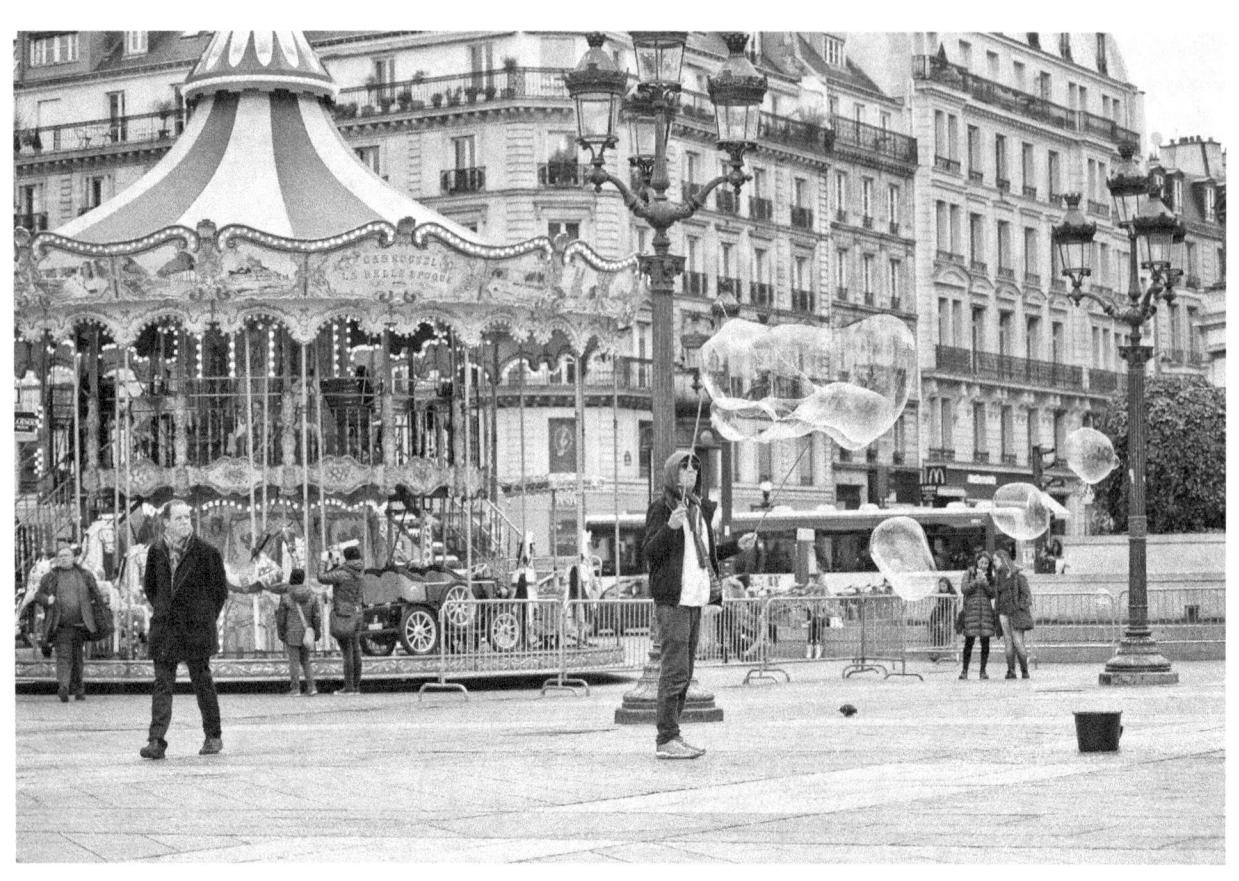

La belle époque, 2016

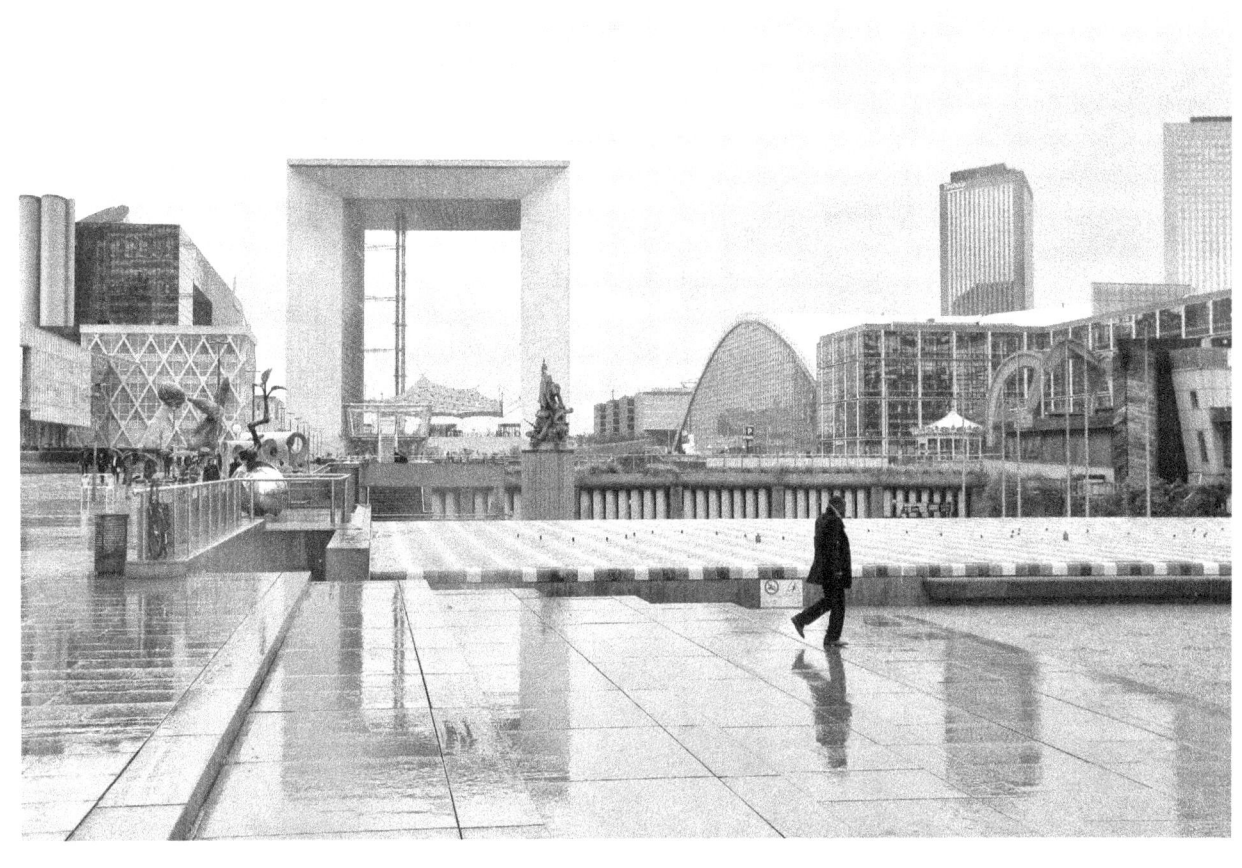

Step into the Future, 2012

www.ingramcontent.com/pod-product-compliance
Lightning Source LLC
Chambersburg PA
CBHW081112180526
45170CB00008B/2820